THE WORLD I FELL OUT OF

THE WORLD
I FELL OUT OF

MELANIE REID

Foreword by Andrew Marr

4th ESTATE • *London*

4th Estate
An imprint of HarperCollins*Publishers*
1 London Bridge Street
London SE1 9GF

www.4thEstate.co.uk

First published in Great Britain in 2019 by 4th Estate

3

A catalogue record for this book is
available from the British Library

ISBN 978-0-00-829137-2

Printed and bound in Great Britain by
CPI Group (UK) Ltd, Croydon, CR0 4YY

MIX
Paper from
responsible sources
FSC
www.fsc.org **FSC˚ C007454**

This book is produced from independently certified FSC paper
to ensure responsible forest management.

For more information visit: www.harpercollins.co.uk/green

To Dave and Doug and all the people forced to live
in the parallel world – I didn't realise you were
there until I joined you.

CONTENTS

FOREWORD
BY ANDREW MARR

If a book makes you cry, properly cry, and if it makes you laugh, repeatedly, both quietly and loudly, then it's safe to say this is probably a good book. This is probably a good book. Melanie Reid is already a star writer for anyone who regularly reads *The Times*. The horse-riding accident which rendered her tetraplegic gave her a ferociously hard, painful and difficult journey; and also, a seemingly inexhaustible subject for brutally self-revealing and often very funny columns. Mel, as her friends call her, is not an excessively inhibited person. She has a big laugh, and a generous, clear-sighted gaze. Here, in book form, you get the full story of her almost mundane accident and its awful consequences. It's her story, of course, with her special particularities – her beautiful remote Scottish house, love of horses, gruffly charismatic husband, and so forth.

But it's also a story for all of us, because we are all vulnerable. Life is incorrigibly random. Broken necks await us on school runs, uneven garden steps, family skiing holidays and at the shallow end of swimming pools; just as major strokes can happen, bizarrely enough, on rowing machines, at the basins in the hairdressing salons, or at either end of an international air flight. You never know. But, as Melanie puts it, our experiences of life are divided into an upper world of unconsciously elegant health and strength, of striding and stretching and elegant gestures we are barely aware of; and the lower, underworld, of the disabled, struggling to dress, and move, to eat and defecate. Anyone of us can be in the upper world, and then suddenly come on a completely ordinary sunny morning, tipped without a moment to complain or protest, into the underworld.

I am not as seriously disabled as Mel, but I have partial paralysis of my left leg, arm and hand and have had to go through, in a minor way, some of the tribulations that she has faced. Her description of the move from the warm cocoon of intensive care into the tougher rehabilitation wards of hospital, a place where the gym, bathroom, functional electrical stimulation and playdough all have a special meaning, returned me immediately to the wards in which I recovered from my stroke almost six years ago. She writes brilliantly about the characters of the different forms of nursing and medical staff, and the way black humour and grim solidarity knits together recovering patients still bemused about what has happened to their lives. (Though when this happens in Glasgow rather than London, the quality of humour is much, much higher.)

For tetraplegics, the road must be particularly rough. The rule she says is adapt or die: 'A rehab ward in a spinal unit is like an under-strength factory floor: too few staff battling to a relentless timetable of feeding, medicating, washing, toileting, dressing and hoisting dozens of helpless carcasses into wheelchairs to get them to the gym.' And then, if you're doing well, come other multiple terrors and challenges of returning home and rebuilding life. Melanie Reid writes sensibly and well about thoughts of suicide, about depression, about the frustration of media-hyped 'medical breakthroughs' that never quite translate into helping you yourself; and unsparingly about the daily frustrations and humiliations of disabled life. For what it's worth, I too have found myself screaming with rage from time to time having dropped yet another utensil on the kitchen floor.

So in that sense, these are really 'Notes from the Underground'; and why would you want to read that? The answer is not only that you might find yourself in just the same place, but that Melanie is such a good guide in how to survive it. She knows that although the subject of disability might seem depressing and offputting, the courage it requires is exciting and inspiring. What she has gone through requires no less physical courage and determination than being imprisoned in a wartime prison camp – a parallel that hovers at times through the writing, but is no hyperbole. She rightly quotes the great English vicar-philosopher Sydney Smith on the importance of taking a short view of life: 'Are you happy now?' She understands the absolute importance of shunning the lethal beckoning poison-fairy of self-pity. As she says: 'you learn, very slowly, to rediscover joy'.

On that journey, here, you'll find some of the funniest and darkest comic scenes you have ever read, from a surreal encounter between the author in her wheelchair and a group of special needs adults, all of them on days out at a bowling alley, while they work out who is lowest on the pecking order. And then there is the scene in the hairdresser's with the colostomy bag ... But I will leave you to discover that for yourself. For what I think has saved Mel, apart from the love of strong people around her, is that she is such a natural and gifted writer. Early on she says, while still in the entrails of intensive care, 'My sanity was ... to make sense of it to myself ... it was good copy.'

And so it bloody well was. The real reason we read is to get an injection of empathy; to help ourselves break out of the shell of our own experiences, and enter other human lives, so that we can understand this business of being alive just a little bit better. To do that we need really good writers on really big subjects. No, this is not probably a good book. It really is one, and reading it will change you.

PROLOGUE

It was a cold, blustery Sunday in late March, ordinary in the way days always are before extraordinary things happen. We had slept late and it was mid-afternoon before we headed to the nearby village for provisions. By then, the sky looked unkind. As we reached the point where our farm track joins the public road, we glimpsed a tall man in hiking gear, carrying a large pack, striding purposefully away from civilisation towards the forests and hills. There was something about him that I couldn't put my finger on, that made me notice him. He had a pleasant face but he looked – what? Anxious? Embarrassed? In a hurry?

'Bit late in the day to be going that way,' I remarked to Dave. Or maybe I just thought it. I can't remember now.

Dropping down into the village, we passed a neighbour out inspecting his hedgerow. A non-gardener, wearing smart trousers and a ski anorak, poking suspiciously at the unforthcoming soil. We slowed to say hallo, holding the car on the brake, not committed enough to put the engine in neutral.

'Just spoke to some crazy foreigner,' he said. 'Lost his way off the West Highland Way. I told him, I said, you're miles off, and he wanted to know what he should do, but I just told him, you'll need to head back the way you've come. Some people, eh?'

I waited in the car while Dave was in the shop. Rain started to blur the windscreen and I felt troubled. For the record, I'm no Mother Teresa. I don't make a habit of picking up lame ducks and I'm ever so slightly impatient with those who do. But there's something about travellers stranded on roadsides by breakdowns, or people who look lost, or in distress, that always makes me falter. Some primitive instinct, which I rarely act upon, makes me want to stop and offer help. Usually I dither, fail to act in case I look stupid, drive by and then regret it: the infinite frozen impulse, the wasted generosity, of the shy. The almost-nearly good Samaritan. Which, if you ask me, is more irritating than someone who lacks the impulse in the first place.

Being truly honest, I was still haunted by an incident from decades ago, when I was inside a tube station in London's West End, rushing for the last train after a show. There was a young man slumped against the wall at the bottom on the stairs, causing people to crush and crowd in their haste to get past. He had a bloodied stump, one leg freshly amputated at the knee, and he looked utterly desperate. He held a piece of cardboard which said: 'Please help me get back to Scotland'. And as I slowed, appalled, wanting to help, my companions grabbed me by the arms and hustled me onto a train. 'C'mon! We haven't time.' And for thirty years I've regretted not stopping to help that boy, often wondering what his story was. Did he ever get home?

This time, though, was different. I knew that road back over the hills was long and exposed and I felt emboldened.

When Dave got back in the car, I said: 'I think we should go and offer that guy a lift.'

'What guy?'

'The walker. The crazy foreigner.'

'You are kidding.' He turned to look at me as if I had sprouted two heads.

'Why?' He wanted to sit by the fire and read the Sunday papers.

'Because it will be pitch-dark long before he gets back to where he started, let alone where he was supposed to be going. It's pouring now and he's ten miles off course in the middle of nowhere.'

'He could be anyone. He could be some Eastern European axe-murderer.'

'Imagine if it was you, or us.'

So we ignored our turning for home and carried on the hill road. We caught up with him toiling into the dusk, a dark figure on a lonely ribbon of tarmac, just before he began the ascent to the moor. He didn't look like an axe-murderer.

We picked him up at the bottom of the hill on the Moor Road.

'Would you like a lift?' we said. 'We heard you were lost.' Speaking slowly and clearly so he could understand.

He smiled and put his sodden pack in the boot and climbed into the back seat, dripping. He seemed profoundly grateful and he expressed it in English. Excellent English, in fact. Our crazy foreigner was a Canadian university philosophy lecturer, a handsome, intelligent man in his thirties with a gentle manner. He'd flown over to attend a conference at Aberdeen University on, and I think I remember this rightly, Thomas Reid, a little-remembered Scottish moral philosopher of common sense during the Enlightenment. With the conference over, our academic had had a few days to play with before his flight home, and had a fancy to try the long-distance footpath that wends from Glasgow into the Highlands. After leaving his B&B in the morning, he'd missed a turning and had walked all day in the wrong direction. Looking back now, I suspect he was a dreamy, erudite man who just wanted to walk in the mountains, rather than a practical map reader.

By the time we got him back to the village where he'd slept, it was lashing rain and almost dark. He was a day out of sync with his accommodation. We insisted on taking him on, by road, to where he had booked a bed for the night. He protested mildly, not disguising his gratitude. When we stopped, at the car park by the shores of Loch Lomond, he got out, retrieved his pack from the boot, and returned to the driver's window. He leant down to thank us. We knew we would never meet again.

'You're good people,' he said warmly. 'Good things will happen to you.'

Five days later I fell off my horse and broke my neck.

CHAPTER ONE

FAREWELL HAPPY FIELDS

Who rides the tiger cannot dismount.
CHINESE PROVERB

I was happy, I do remember that, although those were the days when I rarely stopped long enough to appreciate it. Isn't it always the same old story – that hindsight is the teacher who always arrives too late and says I-told-you-so? We're always blissfully ignorant and complacent leading up to life-changing events.

So, how to pin down those hateful seconds which I will gnaw regretfully over for the rest of my life? One moment I was cantering towards a small-to-medium-sized cross-country jump, relishing the unity with my own, my very own, lovely handsome chestnut Champion the Wonder Horse, high on the hill and the thrill and the freedom and the wind in my face.

I was hearing the little girl inside me crying out, 'Look at me, look at me!' – the next moment I was pinned to the ground with a broken neck and fractured lower back. I was conscious throughout; I knew it was catastrophic. I said, 'Ow!' to myself when my face slammed into the turf, and then I experienced a blinding red flash and felt my whole body suffuse with a most beautiful, intense feeling of warmth; my own internal nuclear explosion; my own terrible mushroom cloud. In those seconds

High on the hill and the thrill.

I was already aware that my life as I knew it had ended. Everything had internalised. The only place where I could survive was in my head. The little girl was dead. Her dreams were atomised. Dust. You stupid, stupid idiot, I heard the voice inside my head. Damn, why did I let this happen to me?

Here are the bald facts. My horse refused a piddly jump, on a piddly little British Horse Society instruction day for piddly middle-aged wannabes playing with their piddly ponies. Harmless, happy people like me, playing at the bottom end of a thrilling, dangerous sport; pretending that I was thirty-two when I was fifty-two. I can still taste bitterness in my mouth, even as I write this, at the unfairness, the bad luck, the every-day, non-earth-shattering mundanity of the whole thing. I was a competent, experienced rider on a competent, steady horse, being coached by competent, qualified people. But horses are horses; they belong only to themselves. That day he didn't want to do it. Jumping stickily. He refused one practice fence. Jumped it the second time. We were still warming up. I doubly committed to go over another jump – 'Kick on, throw your heart over' as the old manuals taught – but he didn't. At the take-off stride, he ducked out sharply, I carried on going. And with impeccable hubris, my pride made me try to stay on by gripping his neck, which was the worst possible thing I could have done. It meant my arms were not in front of me when I hit the ground, so I did a fairly steep, slow-motion head plant. My body and long, long legs pivoted over my neck. 'It just looked like an ordinary fall,' said a friend nearby, shrugging helplessly at the memory. A millimetre or two difference, I would have been fine.

How to pin down the moment when your body deserts you? When you are forcibly divorced from yourself? Wedged face-down, I can taste dry, gritty, late winter Perthshire soil, and I realise I can't move anything but my right arm and my shoulders. My elbows flip-flop a little, like a seal. I reach down and touch my leg – the hand feels the leg, feels the texture of the riding breeches; the leg doesn't feel the hand. Doesn't feel it at all. I can't quite believe it, but I know what has happened. It really has happened – the thing I've always tried to put to the back of my head. The thing I sometimes dwelt upon, ever since I read about how the Hollywood actor Christopher Reeve, a tall, well-built man, had toppled over his horse's ears at a small jump and become paralysed from the neck down.

I manage to lift my shoulders a fraction, and turn my head. My left hand is lying out there, sprawled where I can see it. It responds a bit when I try to clench my fingers. This reassures me, oddly, and I put my face back down in the soil so I can think a bit. In a perfectly cold, logical part of my brain I'm utterly furious with myself. Arrogant enough to think it would never happen to me. But it has.

They have gathered round me by now, my friends, training-day organisers, the instructor. I can't feel my legs, I tell them, please phone for an ambulance. The two nice elderly men from the St John Ambulance, first-aiders in attendance at the course, have arrived. I can hear the anxiety in their voices, their fractured breathing. They put an oxygen mask on me. 'Lie still,' everyone is saying bossily to me, like they're rehearsing a training drill. 'I am,' I say grumpily. Then they start nagging me again: 'Keep talking. Don't fall asleep.' But I am growing weary and want to close my eyes. 'Please phone my husband. His number's on my mobile, in the pick-up,' I tell Helene, one of the organisers. Someone comes back. Says: 'There's an ambulance coming from Perth.' I nestle wearily into the soil. I'm struggling to think straight, but I know I have to try and stay in control. 'Phone for a helicopter too,' I say. Strangely unembarrassed. I hear them, voices off, urgent, ordering a helicopter, giving directions. On stage meanwhile, my monologue is internal.

The brain was still functioning. I held lucid conversations with the paramedics from Perth, who had arrived and were preparing a neck brace. Then, still face down, I heard the helicopter, felt the shock waves of noise, an implacable clatter descending above us. At the time, I convinced myself there were two; could have sworn I heard someone say: 'Here's another helicopter.' What a bloody waste, I remember thinking grumpily. Which was one way of expressing the whole catastrophe, although I didn't see the irony until later. Later the Royal Navy air-sea rescue pilot who picked me up told me I was wrong; there was only one chopper. But that's the tragi-comic essence of disaster: the everyday runs head-on into the bewildering.

They turned me, releasing me from the earth, slowly, carefully – I don't know how many of them, I couldn't feel their hands – onto a spinal board. I remember my vision spinning, the sky suddenly unbearably bright, but my head and neck were trussed with pads, so I could only look straight up, a small dinner plate of vision. My friend Katie was bending over me, telling me that I was going in a Sea King to the Southern General Hospital in Glasgow, where the main emergency specialities were. 'Check out the winchman, he's really dishy,' she told me. 'I'm coming with you.' She always could be inappropriate, but I think she was trying to buoy me up. Of all the emotions, the pressing one in my head was annoyance: one, for causing all this fuss, and two, for not being able to sit up and enjoy my trip in a helicopter. Perhaps shock was setting in.

The inside of the chopper was furiously dark, crowded, vibrating and noisy. I felt sick and claustrophobic, strapped down. Panic started to rise. He was indeed dishy, the winchman, in the rare moments he crossed my limited field of vision. He'd taken off his helmet. Mostly it was his voice I hung onto. I told him that I couldn't breathe and he leant over me, speaking softly but urgently to me above the noise: 'Yes you can. Keep breathing for me, girl. We'll be there in six and a half minutes. Do it for me.' Pure Mills & Boon. It felt profoundly intimate, romantic – but also heart-splintering, because in that same instant, deep down, I knew with absolute certainty that never again would a man lean over me wanting to make love to me. Those paralysed thighs would never part. A brief wave of insight and intense loss washed over me. I can be that precise: in a few seconds, in that maelstrom of noise, my sexual identity died. Lust is only one letter removed from lost.

The crew of the Sea King from HMS *Gannet*, based at Prestwick, treated me as an emergency, aware that with a high spinal injury I could easily lose the power to breathe. The pilot requested a direct route and air traffic control temporarily cleared our path of commercial aircraft so that the helicopter could fly straight to the hospital. In those days, before the Southern General was rebuilt into a high-rise city, the helicopter pad was on the ground, just next to A&E. I remember being transferred to a trolley, remember trying to be polite and thank the RAF crew as they wheeled me away. Already, by then, there was the sense of detachment. This is just too bad; it can't be happening to me, and I felt weary.

Things got a bit blurry after that. Time and cognitive slippage. Apart from everything else, it's very hard to discern what's happening when all you can see is a very small patch of ceiling. There was a warm, pretty female doctor in A&E who bent down to my ear and told me: 'You're going into resus now – it's going to be very noisy, lots happening, but don't worry,' and I clung to her words and her humanity. She had blue eyes and blonde curls. A feeling of almost unbearable loneliness was settling upon me with the knowledge that I was absolutely on my own in this. Only in my brain was there sanctuary.

Snippets only thereafter, those dreadful hours, as shock and morphine kicked in. I was struggling with the unfairness of it; I couldn't believe what had actually happened. Good Friday, it was; how inappropriate was that; and I'd taken the day off work to take part in the cross-country instruction. At some point my poor husband appeared at my bedside, his handsome, ever-optimistic face crushed with shock. Already, I think, he knew more than I did. At one point I remember being slid into an MRI scanner, immobile, staring at the plastic tube wall just a couple of inches above my face. White noise, claustrophobia: the very stillness made my ears boil. I was utterly passive; all will was gone; I no longer had a body. Is this what it feels like, I thought, losing everything?

It was in the scanner, though, that I had an epiphany. So weird was this experience, so unimaginable was it, at the cutting edge of catastrophe, immured like a mummy in a high-tech tube, that I suddenly thought – I've got to *tell* people about this, I've got to write about it. It's just so *interesting*. *Who knew?* On reflection, that point of deliberate detachment from myself was hugely important. It was self-preservation: a way of ensuring I kept control of my emotions. Steel shutters were clanging down in my head: I dared not even think about my son, just emerging from his teenage years, or of my sorry future. But I could safely bear witness and carry on writing in my head. A correspondent from a hidden war.

Another fragment of memory. A consultant came to talk to us. He was an orthopaedic surgeon, the director of the spinal unit. He placed one fist on top of the other, upwards, in a tower, like the playground game one-potato-two-potatoes, little fingers of one hand resting on the clenched thumb of the other.

'Horses, eh?' he said. 'Used to keep them myself. Dangerous things.' He seemed almost cheerful, as if I was more satisfying than a road accident. 'You have fractured your spine at T12,' he said, 'but that's not so important. You have broken your neck at C6; the two vertebrae have gone like this' – he angled his fists, bending the tower in half, 'and compressed the spinal cord on one side and stretched it on the other. That's where the damage is.'

'Is the cord severed?' I asked.

No, he said. And that was all I wanted to know. If it wasn't severed then there was hope.

What I didn't know was that Dave had already been taken aside and gently told to prepare for me being in a wheelchair for the rest of my life. He was to go home, this proud, tough, man's man, and spend the next two nights howling in despair and grief. Who can comfort anyone after news like that? And how can I ever escape the guilt of loading so much pain on him and on Douglas, my son – the two people who love me most in all the world? Even now, that is a kernel of grief which nestles at the centre of my being. I did this to me. But I did it to them too.

While wider family life was in meltdown, the news rippling out, by contrast I was removed to a place of eerie, enforced calm. My first night of my new life was spent in the high dependency unit, doped to the eyeballs on opiates. 'Serious but stable,' said the bulletin released to my colleagues in the media. I would need a delicate operation to stabilise my neck, but my timing had been exquisitely inappropriate: just as I ploughed into the soil, Jesus was believed to be rising from the dead, everyone was on holiday, and no neurological spinal surgery would take place until Tuesday. In the meantime, with a spine unstable in two places, I must be kept totally immobile, nil by mouth, fighting nausea.

The unit was a calm, bewildering, slow-motion cocoon. The room seemed soft round the edges, orangey in colour. I lay and stared at the dinner-plate bit of ceiling available to me, listening to a deranged woman nearby, raving in broad, angry Glaswegian. All I could move were my eyeballs. Hours passed without sleep, while my brain churned with despair. I was dimly aware, though, of a kind presence forever at my shoulder, stopping me from being alone, murmuring kind words. Early in the morning, before I was transferred to the spinal unit, someone – I presumed the same nurse – spoke. 'When you're better, come back and see me. My name is Bridget,' she said. The words strung themselves into a banner in my head, as fragile and as sturdy as Tibetan prayer flags. I grasped them as a lifeline. In the apricot dark, she had given me the gift of human company, connection, hope, a future. One day I would go back. It was the first positive thought I had had.

Years later, by sheer chance, I found Bridget. Who was in fact called Brenda, and it was her co-worker Kate who had sat at my shoulder all night. Morphine turns many nurses, in the perception of their patients, into the Angel of Mons, and many more, unfairly, into Nurse Ratched; but these women were special. What continues to astonish me is that they remembered me amongst the thousands of smashed-up bodies they see in a major trauma hospital.

'You were a fairly unusual case for us,' Kate told me. 'You were covered in mud from your fall. But what I remember was the way you lay awake all night, just looking at the ceiling. I could see your mind turning over and over. And I remember desperately wishing I could do something to put it right, to turn back the clock for you …' her voice trailed off '… but all I could do was sit beside you sponging your mouth. We washed the mud off you in the morning. And I've often thought about you since, wondered what happened to you.'

As I have wondered myself.

CHAPTER TWO

PUT YOUR FINGER IN THE CROW'S NEST

The Warden owns the shade.
LOUIS SACHAR, *HOLES*

An apricot-coloured world, shading to russet, was actually rather an intriguing place to inhabit. You don't sleep, when you're on morphine, you just travel to strange places behind your eyelids, restless journeys through an orange landscape, journeys which leave you exhausted and confused. At night, I frequently found myself at the bottom of a cave, looking up like a potholer at rock faces which were clad with thick, hand-knitted russet wool – chunky cable-stitch, knitted on a giant's great big fat knitting needles, as if to give you hand-holds when you climbed, but I didn't need them because I was on some kind of cherry-picker, floating effortlessly up, up, up, exploring the openings and ledges on the woolly surface. Close to, I leant in and examined the texture, the thick twists of cable stitch. Up, up, I go, high into the stifling dark of orange woolliness.

That was one of the nicer destinations to which morphine took me. Other times, when it was daylight, and I was gazing at the ceiling tiles in the ward, I saw crude graffiti had been scratched. Evil messages to me. I caught the words subliminally. *Fuck off*, it said. But when I trailed my eyes slowly back to look more closely, the words had disappeared. Sometimes the tiles lifted at the edges, and I saw eyes peering down at me – sometimes rats' eyes, other times, illegal immigrants'. Somewhere, in some sane fragment of my brain, I was horrified – my illiberal subconscious was betraying me, my inner *Daily Mail* reader emerging. The other part of me was preoccupied with the need to tell the authorities. Surely they shouldn't be there. Not living in the ceiling. I knew things were bad in the NHS but surely not that bad. I felt under threat. But before I could call out, express it, the morphine carried me away somewhere else, and I forgot.

For three days, over the Easter holiday weekend, I lay motionless in the high-dependency ward of the spinal unit, waiting for my surgery. They had me on a specialist spinal bed, which tilted from side to side, to relieve pressure on my skin, and I was allowed neither to eat nor drink. Every so often the nurses wet my lips with a sponge on a stick. I pleaded for water, but they could not give me any. I pleaded with them to turn my pillow, to relieve the pressure on my head, but they refused to do it as often as I would like, because the neck was unstable. It took three of them to do it – two keeping my head motionless. The other one flipping the pillow. For three days I was unaware of anything else from the real world. I don't know if Dave was there; I drifted.

My only certainty was that the ward was a dangerous, volatile place and I was a silent witness, buffeted and bewildered by the drugs. My instinct was to hang onto consciousness and concentrate very hard on survival. My view, when I was with it enough to open my eyes, was still that bit of ceiling. Out of the dark, in the periphery of my vision, emerged a face. A tiny woman with short grey hair; a kindly, self-effacing sprite whose voice offered me a mooring. 'I'm Christine. I'm your named nurse,' she told me. 'I'll look after you now. Together, we'll get you through this. Things are going to get better.'

The connection she made held me, steadied me, a rope to the shore. She told me she had been a spinal nurse for more than forty years; she spoke with confidence and calm optimism. When she was not there I drifted alone again, fearful. Over the time I spent in hospital, I was cared for by dozens of nurses who were, like all human beings, a mixture of sensitive and insensitive, flawed and uncannily dedicated. With all of them, I sought kindness and a connection; the essence, surely, of any benign human relationship. And with most I found it, with few it was lacking. There was no other nurse, though, who gave me utmost sanctuary in the way Christine did when I was most in need.

Days and nights merged and I was unaware.

I could not feel my body, but I sensed strongly that my legs were raised up in the air in front of me. Floating up high. Later I learnt this was a common phenomenon of a new spinal injury, because they weren't; they were flat on the bed. The other pressing physical sensation was of a steel band tightening around my ribcage, like the hoop holding together a whisky barrel. I could feel nothing else in my torso but that band. Most peculiar. Later I discovered this was my diaphragm. Our bodies, brilliantly evolved to survive, breathe in two ways – via the intercostal muscles around the lungs, and by the action of the diaphragm. The connections for each emerge from the spinal cord at different levels, like a safety net, a fallback system: I had lost the first but retained the second. My injury had paralysed my chest muscles and I was breathing solely by the rise and fall of my diaphragm. Had the break happened a few millimetres higher, both would have been knocked out and I'd have needed a tracheotomy and a machine to breathe for me. But I didn't know this. I knew very little. I had no skin sensation at all … could only feel my head and back of my neck on the pillow. Just to test I was alive, and to release some distress, I chewed angrily at my bottom lip, the only autonomous action left to me. Just then I vividly appreciated the attraction of self-harm. Soon I could taste blood, but felt absolutely no pain. Why wasn't it hurting? Only much later did I realise that this was the effect of the morphine.

Because my neck was unstable, they needed to secure the vertebrae at the front with a small metal plate. Before the operation, there were chats, which I only very vaguely remember, with both the anaesthetist and the neurosurgeon. The operation was tricky because my neck had swollen so much that from the ears down my neck flared out towards my shoulders, like some monstrous steroid-happy body-builder. It looked so grotesque Dave did not allow Dougie to visit me for several days.

'You made an international prop forward look swan-necked.'

So swollen was my throat that the act of intubating me for the anaesthetic was risky and the operation, to plate the front of my sixth cervical vertebrae, took several hours. Afterwards they were worried that my throat would close up with the additional trauma, so they kept me on a ventilator to breathe for me, a big fat air tube in through my mouth and down into my lungs, and I was even more sedated. I couldn't speak. A drip fed my body with fluid; a catheter drained it out. Of all this I was oblivious. I also had a nasal-gastric tube up my nose and down my throat, through which they passed the ground-up drugs into my stomach. When I was with-it enough to cry, the tears ran into my ears and soaked the tape securing the feeding tube to my face. I could do nothing about this; it was the same exquisite misery as when you have a streaming cold but are unable to blow your nose. The only thing to do was try not to cry. Christine had told me things would get better and she never let me down – I just had to take shelter in my head and hang on.

To enable me to communicate while on the ventilator, the nurses hung a laminated card with an alphabet by my right arm. After my fall, Pam, a dear friend of many years, rushed from France to support Dave. I have snatches of memory of them both at my bedside, with me conducting irritable, faltering mime conversations with them, spelling out the words by waving my right forefinger at the letters. My mind – I was convinced – was as clear as a bell; I became increasingly exasperated when they failed to keep up with my slow-motion spelling and grasp the words. They can't be this stupid, I thought crossly. One day they arrived and said happy birthday – I remember feeling a genuine sense of shock and surprise. My birthday was 13 April, surely not yet. But I had lost control of time; I'd been on a ventilator for more than a week and the sound of its rhythm, sucking and sighing, the persistent beep-beep-debeepbeep behind my head, had become the vortex of my entire life. My real world was inside the apricot. I waited, while the scene changes came thick and fast and the only constant was the machine, sighing and pinging apologetically.

Some nights, my bed was in the corner of a room that was being used for a party. They'd opened an Indian restaurant on the ward. There were vast buffets of curry spread out, people came and went, laughing. My bed kept being moved. Every day I was in a different room and strived to orientate myself. One night I had a bird's-eye view overlooking a city, which lay across the curve of a bay. In the dark the lights of the city were twinkling, reflecting across the water. Another night, workmen, wearing high-vis jackets, were digging up the floor around me. Then my bed split in two across the middle and I was sliding down into the gap, suspended over dark, deep water, and I kept crying out to the nurses to tell them I was going to drown, but they didn't understand. One nurse was lying on the floor behind my bed snogging a workman. Another night, I was kidnapped – strangers used a fork-lift truck to take me, on my bed, out the back of the ward and stow me in a horsebox. They wanted me to go back to the cross-country course and testify that my accident was not their fault.

A family game from childhood haunted me, the rhyme shimmying around in my head. It had come from my mother, who played it in Northern Ireland in the 1920s on the way to picnics on the beach, sometimes Tyrella, sometimes Ballywalter. We played it too, obediently, on the back seat of the car. You crossed two fingers from one hand, opened a little, over the two fingers on the other hand, creating a neat, square, inviting hole in the middle. As you offered the gap to the person next to you, you chanted:

Put your finger in the crow's nest
The crow's not at home
He's gone to Ballywalter to gather shelly stones …

And then, squeezing on the other person's finger, you shouted:

He's coming
He's coming
He's nipping!
He's nipping!

And you squeezed and squeezed, and held them, trapped tight by the finger, until they squealed for mercy.

At one of the ward rounds, in a window of comparative sanity, I remember meeting my consultant for the first time. Mariel Purcell was young, a tall cool stylish Irishwoman, with long dark hair she wore loose. She wore sassy dresses and high heels. 'We are keeping you on the ventilator,' she told me. 'You have a lung infection and we are giving you antibiotics.' Later, when I was off the ventilator, she was more expansive. It was pneumonia. I was strangely thrilled, in the way you are when you're a kid and you're going to have something to boast about when you go back to school. It was like being eight again, falling off roller skates and cracking a bone in your wrist. But at that point I was just frustrated. I'm fine, I tried to tell her with my eyes. The purgatory of the ventilator jammed in my mouth was becoming unbearable. I wanted it taken out. I pleaded with the nurses on my alphabet card. W-H-E-N? T-O-D-A-Y? At the weekend, they said. Soon. They lied. Lied repeatedly and prodigiously.

The weekend never came. Day followed day. I inhabited some lost bit of space, some cul-de-sac on the dark side, all alone, floating along in my own ghastly spaceship of tubes and sighs. Beep-beep-debeepbeep. Beep-beep-debeepbeep.

I remember when they took the ventilator out – there was an unpleasant rippling sensation as the corrugated ridges of the tube were withdrawn from my throat, I had a fleeting vision of those perforated blue drainage pipes, the kind you dig into the soil of your garden. Then it was over and I was drawing in my own air, could talk again. My jaw and my ears ached, despite the morphine, my tongue so dry and fat I was barely decipherable. I pleaded for a drink, but they refused: it was still too dangerous for me to try swallowing. At one point Christine moved across my line of vision, dragging a machine on wheels.

'You don't know this, but today is a very good day, a very significant day for you.'

I looked quizzical.

She smiled her shy smile. 'I'm taking the ventilator away from your bed space. You're making real progress.'

At some point during that time, on a morning ward round, the doctors clustered inside the curtains round my bed and asked to do an anal examination. What I didn't know was that this was the test to see how paralysed I was. The spinal cord ends in the perineal area, your bottom, and if you have sensation in your anus, it indicates how badly injured your spine is.

I was rolled on my side and they stood behind me. Can you feel that? Can you clench your bottom? No, I said. Nothing. They were silent, grave. I decided, in my morphine haze, to be a good hostess and fill the silence to cover up any embarrassment. After all, my body was the party, wasn't it? 'That's the nicest anal examination I've ever had,' I said in a jolly more-tea-vicar sort of voice, trying to lighten the atmosphere, turning my head so I could grin at them. I didn't understand why they didn't smile back.

The severity of a spinal injury is measured on a scale developed by the American Spinal Injury Association – the ASIA impairment scale. If you are Asia A, you're completely buggered, basically: you have no power or sensation preserved below the injury to your spine. You will not recover function. Asia B, you have sensory feeling below the injury but your muscles don't work. Asia C, some muscles do work but they're very weak. Asia Ds have muscles, at least half of which have reasonable strength and they can walk. And Asia Es, lucky creatures, are normal healthy people.

I was diagnosed Asia A. Completely buggered. They didn't tell me that. Not then.

Only the ward was real. My other life had receded to some distant place. My sanity, my compensation, was to pretend I was indeed that war correspondent on the front line, compelled to start recording this crazy story, to make sense of it to myself. Besides, it was good copy. I was finding things quite fascinating, in a rather grotesque way. By writing, I figured, I could justify my absence to my bosses at my newspaper, *The Times*. It's peculiar how much of a priority this felt at the time – a measure, I suppose, of my desperate determination to hold onto something familiar and re-establish some control. Work could save me, keep me viable. At the same time, it represented escape from emotional anguish. Very few things made chronological sense to me. Unbeknownst to me, Dave came every day. Other visitors were discouraged by the hospital and he was like a Rottweiler keeping people at bay. Later I heard some of the details of events outside: Dougie had been away on an Easter ski trip in the Alps and apparently it took him a couple of days to get home; his mates performed a heroic drama-filled dash to get him to Geneva. I honestly don't remember the moment when I first saw him at my bedside; grief and morphine have kindly erased the memory of the encounter. I hope he has forgotten too: but even now, years later, I am unable to ask him, in case I reawaken the pain. In some dark corner, I have a terrible memory of trying to give him a thumbs-up gesture with my right hand as he left, and realising with shock that I couldn't; my thumb wouldn't move – simultaneously realising that he had perceived the same thing. At the time I was aware only of the unbearable hurt I had inflicted on my child ... and him being extraordinarily brave and composed and trying to comfort me.

Dougie's best friends from university, I much later discovered, came to stay at our home with him to comfort him during the first couple of weeks. I thought that was wonderful, that he had friends as fine as that. He was always more of a doer than a dreamer and I realised after my calamity that he was happiest when I asked him to do practical things; it was welcome distraction. When he knew I wanted to record what was happening to me, he brought in his Dictaphone. After he had gone I asked the nurses to place it beside me on the pillow and switch it on. I spent half an hour or so rambling gently about how I'd got here, trying to be professional, coherent. I had a job to do. A job to try and keep. I expressed anger at my own stupidity in falling off. Then I ran out of energy and the machine kept running, recording my breathing and the voices of the visitors in the bay opposite mine. Perhaps in my head that corner of the ward was still a curry shop at the time, or maybe by then I was at the stage of being convinced that a crowd of football casuals had got in and were trying to steal from my bedside cabinet. Shimmying between sanity and madness, I managed to summon the wit to ask a passing nurse to hit the off switch.

The next day Dougie took the Dictaphone and promised to email the recording to London.

They must have transcribed it and put something in the paper because at one point Su Pollard phoned the ward to talk to me, which was precisely the moment I knew my spaceship had landed on another planet. Su Pollard, for those under forty, is a wacky English character actress best known for a sitcom in the 1980s called *Hi-de-Hi*, which I had been aware of, as a young twenty-something, as a piece of cheesy middle-brow telly for my parents' generation. A totem of its time, like Morecambe and Wise. Su is famous for eccentrically outsize glasses and a funny voice. Good-humoured Eighties kitsch. I had never met her in my life.

'Call for you,' said a nurse, holding the phone, eyebrows raised, a rather amused expression. 'It's Su Pollard.'

It must be a morphine moment. She would drift away in a minute.

'THE Su Pollard?' I said.

'Sounds like her.'

'But I don't know her.'

'It's you she asked to speak to.'

Of all the people I least expected to discuss my plight with,
it was Peggy Ollerenshaw.

Too random. Had to be opiates. The nurse held the phone
to my ear and I had a short, apparently lucid conversation with
someone who sounded exactly like the hapless holiday camp
chalet maid Peggy Ollerenshaw whom I'd occasionally seen on
TV thirty years ago.

'Your article moved me so much I had to phone you and
speak to you. You're very brave and I send you lots of love,' she
said.

'That's really sweet of you,' I said lamely.

'I'm rooting for you.'

'Thank you.'

I still don't know if it really happened or not.

At night, I experiment with the only bit of my body that still answers me, that has a glimmer of feeling. My right hand, weak and floppy and fast becoming numb, fumbles down past layers of exhausting obstacles, past sheets and tubes and swaddling gowns to reach the bare skin of my hip. Exploring in the dark. The one-way sensation of touching my own warm skin, and feeling nothing back, is most peculiar, as if it is an alien I am attached to. My fingers are not giving me trustworthy signals, because their nerve connections are damaged too, and retreating further into shock. What's so devastating is that the skin I touch feels fleecy, beautiful, devastating; all these things at the same time. Because it belongs to me but it doesn't belong to me. It's someone else's; it's like reaching down and touching your lover's body in the night. How peculiar. Four-fifths of my body has divorced me, but it's still attached to me. I'm two people – me and the rest of me. I am eerily still … but inside I'm screaming and waving. I'm helpless as a beetle on its back, except my legs don't even wave to express it. My name, it would seem, is still Melanie and I am a doubly-incontinent tetraplegic. Where do I go from here, seeing I have already blurted out something about Switzerland and Dr Purcell didn't respond?

The movie *Trainspotting* was really accurate, you know. The stuff about coming off morphine, when your body is a seething rats' nest and nothing will calm it. Although I didn't realise what was happening at the time, because I didn't even know I had been on morphine. All I knew was that it felt worse than anything I'd ever experienced. Even though my body was paralysed and insensate, I felt that it was jangling all over, itching, shivering – compelling me to cry out for relief, for death, for anything to make it stop. Inside my brain, restless leg syndrome multiplied a million times, ants crawled inside my skin, devouring me from within. One vivid day I became convinced my bedding was soaked. The mattress and bottom sheet were sloshing in icy water: I was certain I was freezing alive, shivering, nagging for more blankets.

'I can't give you any more blankets,' said the nurse. 'You're not cold.'

'Please, I'm freezing,' I wheedled. 'Please. Be kind.'

'Kind?' she said. 'Heart like a swinging brick, me.'

She wasn't joking. She was on duty one weekend morning when they were desperately short-staffed – they often were at weekends – and running very late, taking hours it seemed to me to attend to each of us high-dependency patients in turn, log-rolling us to wash us. The morphine withdrawal must have been at its peak, for I started crying out from the sensations in my head. Outwardly motionless on the bed, I was inwardly consumed by chemical distress and bewilderment. I could see them log-rolling someone else in the distance; although I must have been imagining it, because the curtains were always closed when they were washing someone. The room kept changing in shape. I shouted again but still no one came. Of all I had experienced after my accident, in its totality, that was my most desperate lonely moment, the point when I couldn't go on. Like someone near death, my instinct was to shout for my mother. But she was dead, I knew that, so I shouted for my sister. She lived in France and I had not yet seen her, but I had regressed to childhood; my big sister would make it better. Lindsay would make them help me.

'What d'you want?'

It was Swinging Brick and she was pissed off.

'I feel awful,' I said. 'Please …'

'We're busy with other patients. We'll get to you when we can.'

I never cried out again.

Lots of other patients vocalised their distress; I listened jealously to them screaming and yelling, calling out repeatedly. I was too repressed, too polite. Posh girl in bedlam. It's only funny now, much later. How I used to envy them their release, these unseen uninhibited souls who raged aloud, who set loose their pain upon the world at large. I wished I too could wail and curse. The way I'd been brought up, you suffered in silence, you were never rude, never made a fuss. There was one voice I often heard shouting at night – a young argumentative male who roared with anger and rage, despair coming from the deepest, darkest torture chamber. 'Why?' he used to shout. 'Why can't I fucking move? Just tell me why.'

I asked Christine about him.

She sighed. 'Oh, that's Snafu. He's one of mine too.'

'Is he OK?'

'He's finding it hard.' She sounded sad. She didn't say any more. I would find out later for myself.

In general the cursing was epic. Legendary. When West of Scotland working man meets catastrophe all he needs is a victim to let rip upon. The spinal unit had a resident psychologist, a gentle New Zealander, a bit of a waffler who must have helped some people lost in the shock of paralysis, but I found him irritating. Everything he said seemed anodyne. But then who wouldn't seem ineffectual, with the unenviable job of counselling people in the rawest of grief? We existed in a world beyond platitudes, beyond consolation. On the ward, I still couldn't raise my head to see anything but I lay and listened, as would a blind person, to the voices and the noises.

The darkest of five-star entertainment came one afternoon when the psychologist was sent to counsel an older man who was refusing to cooperate with the nurses. Grunt was a tiny Glaswegian hardman, paralysed from the neck down, who was taking his plight as a personal insult and was either beyond or incapable of reason. He launched a verbal assault upon the hapless Kiwi, a tsunami of violent Glasgow kisses which no curtains round a bed could confine. His tirade was loud, sustained, fluent, uninhibited and utterly priceless: the hair-dryer treatment, poetry of the utterly profane, articulating all the pain and fury inside him. Grunt was no doubt a talented curser already, but neuroscience shows that swearing actually helps people biologically to relieve extreme distress, and he was going for it. The caress of the damned, it occurred to me.

'Fuck off. Who the fuck are you? Jesus fucking Christ what's it to you? What the fuck do you fucking want? Yer fucking useless waste of space, yer fucking stupid idiotic cunt, nah, nah, get out of my fucking face yer fat cunt and leave me alone.'

'Now I git it why you're upsit,' said the Kiwi, his voice high and mild.

'Upset, you useless piece of shit? I'll give yer fucking cunting upset, you bastard.'

'B-b-but it would hilp to talk, chick out some thoughts, it's nicissary for you to ixpress yoursilf …'

'If I could fucking move I'd fucking express maself, I'd wring yer fuckin neck. Just get to fuck … right?'

'Yis, Grunt … I understand.'

'Away back to Australia yer stupid speccy bastard, yer useless cunt. Someone should have drowned ye at birth.'

And so it continued. Lying on my back, silently chortling, I was joined by one of the nurses, who dashed in behind my half-pulled curtain, stuffing her apron in her mouth to silence the giggles. We shared a wonderful private, silent moment of hilarity. It was the first time I had laughed since the accident.

Perhaps it was the third week in high dependency when I became aware lots of things were starting to happen. I'd regained the breathing; now it was basic stuff like drinking normally. Previously, much as I had pleaded, the specialist designated two-woman swallowing team, who came round and judged these things, had deemed me unfit to do so. They were the Fat Controllers of the gullet: at one point, they tested me with a sip of tea from a straw while they stood and watched, unsmiling, pens poised over clipboards. They seemed spectacularly humourless, these specialist teams. I sucked with a degree of arrogance. Of course I was fine! But much as I craved it, drinking was weirdly difficult. I found myself spluttering, coughing, and they shook their heads and took the tea away.

After that, I stopped pushing against the system. A few days later, they granted permission. A kindly staff nurse, to whom I had confided my fantasy about a latte, went and bought me one from the café. But what I had yearned for tasted acrid, strong, too hot. I turned instead, gratefully, to sucking weak, tepid, milky NHS tea – baby tea, they called it – through a straw, as she held the cup. I couldn't believe that I couldn't hold a cup by myself, but then I had not even started to address the size of physical loss which I faced. Denial piled up on itself; like bricks in a wall. I had nowhere near yet exhausted what Brian Keenan called the strategies of denial, convincing myself that if I could just take back control and start doing things for myself, then all would return to normal. I thought my hands would work if I really asked them to – of course they would! – so I asked the nurse to leave that day's pile of greetings cards upon my bedclothes in front of me, rather than set them aside for Dave. Anyone can open an envelope! Surely! I tried to pick up the top card and watched with bewilderment as my fingers refused to grip. I didn't even get to the stage of finding out they couldn't rip paper. Then the cards slid slowly off my chest onto the floor and I watched them go, passive and helpless. So much for Get Well Soon.

My right wrist, though, had something still going for it. There was still strength there. The hand therapist Leslie had come to see me and, upon her instructions, Dougie went shopping and found me a travel cup with the handle open at the bottom. I could wedge my palm under the handle and lift a mug of that precious baby tea high enough up to drink through a straw – my first independent action. Likewise, when the Gullet Controllers had carried out Protocol Two Testing, Permission to Take Solids, I was given yoghurts and found I was just about able, by myself, to dig in a spoon and then transfer it to my mouth. The feeding tube, a ghastly uncomfortable thing that had been strapped to my cheek and down my throat for weeks, was withdrawn – a peculiar sensation as the nurses reeled the long, thin pipe out of my stomach via my nostrils, as if hauling in the garden hose. At the time I took little notice of such progression, unimpressed, impatient merely that I was so feeble at simple tasks. As I mocked and fretted, denial built. Only later, wiser and humbler, did I come to understand the extraordinary significance of this hand–mouth coordination, and how lucky I was: so many people with broken necks, several of them in the unit with me, could not do this basic task and were doomed to total dependency in order to survive. Others needed months of hand therapy, and specially adapted implements, to be able to drink by themselves or reach their mouths with food.

Time to sit up a little, another milestone. I was fitted with a white collar, like a Star Wars Storm Trooper, so that my neck was supported when my bedhead was raised a few degrees for the first time. This meant my first view of the new world. It also meant I saw my legs for the first time. Not good. Nothing – nothing at all – can prepare you for the appearance of those paralysed limbs, sprawled where you do not feel them to be on the bed, lifeless and somehow deeply misshapen. Someone else's legs, not yours. I felt physically sick. They looked like the Guy Fawkeses we made as children for bonfire night, newspaper stuffed into an old pair of tights, puffy and lumpy in the wrong places, knees and ankles askew like scarecrows. These weren't my legs at all; they were horrific, alien objects.

Perhaps that's what happens when you face sudden, extreme disability as an adult: a sense of disconnect, of disbelief, which I can best describe as a compound fracture of the soul. Losing the use of one's legs is profound, an event so fundamentally wrong that it catapults you through a door which no one else who has full function can possibly enter, into a place which often is the loneliest place in the world. Humans were not meant not to be able to walk; we are hard-wired to move, and at the deepest level we understand that in movement lies our ability to survive, to feed, to keep warm, to seek shelter, to procreate, to interact. Mobility is caveman stuff – we are programmed to understand, somewhere in our ancient genes, that those who cannot keep up are left behind to the wolves. When wild animals and primitive people fall ill, or fail with age, or grow lame, they drop back from the herd. It is natural. Those who cannot walk are left behind; they become isolated; their weakness overtakes them; they stop, lie down and die. Elephants do it; sheep do it; Native American people did it. By allowing the healthy to move on, unburdened, nature ensures the survival of nature. Walking therefore has a grip over our imagination, which helps to explains healthy people's subconscious prejudice against wheelchairs, manifest in their impatience and irritation and sometimes open hostility. Civilisation in certain instances can desert us in a flash, because deep down it's about life or death. Walk and win. Go off your feet and you're history.

Now I'm sure everyone, should they ever be forced to part with them, would be partial to their own legs, but I'd always been particularly attached to mine and my initial feeling was absolute bewilderment. They weren't slim or beautiful, my legs, but they were so unusually long they defined who I was: a thirty-six-inch inside measurement, longer than most men's, making me over six feet tall without shoes on. I liked that. They

Long legs were good for skiing. In the Alps in the yuppie 1980s.

gave me scope, shaped my identity: in their time they had pogoed to punk bands, skied down black runs, ran half marathons, walked up mountains and done crazy charity endurance stunts. This is humblebragging, isn't it? I'm boasting, pathetically, about something I don't possess any more. But it is the only way I can plot the scale of my loss. My legs were my closest allies, my ever-ready Amazonian accomplices, enabling me always to skip away from bores and bossiness and bureaucracy. Catch me if you can. All of which made my present situation even more difficult; the sense of bereavement even more profound. Without my legs, I was baffled. What now? I'm sure every sporty person, every individualist and risk-taker who has ever damaged their spine, feels the same. How did we bridge the imagination gap between what was, and what is? Who was this godforsaken new person who could not move?

I did not know them. Nor did I know what they might become. Nor, quite frankly, did I have any intentions of finding out. I was going to get better.

Paralysis. The Venerable Bede prescribed a cure. 'Scarify the neck after the setting of the sun and silently pour the blood into running water. After that, spit three times, then say: "Have thou this unheal and depart with it."'

Paralysis. According to Wikipedia, defined by the loss of voluntary movement or motor function. A late Old English word, via Latin from Greek *paralusis*, from *paraluesthai* 'be disabled at the side', from *para* 'beside' + *luein* 'loosen'. A term used figuratively from 1813.

Paralysis. According to the Egyptian physician Imhotep, 3,000 to 2,500 years BC: 'If thou examinest a man having a dislocation in a vertebra of his neck, shouldst thou find him unconscious of his two arms and his two legs on account of it (and) urine drips from his member without his knowing it, his flesh has received wind, his two eyes are bloodshot … he has an *emissio seminis* which befalls his phallus, thou shouldst say concerning him, "an ailment not to be cured".' Give or take the phallus, old Imhotep was spot on.

Paralysis: all in all, a complete bastard of a word.

The human skeleton is designed to protect your core nervous system at all costs: the vertebrae link like chain-armour around it, grow bony spikes on the outside to foil intruders. The spinal cord is the wiring from central command and control; it is the engine of your free will; the power and pleasure of your flesh. When the spinal cord is damaged, it is indeed like a nuclear attack, the ultimate hit. Your body does everything it can in defence: it shuts down, retreats into itself, sends fluid to the site of the injury. Every resource available goes to the core and the extremities get forgotten about. The surface of your hands and feet become thickened and leathery with excess skin. Your heart rate slows, you start to retain litres of water and swell all over. The body remains in a state of suspended animation for four to six weeks, during which time accurate diagnosis of the extent of your injury can be impossible. Some weeks after my accident a deep ridge started to emerge from the cuticles at the bottom of my fingernails and slowly grew its way up: a tremor in my body's rock stratum; a record of the geological seismic shock within me.

They don't hang about on the NHS. As soon as my neck was judged suitably stable, they started to hoist me into a wheelchair. There is a set regime to protect the skin on your backside from pressure sores. You start with half an hour a day in the chair, then an hour. You build up. You carefully toughen your epidermis to its new weight-bearing role in life. Overnight, your buttocks have become the soles of your feet. When you accustom the skin to that fact, you've reached the magic goal in spinal rehab of 'up as able'. You're then allowed to sit in your chair all day. This process takes weeks.

Getting up was a ritual like preparing a medieval knight for battle, a fairly accurate reflection of the pace of life with a spinal injury – achingly slow, with progress measured on a scale too tiny for the able-bodied to contemplate. Understand the mammoth effort, you able-bodied, and you will never again take for granted the fast, fluid ability to sit up in bed, swing your legs over the side, and stand up. First, the nurses have to dress you. It feels like they are stuffing a giant sausage. No underwear, just the baggiest T-shirt and joggers you possess. I had asked the boys to bring me in one of my 10k race T-shirts and the nurses cut the neck to widen it. It was a symbol of who I really was and my statement of intent – a sporty person who shouldn't be here. Mistaken identity. As reality bit, I felt embarrassed and threw it away.

Then they put on my high, choking collar and they rolled me on the bed into a hard white plastic shell, a back brace, to protect my lower-down fracture, until, trussed, I resembled a Storm Trooper even more closely. Why was I so miscast? Didn't they realise I was actually, in my past life, a female Jedi warrior? The brace on the collar extended down my sternum; the body brace came up to meet it. Thrust up into the gap between, elevated like some spoof medieval embonpoint, came my breasts. They sprouted, insensate, near my chin.

'Jesus, your tits look amazing,' said a male colleague who came to visit me a couple of weeks later, 'like they're peeking over the garden fence.' Never was there a less sensual image.

Only then, fully armoured, was it time to be hoisted into a chair. Lack of balance and orientation from weeks spent lying flat, plus the low blood pressure endemic to my injury, made this an ordeal. Seasick and head swimming, headsick and seaswimming, I was rolled to get the hoist cradle under me, and then lifted up to dangle for all the world like a dead cow in an abattoir; whereupon they lowered me into a wheelchair, rocking me forward and back until my weight was centralised. The whole process was exhausting, lengthy and discombobulating. That first time, I cried out in fear – I had a terrifying sensation that my head was loose and was going to fall off backwards, so

the physiotherapists fashioned a temporary cardboard extension to the chair back to comfort me. They told me my neck
was completely stable and things would get easier but I was not
convinced. Inside, I screamed at the indignity and the horror
of it: outwardly, I put on a grim smile and told myself sternly
that this was progress. This was how to get better. First goal, get
used to the chair. Then begin the recovery.

Once in the chair, I could resume some adult responsibility.
My immediate boss at *The Times*, Magnus Linklater, had been
one of the very few allowed in to visit soon after the accident.
He had told me not to worry, and kissed me on the forehead.
The kiss struck me as terribly kind but rather worrying. Was I
really so ill? It was evident to all but me. Then Anne Spackman,
the comment editor, who told me she had wept as she transcribed that initial tape recording, flew up from London. I
showed her how, now I was up, I could use a laptop with one
finger. I couldn't grasp why everyone seemed so surprised about
my determination to try and get working again. Anne was
followed by the editor of *The Times* at the time, James Harding.
The nurses arranged for me to meet him in the conference
room. Hazily fearful, I think I expressed my insecurities about
the future. He could not have been more supportive. Could I
continue to write, I asked hesitantly. The professional editor in
me, despite the madness of the morphine, smelt a source of
good copy. Of course I could, he said. In fact, he wanted a
weekly column about my recovery, to be published in the
Saturday magazine. My heart, I remember, leapt.

'The only thing is, we don't know what to call it.'

'Oh, I've already thought about that. What about "Spinal
Column"?'

Did he know, this most human, warm, sophisticated man, that he was handing me a precious lifeline? Not just in terms of my family's future, but of my psychological survival. Here was a chance for me to create my own biographical narrative, to write towards some kind of redemption.

Labouring under many illusions, and feeling quite breezy – I do think the opiates were largely to blame at that stage – I then tackled my first session in the gym, which swiftly brought home the brutal realities of my situation. The cruel parallels of two worlds were beginning to impact on me, old and new crushing me between them: the gyms as I had been familiar with them, Lycra-ed temples of beautiful fit bodies in motion; and gyms, paralysis-style, where broken, frozen people were propped upright, in various stages of disorientation and bewilderment. Plus, there were unseen horrors to discover. I was about to have a crash course in the reality of paralysed bowels. As two physiotherapists used a hoist to lift me from wheelchair to specialist rehabilitation plinth, gravity struck. My bowels suddenly and involuntarily emptied. The only way I knew was by the sound and then the nostril-fluttering smell, which trapped me in a ghastly freeze of humiliation. What was the famous Nike gym slogan? Just do it? Well I just did. 'Uh-oh,' said the physiotherapist at the wrong end.

Too upset even to cry, I could only stammer my apologies, but they were totally nonplussed, matter-of-fact. Don't worry, they said. Part of the job. Happens all the time. For me it seemed catastrophic. My first morning in the gym, when I had planned to hit the machines, develop sizeable shoulders and start my legs moving again, all within the space of an hour, and there I was being lowered, stinking, onto pads on the wheel-chair, hurried back to the ward, laboriously hoisted again onto a bed of pads and rolled and cleaned like a baby. I was getting an inkling of what exactly paralysis entailed.

Over the next few days, I had a few more brief sessions in the gym when, thank God, my bowels did not betray me. The gym offered a welcome distraction from reflection. It wasn't wise to sit and dwell on your plight. 'Gym,' one cynical spinal consultant once muttered, 'is really only there to take people's mind off things.' You hid your despair as much as you could, if only because too many tears invoked a dreaded visit from the Kiwi psychologist, whose amiable 'Have you got time for a chit?' confirmed to you that matters really were wrist-slittingly terminal.

The gym in fact, became all-consuming. I got my first taste of what it would take to strengthen my arms and shoulders and returned to the ward furious at my own weaknesses. Where was bloody superwoman now? Ten minutes on the handcycle – where my hands were bandaged to a set of handles rotating at shoulder height – left me puffing as I would once have done running on a treadmill. Another big test was to propel myself for the first time in a chair. It sounds so easy but it was such a ridiculously difficult, slow-motion challenge, even just twenty yards down the hospital corridor, that when I made it back to the ward I was totally drained. My right hand, because my wrist was strong, was good at pushing but the left, a bunch of stone bananas, couldn't grip the chair's push rims and the imbalance made me zigzag across the lino. To compensate, I turned my left hand and elbow outwards from the shoulder, like an injured bird, and propelled with the edge of my palm and wrist. There was some residual power. Life, it occurred to me, in an image which would be repeated, honed to perfection over the next decade, was beginning to feel exactly like one of those sadistic TV game shows made famous by Clive James in the 1980s. It was the genre of humiliation as entertainment, which began on Japanese TV and in Britain evolved into *I'm a Celebrity Get Me Out of Here*. And that was exactly what it felt like for me, that world of crazed, pointless challenges tantalisingly just beyond the contestants' grasp, the stream of filth and cockroaches cascading over their heads. And the celebs had it easy: they went home after a month.

With the ability to push a few yards came a tiny amount of autonomy and I started to explore the corridors around the high-dependency unit, like a toddler exploring her home. I would reach a big window, or a glass door, and peer out at the sky and a bit of treetop behind the roof. Sometimes I over-reached myself and had to sit for five minutes, resting, at the corner until I was strong enough to turn. Five minutes ... the most inconsequential flick of time in a spinal rehabilitation ward, where snails moved faster, their goals better defined. David Allan, the director of the spinal unit, the man who had clenched his fists in A&E for us to demonstrate what happened to my neck, had already warned me my rehab could take over a year. When he had said it I was aghast; now, reluctantly, I was beginning the process of understanding.

The awakening consciousness, the struggle to regain some form of control over my life, was encapsulated by my tragi-comic battle over my hair. When you break your neck, you are condemned to have the back of your head set on a pillow for, well, much of the rest of your life, and in the shorter term to wear collars for several months. My thick, wavy hair was problematic. Too short to be tied on the top of my head in a pineapple – the only place where it would be out of the way – but long enough to snag and mat like the fur of an abandoned dog. And it hurt. Being unable to raise my head was ordeal enough; having the elastic straps from oxygen masks to tug my scalp, tubes to stick in the hair, tears to dry in it and a collar to catch it made my daily existence more miserable. The back of my head became a hot, itchy torture and just as I had earlier obsessed about drinking a coffee, so I now fantasised about having my hair shaved like a GI. Cut it off, I commanded the most friendly nurses. They laughed at me. I blustered that I would do it myself, but of course in reality I wasn't able to raise my head unaided, let alone lift my arms behind my head, or wield scissors. I ordered Dave to send for two of my most resourceful friends. I demanded my human right to have my hair cut.

But my husband, less impulsive than me, was concerned it would be against hospital rules or might injure my neck. He refused. I tried again with the nurses, they asked the ward sister, but she too had a touch of the Fat Controller about her, and forbade it – some specious excuse … health and safety, infection control, possibility I might sue them – and I lay and seethed with impotent fury as my Rastafarian mat hummed behind me on the pillow. I remember eyeing the sister balefully as she stood at the nurses' station. Bloody jobsworth, hidebound by rules. Totally exasperated at my lack of control over something so trivial, I resorted to asking my consultant on the ward round. Dr Purcell raised a cool eyebrow and agreed a family member could cut it. So it was that my sister Lindsay, over from France and armed with a pair of blunt disposable NHS scissors, gave me the best cut of my life – hacked short and choppy up the back of my head. She insisted on leaving the length on top. The result was Simon Le Bon circa 1983 but I felt so free and cool and happy I couldn't have cared less. My appearance, I had at least twigged, wasn't going to matter that much for a while, if ever again. I had bigger priorities ahead.

Around then the doctors finally took me off tramadol and I experienced my first proper sleep, morphine-free. I remember waking with a sense of profound joy, awash with the novelty of feeling deeply rested. Unbelievably restored, at peace. All traces of the orange cable-stitch wool had gone away and the sunlight was streaming through the thin patterned curtains around my bed, a pattern of blue oblongs and squares which I had, it seemed, been studying and reinterpreting for years. For the first time the material looked fresh, normal – just cloth – not an omen, or pictures, or a metaphor, or a maze.

It was time to move into the unknown.

CHAPTER THREE

SWALLOW DIVING FROM THE SEVENTH FLOOR

What hath night to do with sleep?
JOHN MILTON, *PARADISE LOST*

The rehab ward was no place for sissies. I learnt that in the middle of my first night, woken from sleep as if for a hostile interrogation. Two nursing assistants arrived in my bedspace with a flourish, switching on the full-strength fluorescent examination light overhead, pulling the curtains noisily shut behind them, stripping back my blankets. It was somewhere in the small hours; there were other patients asleep a few feet away in the same room.

'What's happening?'

No reply. They were talking, but not to me.

I was bewildered, dazzled, disorientated. They were putting their hands under me, moving me across the bed. Maybe this was another fantasy kidnap.

'Please, what's happening?'

One of them broke off from their conversation.

'You need turned.'

He reeked of cannabis. Dougie always said I had a nose like a bloodhound but this guy was in a different league. You could almost taste it. Together they worked like a Formula One pitstop team: rolled me onto my other hip, wedged a pillow behind my back to keep me there, placed another pillow under my top knee, and switched my overnight urine drainage stand, attached to my catheter, to the opposite side of the bed. It was done in seconds, a slick, well-practised manoeuvre. Wham bam, wheelnuts tight, off you go, Sebastian Vettel, back out of the pit lane.

'OK,' Doobie said. It wasn't a question. They switched off the blinding light, pulled back the curtains, and moved to the next bed. Click, swoosh, gone. Not remotely cruel, but not remotely kind either. Disengaged, impersonal. I wasn't a person; I was a task, one of dozens of four-hourly turns they had to perform through the night. It was an attitude I was to become deeply accustomed, and eventually immune to. But right at that moment, I had never felt more alone, more insulted by the stench of cannabis, or more acutely aware of what a sheltered, precious, middle-class prat I was to feel so offended. Later, when I got to know Doobie better, I became quite fond of him. But not his smell.

Way back in the beginning, hospital was a sanctuary. Like driftwood washed to the top of the beach by a high tide, salt-bleached, splintered by the storms, you just rest awhile, nestling in the sand. Something terrible has befallen you, but if you lie very, very still, you will be safe. Nothing is asked of you. Hands which you cannot feel will gently position you; quiet voices address you. In intensive-care and high-dependency wards, they turn you frequently in the night to protect your skin from pressure sores, but they do it discreetly and by torchlight in order not to wake you. When you cease to be acutely ill, and move away from those remarkable acute areas where the staff ratio is generous and the NHS functions at its very best, things change. The nurses in high-dependency tried to warn me about the difference in ethos awaiting me. 'It's different next door,' they said. Next door was the adjoining corridor, the forty-bed spinal rehabilitation ward, where, having had your spine stabilised, you would be schooled to cope with your condition. Weeks later, Euphorbia, one of the senior rehab nurses, proudly shared with me the standard joke about the transition.

'Like going from the Ritz to a Travelodge,' she said. And laughed. Took me a while to find it funny, but I did eventually.

The ward seemed more Guantanamo than Travelodge, though, that first night after the interruption, as I lay with a thumping heart and retinas imprinted with the white-hot square of the ceiling light. It struck me, as I struggled to take in the rules and understand the rhythm of the ward, that this was what being dumped at boarding school must have felt like to a sheltered child. A doctrine of tough love with the love taken out. Newly paralysed, I was exquisitely powerless to do anything but watch and listen. Once again, I garrisoned myself deeper and deeper in that only safe place, my head. Once again, it came down to survival.

And boy, imprisoned, motionless, I really did feel my spaceship had landed me on yet another alien planet. I had to learn fast. There was something almost Darwinian about it. Sink or swim. Adapt or die. A rehab ward in a spinal unit is like an under-strength factory floor: too few staff battling to a relentless timetable of feeding, medicating, washing, toileting, dressing and hoisting dozens of helpless carcasses into wheelchairs to get them to the gym. I guess it's a bit like a geriatric ward only there's more shit and less dementia, and I'm not sure, from a nurses' point of view, if that's a wholly desirable payoff. The operation was geared to through-put. The aim was to get us wrecks into the best possible state of semi-independence as quickly as possible, aware and able to self-manage, so we could be returned to our homes. It was noisy, smelly, shitty, relentless hard work for the nursing staff and a slow, tormented awakening to reality for the carcasses, many of whom lacked even the motor function to press their call buzzer for attention. But it was functional. Something had to be done with us.

Things, I swiftly discovered, wound themselves up from 6 a.m. onward, in preparation for the 7 a.m. handover, when the nurses' twelve-and a half-hour-night shift switched with the twelve-and-a-half-hour day shift. There is a grim unforgiving routine when you have paralysed bladder and bowels. Conveyor-belt stuff. The nurses detached our overnight urine drainage bags, great wobbling two-litre plastic bags of yellow fluid collected from indwelling catheters, and emptied them down the loo. Before handover, in the dawn light, they would leave us our little morning package of delight, anal suppositories wrapped up in an incontinence pad, on the ends of our beds. 'Are your supps in?' echoed the cry.

Paraplegics, whose arms and hands were not paralysed, were taught to reach behind their backs to their bottom and shove their own up. Tetraplegics like me, who could neither hold nor reach, had to wait to have the nurse do it. A few minutes after insertion, as the suppositories began to do their work, our semi-naked bodies, big, small, and everything in between, were hoisted onto commode-style shower chairs and wheeled into the bathroom one after another, to be poised over the loo until our bowels delivered. There was a critical time balance as to how long you waited. Left in bed too long, you would poo on the sheets or, worse, in the hoist; or perhaps even dump upon the floor through the hole in the shower chair seat en route to the bathroom. Too short a time, and you would sit for what seemed like hours over the loo, waiting for the splash that told you something had happened. It was the only way to tell. You had no feeling.

Eventually, a staff nurse would come and use a gloved finger to check that your bowels were empty; and then you would be showered. Often your bowels didn't oblige and after half an hour or so, with you cold and acutely miserable on the hard plastic split seat of a shower chair, a staff nurse would come and put their fingers up your anus, stimulating the rectum until it released. Some nurses were better at it than others. They were the ones you loved because they were fast, efficient and gave you confidence that you would last the day without an accident. The ever-cheery Rosebud, one of my favourites, used to waggle her index finger and joke that she should have it insured as one of the best in the business. Without the willingness of spinal nurses to put their hands up dozens of backsides a day, closing their noses to the smell of faeces, the paralysed would die. It's as simple as that. Perhaps it's no surprise that death rates for spinal injuries improved after the invention of the disposable latex glove in the 1960s.

They gave as good as they got, those fast-talking, insouciant Glasgow girls. Lupin, her uniform straining over her fabulous bust, had spent the morning crouching on the floors of bathrooms, beside arse after arse, evacuating poo. Later she sounded off to some of us, the patients she trusted, about being criticised by one of the consultants.

'He's like complaining it was too smelly when he was doing the ward round.'

She threw her hands out, paused for effect.

'I'm like, "No shit Sherlock!"'

'Did you really say that?'

'You kidding?'

For us, new trainees in the hard school of double incontinence, this was the start of an entirely different way of life. We laughed about our plight when things went particularly wrong, forged together by the dark humour, the dry-as-dust jokes, the human condition stripped to its most primitive. It was, I guess, like a PoW camp. With it went an undercurrent of real camaraderie, a shared acknowledgement of our common misery. Up and dressed one mid-afternoon, a dozen or so of us were parked in our wheelchairs in a polite semicircle, staring at the wall onto which was projected the first slide of a PowerPoint presentation. And one of our number, a distinguished man who had boarded a plane at Heathrow but when it landed was unable to stand up because he had suffered a spinal stroke, leant over from his wheelchair towards mine and muttered:

'Did you ever imagine a situation where you would sit gazing intently at the words "Bowel Management"?'

Indeed, there were far too many things beyond the power of imagination and they were pressing in on us. We got detailed tutorials. We were as mordant as we could be, for without a highly developed sense of the ridiculous, how else could we cope with bleak forty-five-minute lectures about suppositories, peristalsis and sphincters; or indeed, in subsequent sessions, about pressure sores, catheterisation techniques and the risks of a deadly condition called autonomic dysreflexia? We were awake yet trapped in an undergraduate's anxiety nightmare, where you dream you've committed to study entirely the wrong course. There had been some terrible mistake. You wanted to do English Literature; you were stuck in theoretical astrophysics. And in this university there was no dropping out, no transferring. To this day, I have lodged in my memory one particular giant image of a bedsore on a buttock which was displayed on the wall for us during those afternoon education sessions.

'This sore is the size of a plate,' warned the nurse in charge.

'It had to be packed every day and the person had to spend two years in bed before they were able to sit up in a chair again. It is what can happen if you do not check your skin and take efforts to relieve pressure points.'

I looked at plates differently after that.

Most definitely beyond imagination were the backstories of my fellow patients: the extraordinary mixture of bizarre and mundane which had brought us together. We were a community bound by the common possession of crushed or severed spinal cords, but the disparate tales of how it came to happen were far, far stranger than fiction. Any woman who has given birth in an NHS hospital will know what it's like to share a ward with the fantastic, comic mix of rough and ready, posh and precious, and every kind of female in between, whose only common bond is the ability to have a baby. Well, breaking your back is like that but magnified a millionfold. If you tried, you could not have made us up. Academics, labourers, wasters, tradesmen, accountants, failed suicides, business managers, teenagers, drunks, cyclists, stuntmen, farmers, speedway riders, criminals, jockeys, teachers, police officers, motorbikers, dog-walkers, golfers, drug addicts, teachers, pensioners and more congregate in spinal units. We were young, old, decrepit, well-groomed, inarticulate, intellectual, deranged, gay, straight and transgender, condemned to our wheelchairs by road accidents, falls from bikes or horses or walls or beds or cliffs or balconies, stumbles off kerbs, trips over slippers or coffee table or dog leads or manhole covers, crashes on the piste, dives into swimming pools, rugby tackles, violent assaults, attempted murder, war, vascular incidents or complications from tumour operations. Several were victims of slipping on ice. Men outnumbered women by almost ten to one. Every one of us had our own bitter misinterpretation of risk to reflect on. What we had in common is that life, quite simply, chose to leap out and attack us. As one nurse put it: 'When I first came to work here I was terrified of the chance of spinal injury happening. Then I saw that it can happen to anyone, in any circumstance. It is completely random so I stopped worrying.'

This did not stop us, as individuals, in private moments, being haunted by our 'what ifs'. What if I'd left the bike at home. Or pulled up the horse. Or not got in the car. But such thoughts were entirely pointless, jousting with the random essence of existence. Meantime, I decided, even if I couldn't move, there was at least some fleeting entertainment to be had watching and listening to my fellow travellers. It was, I supposed, like being on a cruise ship.

The rehab ward was subdivided into rooms of four or six beds. One of these, opposite the nurses' station, was a dedicated respiratory section for those poor sods who were on tracheotomies in order to breathe. They remained strangers to most of us, as they never rose from bed to wheelchair, and were too sick and dependent to reach the gym. People with such high-level neck injuries stayed as long as it took to stabilise them and arrange the massive twenty-four/seven care packages they would need at home. Then they were taken away at quiet times: still, distant figures upon stretchers beset by tubes and ventilators.

I remember catching a glimpse through the internal ward glass of one occupant: a morbidly obese man, not old by any means, who lay like a mountain upon what seemed an impossibly small bed, the tubes through the front of his throat, his face turned impassively towards the outside window. He did not live long enough to go home: one morning the staff came and drew all the internal curtains in the wards, shut the doors and hushed our buzzers, because his body was being removed and we were not to see. His accident had probably been caused by a fall – the most common cause of calamity. But oh what variety was contained within that tiny little word 'fall': it included everything from failed suicide to a trip over the coffee table in the living room after, or even before, a glass of wine, or sometimes six. All of human life was there in the lurid, eye-popping diversity of falling. There was Del, a part-time brickie and a full-time wild man, who had swallow-dived from the seventh floor on holiday in the Costas, convinced by drugs and alcohol he could fly. Despite his injuries, I think he still thought he could. He also thought he was irresistible to women and was famous for making lecherous comments to staff and female patients. Some weeks later, when I was upright in the gym on a static wooden standing frame, braced upright between foam knee braces and leather straps behind my bottom, I became aware of Del in his wheelchair at my right hip, leering.

'You look OK standing up. For an old bird,' he said. 'I'd have a bit of that.'

'In your dreams,' I said as haughtily as I could, trying not to laugh at the pitch-black irony of a pick-up line from one deranged tetraplegic to another marginally less deranged; indeed, at the very suggestion either of us had sexual currency of any kind. How to plumb the depths of bitter-sweet. Later I rationalised that as offers went, given my condition, it was probably the best I was ever going to get.

He cackled and rolled off to pester someone else. I felt as if I had joined some hilariously macabre list of Dickensian characters. Tenement had done much the same thing as Del but on a lesser scale, a chronic alcoholic who had lost his house keys and fallen while trying to climb in the window to his third-floor flat. If his life had been chaotic beforehand, it was hopeless now. His hands jangled like a medieval palsy sufferer's, and it was nothing to do with his broken spine. The stuff his girlfriend smuggled in for him could only assist. Despite encouragement he never showed up for gym sessions; he preferred to go outside and join the smokers, the small band of paralysed who huddled their chairs near the entrance to the spinal unit. Out there too was Steroid, a scaffolder who told the doctors he had tripped but confided to us in hand therapy, where he was learning to feed himself, that he'd run into a wall in a drug-induced rage and broken his own neck.

'At least I think I did,' he said. 'I was aff ma fucking heid at the time.'

Right outside the front door, just through the underpass, lay the streets of Govan, an inner-city Glasgow ward which persistently featured in all the indices of deprived Britain. Like urban foxes scavenging, the occasional local street dweller or small-scale drug dealer smelt out the needy patients and would drift by in the evenings, offering an anaesthetic of fags, booze, dope, pills, harder stuff. Here was an eager market; and usually with cash stowed in their zips and pockets. But nothing is successfully furtive when you cannot use your hands and slow-motion drug-dealing with cripples in the dusk was worthy of the blackest of comedy scripts. The dealers – though the name makes them sound more glamorous than they were – would hand over their booty and watch as the paraplegics, whose hands worked, fumbled in the pockets of the joggers of the tetraplegics, whose hands didn't, to get their money out for them. That was the unwritten code with a knackered spine: anyone who had a less severe injury and could do something, helped out anyone who couldn't. If your hands didn't work, you found a mate whose hands did, and you locked your wheelchairs together in a macabre mating while they reached over and retrieved what you needed. For the scavengers it was a rare encounter with people far lower down the pecking order than they had ever met before.

Although the authorities alerted the police regularly to drive away the dealers, these transactions were fairly unstoppable. Anyone caught using or in possession of drugs inside the unit was expelled, and some were when I was there; but who was to ban patients from smoking outside the hospital doors? Morally, these were the entitlements of the damned. Down among any dead men – the traitor before the firing squad, the poor sod in the trenches with his torso blown away, the young paraplegic whose penis would never feel again – a cigarette was an emblem of compassion. Who would ever deny the needy whatever tiny pleasure was possible? Certainly not the occupational therapists, who would on the quiet craft ingenious devices to allow tetraplegics to continue to smoke – hand straps to let them grip fag packets, a length of wire with a loop on the end to hold the cigarette, so they could reach it to their mouths. There were no pious bleats about being forbidden to facilitate patients' smoking, just discreet pragmatism and an absence of judgementalism. The bosses looked the other way. I loved that, even if it was just one more measure of how great a catastrophe had befallen us.

In my ward there were six beds and slowly I began to find out about the people around me. Next to me was Karen, who was the same age as me. She was a fall statistic. An innocuous tumble in her house had mysteriously paralysed her: only when she was X-rayed did she find out that she had undiagnosed arthritic deterioration in her neck which, in a stroke of appalling bad luck, had pierced her spinal column. Her injury was at a roughly similar level to mine, but I was the luckier: she had less movement in her arms than me and her fingers were permanently bent shut. If she envied me, it never showed. She never knew, either, how much I envied her calmness and realism: while I was gung-ho to fight my way back to total fitness through blood, sweat and tears, her ambitions were simply to be able to hold a mug, feed herself, and apply make-up. Guess who was the wiser?

With us in the room were two teenagers, one who had dived into the shallow end of a swimming pool on holiday, the other who had her back broken in a car accident. For months, lying listening to those kids learning their new realities, hearing them sobbing behind the thin curtains, or being taught how to catheterise themselves, or sitting their national school exams with an overwhelmed-looking adjudicator, was a profound lesson in how fortunate I was to have lived a lot of life before this happened. Later I shared a room with another little girl, and felt silent anger flare when Snapdragon, a senior nurse, insisted that her teddy bear was an infection control risk. Normally the bear would have had to go but, announced Snapdragon, glowing with the warmth of her own magnanimity, she'd make an exception as long he was kept wrapped up in a sealed plastic bag. Teddy sat there on the bedside cabinet, asphyxiated, head forced sideways, nose crushed against the plastic, pleading black button eyes, until the child went home.

In the far corner of the room was a mysterious patient who never got up: she was ensconced in a vast, high, warm sand bed, the size of a car, which shifted and vibrated constantly to heal long-term pressure sores. The bed, with its noise and warmth, had a strong presence of its own. Its occupant, an older woman, did not interact with us. Apparently her spinal injury was not new, but she had been unable to look after her skin for some years, and had developed a sore so bad she had been brought back in. Plates. The warnings resonated.

As a rule, the higher the neck injury, the more one's hands were impacted. So every morning at 11 a.m., after our previous joyous two hours on shower chairs, us high spinal cord injury patients – the young, the old, the sporty; you might call us an elite of misfortune – congregated in the manner of elderly tortoises around the hand therapy table in our wheelchairs.

Most of us wore the same severely restrictive collars, making us even more tortoise-like, so we greeted each other without full eye contact, nodding and squinting at midair, and then taking our places, waiting for our pots of hand putty to arrive. It resembled an early learning centre, but we were far more placid than toddlers. Left in peace long enough we would start to snooze, our heads drooping onto our collars.

There was Karen, wry and cheerful as ever, learning to hold her mascara brush. And Nevis, a high-flyer businessman who'd broken his neck ski-mountaineering, a silent man with the

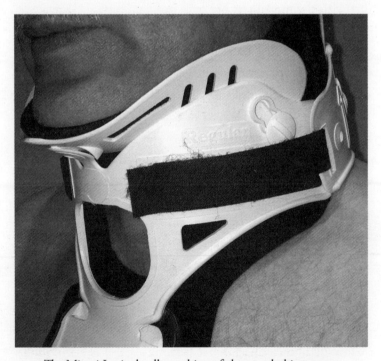

The Miami J spinal collar, a thing of claustrophobic torture, smelling of sour milk, and worn every minute of the day for three months. That's not me modelling it, that's one of my mates from the spinal unit. Looking only a little bit porny.

most harrowing thousand-yard stare I witnessed on anyone in the unit. Hand therapy was a misnomer for him: his hands were lifeless. Instead his arms were put in slings suspended on metal stands, the kind used to hang saline drips from, and he was trying to move his shoulders enough to be able to make them swing. If he could get enough motion, his insensate fists would brush hard enough across the pages of a magazine to turn them. The Professor was an elderly scientist who had been pulled over by his dog while out walking and broken his neck; he told whimsical, erudite stories and charmed everyone.

We had some laughs, most in very bad taste. Joker was a serial offender with velvet brown eyes and winsome long eyelashes who had broken his neck falling through a roof. He was one of the brightest people in the unit, subversive in a way that challenged common perspectives. He just didn't care about anything or anyone. He said he quite liked having a broken neck because it meant that he got looked after.

'I've been in Y— [a young offender's institution] thirty-seven times,' he announced one day, sitting opposite me and flapping his elbows for balance as he reached up to try to rearrange an abacus.

'Ooo,' I said. 'What for?' My tongue was sticking out with concentration. I was doing my best to play Chinese chequers with rubber bands around the wooden pegs for grip.

He looked pityingly at me, across our different worlds.

'Stealing cars.'

I found him fascinating. He told me the best makes to steal and how easy it was. He said it had been fun for a while but then it got boring and he didn't like being on the streets, so he would steal a car deliberately to get caught, knowing it meant a warm bed and hot food. I always feared he would take his own life when he left the unit, but in fact, with proper care in place for him and a new sense of being valued, he forged a career online.

Joker had about a year's seniority on Kindle, another of my contemporaries, a brilliant schoolboy whose parents' car had skidded on black ice. Kindle did his Highers, the Scottish equivalent of A levels, in the unit and went on to Oxbridge. He carried a tablet in his sweatshirt, and read compulsively, even on the standing frames. Both young men broke my heart: just boys at the start of their adult lives, making the best of the cards they had been dealt, from different ends of the pack.

And so we gathered every weekday morning round the white melamine tables, and while those with no movement in their hands were put into arm slings, those of us with semi-viable hands had to start on our own personal lumps of hard, blue putty. This was our warm-up kit – we must mould and squeeze and grip and shape the putty, flatten and separate it into tiny balls and roll it into long sausages, all the while strengthening and suppling our hands. Cars droned past on the arterial city road outside, and the wider world was turning, but in our bewildering new pre-school this was the only task which must concern us. Here I was, I reflected, former mistress of my universe, member of the chattering classes, mover, shaker and regularly responsible for editing a national newspaper, here I was struggling to cope with playdough. It required astounding effort. At the end of the exercise you returned the putty to a big round ball, which you pressed into the table with the heel of your hand. Then you sat and panted for five minutes, wiped out by the effort required.

My hands were more damaged than I liked to admit. Both were very numb. The left, in the beginning, badly swollen, flopped heavy and useless on the end of my wrist. I clocked myself in the face with it several times. My right, although fairly normal-looking, with a relative range of movement, had almost no power at all. My grip was gone. But the hand therapists, positive, cheery people, kept at us. The nicest times were when they took our hands and smoothed and massaged them within their own, so warm and active and normal. Leslie the senior therapist would take my hands, grotesquely white and crusty with dead skin, and soak them in a basin of warm water for ten minutes, and then scour off vast amounts of lizard-like scales with a coarse NHS towel. The result was extraordinary – the palms and the fingers felt liberated and free to move again. Then there were more tasks to fulfil: Connect4 to complete, tiny plastic cones to be lifted onto other cones; hoops to be taken off one peg and placed upon another. One fiendish challenge was a tall wooden stick, a tree with pegs instead of branches, upon which we were to hook discs with corresponding peg-sized holes – the sort of thing a bright three-year-old would manage in seconds. Actually, a two-year-old. First we had to reach up and hang the pegs on the top branches. Then, try and lift them off. Trying to balance my torso, extend my arms above my shoulders and grip, simultaneously, took me to my physical limits. If I managed, I was left exhausted but ridiculously pleased with myself. I saw the same sense of elation on the faces of my fellow patients. This was like climbing Everest for us.

My frequent challenge was a game for children aged five plus using a pair of tweezers to lift tiny coloured balls of plastic,

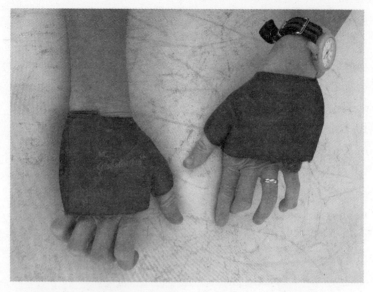

My distorted hands in leather pushing gloves. This is after the
swelling went down. My fingers soon froze in this shape.

1970s love beads, and place them on equally tiny pegs. With
enough concentration, to my amazement, the thumb and
middle finger of my right found the infinitesimal amount of
squeeze needed to do this. I even managed a few with my left
hand as well. I glowed with the achievement.

Frequently we had FES – functional electrical stimulation.
Electrodes on our wrists, wired to a battery unit, sent pulses
which made our fingers lift and straighten. And strengthen. The
electric pulses replicated the nerves which had been destroyed.
The effects were remarkable. Leslie fantasised about putting
newly spinally injured people in all-over FES suits, to kick-start
everything. She focused heavily on making my left wrist flex
upwards. This, I was to learn, was critical to my future.

* * *

Oxbow the ecologist had been cycling to work when his front wheel hit a pothole and he broke his neck. He could hardly move anything; his elbows were supported in slings in hand therapy so that he could try and regain a scintilla of shoulder action and be able to work the joystick of a power wheelchair. Barnaby was an older man, a former ship's officer, desperate only to learn to feed himself so he didn't impose on his elderly wife. He had fallen at home. He would sit, his forearms in yet another kind of sling, waving with a spoon at a bowlful of apple segments. Occasionally he hooked one and got it as far as his mouth, and his face cracked open with satisfaction as he munched.

Stoical the businessman, who had slipped on ice crossing a supermarket car park and suffered cervical damage, had, like all of us, numb fingers. But his numbness was combined with painful hypersensitivity in his fingertips. Every single session he sat, like a man on a lifelong mission, methodically scouring away at them with gentle sandpaper, desensitising them. I envied him his calm.

Priceless was an older, educated woman, a tourist, who had fallen and damaged her neck after drinking a glass or three of wine. She could still walk and her injuries, compared to the rest of us, were about as bad as a summer cold, but she was oblivious to this. Her lack of self-awareness, common tact even, was breathtaking. Viewed through her eyes, her plight was monstrous – her holiday had been ruined and her elegant hand-writing was affected. She demanded the hand therapists help her restore it; she complained loudly about the nurses on the ward who refused to help her wash and dress, the state of the food, and the fact she was in pain. She was one of the very few patients who didn't either touch or amuse me; it took me several years to understand the truth that she embodied. Everyone's handicap is relative. We are all entitled to our own perspective on how badly we are injured. What seemed trivial to some was life-changing to others, and vice versa. The ownership of that grief belonged entirely to her; that was her right. Its impact upon her was not for others to judge. At the time, though, I just wanted to tell her to open her eyes and look around at the rest of us. And if I'm honest, I still experience a similar stir of exasperation when I am corralled by some old dear who wants to tell me how bad her sciatica is. I have learnt to smile and nod, detach myself from judgement.

After a couple of weeks, the intensive hand therapy began to reap rewards. My left hand became less stone-like, and the thumb and fingers were starting to wiggle. The wrist grew strong enough to prevent it flopping. My right hand was definitely more powerful and I could grasp an old-fashioned phone receiver, something I couldn't have done a fortnight ago. Dave and I managed our first telephone conversation, home to hospital, which made both our hearts sing. Eventually, in hand therapy, I even managed to open an envelope, a major victory. To do this, I had learnt how to use my teeth, my invaluable third hand from now.

Afternoon gym was also becoming less unfamiliar. I was starting to recognise faces and understand the rhythm of therapy. The gym was two large spaces linked by a glass divide, and equipped with about ten pale blue physiotherapy plinths, which raised and lowered electronically. To a layman's eyes, the landscape was hard to interpret, more like a medieval torture chamber than anything. There were standing frames and tilt tables beribboned with heavy-duty Velcro straps to bring para-lysed people upright, jutting pulleys for carrying arm and leg slings, hooks hanging from mesh cages suspended over more plinths, two sets of parallel bars, a conveyor-belted machine with robot legs and a harness suspended over it, and various arm and chest weight machines. Plus, splendidly, like a piece of modern art, half a car – a Fiat cut off in front of the windscreen, which was attached nose-in to the glass partition. That was for the future, for those of us who were able. We could learn to transfer into driver or passenger seats, practising for a life outside.

Everywhere I looked, I saw devices I could not understand but was desperate to try. My desire to get better was atavistic.

Resting on one of the plinths while my physiotherapist attended to another of her patients, I could observe fellow inhabitants who were learning to mobilise their bodies and cope with their new lives. I felt all of eleven years old, wide-eyed, evaluating my new classmates at the big school. Who would be a kindred spirit? Who would have a sense of humour? Swiftly you learnt who to seek out, who to avoid. Fetlock had also fallen off a horse; she'd had a close escape, was walking wounded and would be going home soon, but she wanted to tell me, in great detail, in the way only horsey people do, about every wisp of hay and variation of snaffle bit she had ever seen. I shrank inside myself when she walked – walked, damn her – over to me, and I could not escape, because I was not in my chair.

'So what horses have you got? I've got three – my old mare and my young one – it was my young one that dumped me

– and then there's my pal Sheena's pony, I have him too, but he pulls like mad and he's a bugger to catch and keeps ripping his rugs and I have to soak his hay. Do you keep yours at livery?'

Like I'm going to keep any horse, ever again? Please go away, Fetlock. I don't wish to be cruel, but don't you realise that my dream has ended, that you're shooting holes in my soul?

I smiled up at her, and made some anodyne reply. On a cruise ship, be tolerant. Keep your own counsel.

Wee Jimmy had been shot in the spine, for all sorts of alleged reasons. You never asked too many questions. Some said it was revenge for a murder by his uncle Tam-the-Hatchet. In that sense the unit was akin to a church, a place of sanctuary where you accepted people for their needs rather than their deeds. Jimmy was gangly, mild-mannered and wary. He had the air of someone faintly bewildered as to why the staff were being so nice to him and he tried hard in rehab. He gave everyone on the ward a slice of his birthday cake and when he left hospital he made the front page of the tabloid press. As well as their victims, every now and again you got criminals in the unit with broken spines. Big Willie, one of the physiotherapists, a benign sixteen-stone barn door of ex-rugby player, remarked that over the years he'd had several as patients but only realised it when he read about the court cases in the paper afterwards. One man was later convicted of organising a murder.

'Honestly, you couldn't have met a nicer guy,' said Willie, shaking his head.

Mostly we were innocent, life's fallen jesters. Cycling and sports injuries were common. Cog was a mountain biker from down south who'd gone over the handlebars on a boys' biking weekend in Scotland. He was semi-dazed and nauseated by tramadol. I remembered its ghastly nausea-inducing and head-fugging qualities. Taking tramadol, you were in the world but not of it. Pretty soon Cog transferred back down south, still looking grey and confused.

Tourette was a middle-aged man who had had a stroke that damaged his speech, long before a car accident broke his back: he was in a wheelchair and came to the gym but could only shout 'Fuck Off!' or 'Pish!' Again, his ability to swear endured, although his brain had closed down more sophisticated speech circuitry. Tourette looked like Waldorf from the Muppets, his mouth set in a determined upside-down U. Despite appearances, he was very cheerful and seemed to enjoy amusing the rest of us by cursing inappropriately. Spatula, the chef who'd broken his back in a drug-addled suicide attempt off a cliff, befriended him, and the two of them sat outside and smoked, mostly in silence but for the cursing. Spatula could stand, and mobilise a little, and could have improved, but he stopped coming to the gym and the rules were strict. If you didn't buy into rehab, you had to leave.

And then there was Grit, a former soldier, five-foot-two tall and as hard-boiled as a twenty-minute egg. I loved Grit. He possessed very little in the world but an outsize sense of decency; his flat in a Glasgow high-rise had been broken into and when he challenged the suspected culprits, they stabbed him. One knife wound pierced his spinal column and he was paralysed down one side. Grit had been treated with little sympathy by the police and had languished without expert care in another city hospital – just one more knife victim with the wrong post code – until a doctor had recognised the seriousness of his injury and got him transferred across the city to spinal. He couldn't believe how well he was treated in this unit by comparison.

'Night and fucking day, Mel,' he told me. 'They're just fucking angels here, the nurses. The doctors listen to you. They just didn't care in the last place. Not fucking interested.'

Grit and I were mates from the days of high dependency when we'd had beds in facing bays; I told him he'd be walking soon and so he was, within a month, so he took to calling me Crystal Balls. He had a lot of mates, hardmen like himself, who crowded round his bedside and told him how his football team was doing and discussed the people who'd stabbed him. They knew fine who'd done it.

'Fucking terrible, sure it is. You should see what the dirty wee bastards are getting away with now.'

'We'll fucking get them for you, Grit, we will.'

Sometimes the crescendo of cursing got so bad that my husband, a man not unknown to swear himself, would turn his head and lift an eyebrow. Grit would clock it, and his natural courtesy would kick in.

'Listen Dave, big Mel, ah'm sorry, ah cannae stop fucking swearing. Lads, tone it down. Stop fucking swearing so much. Youse are upsetting people.'

Weeks later, in the gym, when Grit was getting around, first on crutches, then a stick, he busied himself bringing cups of water from the cooler to those of us stuck on machines. One day I was strapped upright, my head at least twelve feet in the air, on a tilting table with a mechanism which moved your feet backwards and forwards – towering like some ghastly human sacrifice over everyone else in the gym. Grit, who couldn't reach high enough to put the plastic cup of water in my hand, put down his stick and starting climbing up the frame to give me the water. Only one side of his body worked, and he was utterly precarious, but he made it up and down safely and glowed with paternalistic pride as he watched me.

'Fucking brill, big Mel. Youse are doing great, Crystal Balls.' In the land of the blind, the one-eyed man was king.

There were Buddhists, and poets from the Scottish islands, there were heroes and villains. There were several patients with old injuries, returned for treatment, whose voices we only really heard if the drugs trolley was a few minutes late, which it often was, and they would ring their buzzers crying for their methadone. Had their injuries made them opiate addicts? You could not ask, and no one would ever tell. Nor would judgement ever be passed. We mostly lived out our private lives in public, but we gathered into ourselves what scraps of dignity remained behind those grotty thin curtains, and kept some secrets. There was a policeman who had had his back broken by a getaway car; he often rehabbed on the plinth next to a stone-mason whose bungee jump had gone wrong and whose mum kept complaining about the quality of the food. Mrs Bennet, a school dinner lady, didn't come to the gym often – hurt in a fall, she seemed to accept her fate with remarkable good grace, though I suspect it was partly to do with the amount of tramadol she took. She was not at all unkind, but very lazy, and liked to know everyone's business. Had there been a God, she would have had several unmarried daughters, and an acerbic husband. And who could forget Passion, the Brazilian stallion, whose spinal operation had not been successful? He fretted very publicly about whether he would still be able to have sex and boasted that his body would be perfect again soon. Very swiftly he earned a reputation for commandeering the communal bathroom when his wife came to visit, presumably so he could check out whether things were really as bad as he feared. He was ignorant, and sexist, and thought nothing of making insulting remarks to female patients, me included, but I watched him on the parallel bars one day, straining to make his steps fluid, trying to convince himself he was winning, the beads of sweat glistening on his upper lip, and felt sorry for him. We were all in our own ways trying to kid ourselves.

So I began my rehabilitation, trying to ride that ghastly non-compliant new horse which was my body; a terrible physical challenge that bucked and threw me contemptuously, time and time and time again. They had given me a wheelchair with the brand name Quickie and in it I learnt a new definition of slowness. My nails grew faster than my progress down the corridor. Somehow I had to learn to exist again; my arms had to learn to support and move me; my hands, the fingers now tightening, clawing into stumps like decrepit Trafalgar Square pigeons, had to learn how to hold a kettle or a toothbrush and bear the pain of the push rims of the wheels on my palms. I was given thick leather mitts, which fastened with Velcro and were specially designed for easy use by tetraplegics, to protect the skin (see photo on page 58). One day, trying to come back from the gym along the carpeted stretch of corridor – installed, sadistically but sensibly, to prepare us for real life – my arms gave up and the pile of the carpet steered me into the wall. I sat quietly weeping in frustration until a nurse took pity on me and pushed me off the carpet.

In the gym my routine was simple: arm exercises first –
twenty minutes on the handbike, then biceps curls and triceps
lifts on the weights machines. Then, hoisted onto the specialist
plinths, I began the process of coping with the appendage
formerly known as my body. Propped in a seated position, my
feet on the floor, foam wedges behind me to catch me if I went
backwards, I started to learn how to balance sitting upright.
How peculiar it felt. Because I could not feel my backside in
contact with the plinth; I had the sensation I was a head and
shoulders poised on wobbly air. I swayed like a blancmange,
only staying upright because I could grip the edge of the plinth
with my crocked fingers and lean back on my arms.

Next, from the same seated position, as my left wrist
strengthened and began to hurt less, I was told to place my
hands beside me on the firm surface and try and lift myself.
Impossible. But critical to the future. When your body is paralysed and you try to lift your own body weight solely with your
unaccustomed arms, you cannot believe how hard it is. The
movement starts in your brain with a huge heave and ends, if
you're lucky, in a flicker you barely perceive. The physios put a
bench in front of my knees so that if I toppled forward, I would
not go onto the floor. And there I sat, for perhaps forty minutes
at a time, hands aching on the blue plastic, wobbling, tilting
forward a little, bracing through my shoulders and arms, trying
to heave. Did anything happen that time? I could only tell by
peering down, trying to imagine a sensation of lightening. It
was exhausting. And I couldn't kid myself that I saw anything.

*　　*　　*

The gym had a radio, with notoriously bad reception, tuned by whichever member of staff got to it first in the morning. If Big Willie switched it on, we had Radio 2, because he was addicted to trivia and knew the answers on Pop Master. Margaret, the lovable, warm-hearted physio assistant, upon whose shoulder I often wept, preferred Smooth. And Susan, my own physio, a feisty rock-chick with a tongue stud and attitude, the woman who became the focus of my world, always went for Rock Radio. Somehow, as the weeks stretched onwards into summer, and the hours spent in the gym fused into one another, the only tune I can remember, throbbing fuzzily, flatly, over and over and over again, was 'Heartbeat' by Enrique Iglesias and Nicole Scherzinger. The more tinny and unmoving, the better, as far as I was concerned. Only in the gym could I bear music, where there was company and distraction. On my own radio, in the intimate surroundings of my own bed with an earpiece in, I never tuned to music stations. Only talk could I cope with. Current affairs. Hanging onto the familiar voices of the Radio 4 Today presenters, friends from my lost past, discussing current affairs that used to matter. When I was surprised by snatches of music or songs, especially those that meant something to me, the violence of my grief was overwhelming. Music released emotion. In order to stay strong, I had to shut it out.

About six weeks after my accident, the staff took us out of the unit in a minibus to the local shopping mall to play ten-pin bowling. It was my first time out in the world in a wheelchair and I found it brutal – physically alarming (would my head stay on going round corners?) and emotionally souring. Glowering from the minibus windows at the drivers zooming past in their busy, able-bodied lives, I cursed the bad luck that had put me here, in crippledom, in what felt like the Sunshine Variety bus, rather than where they were.

At the giant shopping complex, I struggled with everything – the fresh air, the searing daylight, the tiny gradient up to the entrance, the sight of people, people, people, effortlessly doing all the things I used to do, getting out of cars, rushing into shops, window shopping. The sense of dislocation and loss was profound and I felt so small that I wished I could disappear, swallowed up in my own tears of self-pity. Weeping defiantly, I inched my way along the fronts of shops full of clothes designed to look good when you're standing up, cursing them as well. As I was by far the weakest wheelchair pusher there – and it's a tough school, spinal physio; you have to push yourself – I was trailing a long way behind the others by the time I got to the bowling alley at the end of the mall. Black humour is possibly the very last lifebuoy left in the sea at times like that; it certainly came to my rescue that afternoon.

The spinal outing had coincided with that of a group of special needs adults, who were clustered around the arcade games at the entrance to the bowling alley. Severe Down's syndrome, people with growth deficit, damaged bodies and all degrees of learning difficulty, enthralled by the flashing lights and the buttons to press. Then they saw me coming. I guess I was some sight: a kind of Ninja Turtle moving very, very slowly on wheels, encased in black and white plastic from chin to groin, flailing elbows, funny gloves, red eyes, a yellow bag of urine and its valve trailing mysteriously from under my trouser leg. They all turned, entranced by the vision. At the entrance, just where the arcade machines were, the shiny floor of the mall turned to carpet and upon it I stuck, becalmed, and my legs went into spasm.

Oooooh, said the army of little people, and they forsook the flashing lights and motorbike simulators to gather around me. They inspected me at close range with grave, uninhibited curiosity, fascinated by the alien on wheels flailing weakly in front of them. I smiled and nodded at them, foolishly trying to protect my dignity. They didn't care. They weren't being judgemental. I realised that they had instinctively identified someone who was as low down the pecking order as they were. I was one of them, but I looked a bit funnier. I might even be lower down the order than them. Indeed, most of these solemn-faced souls were taller than me, and much more mobile. I felt as if I had been cast in one of Alan Bleasdale's black comedy dramas. They were still staring, gently but persistently, when a nurse came to my rescue and pushed me onto the carpet towards the bowling alley, and balls I could neither lift nor bowl.

During those early days in rehabilitation, I got to put a face to Snafu, whose angry, distressed voice had echoed round my nights in the high dependency ward. Everyone adored Snafu – male and female patients, nurses, physiotherapists, his mum, his sisters, his Army mates, his five thousand ex-girlfriends: he was a tough, outrageous, larger-than-life character, as wild as a semi-domesticated polecat, as sharp as any stand-up comedian, as mature as he was vulnerable. Then nineteen, he had been shot in Helmand, Afghanistan, when a sniper's bullet sneaked into the sleeve hole of his body armour, hit his shoulder blade and ricocheted through his spine at the top of his chest. He reckoned the Afghan was a rubbish shot.

'If he was any good I'd be dead, wouldn't I?'

As he lay on the ground, fully conscious, he remembers bantering with his fellow soldiers. He thought he was dying, but decided he might as well go with a smile on his face. His mates told him what soldiers always tell their dying comrades – that he'd be all right; that he'd be in the pub in no time. He was helicoptered to Camp Bastion, thence to Birmingham, and soon to the spinal injuries unit in Glasgow, to be nearer his family. The six-foot-four, fifteen-stone soldier morphed into a skinny, laconic, blue-eyed tetraplegic playboy, soon well enough to dance around the gym on the back wheels of his wheelchair like a trick cyclist, chatting up all the girls, amusing everyone with his antics. Either that, or he indulged in a soldier's favourite game of mooching, fag in hand, at the door, trading profane insults with anyone brave enough to take him on.

During the Pope's visit to Glasgow in 2010, Snafu appeared at one end of the ward, as if in a vision, a mitre fashioned from a pillowcase stuffed with cardboard upon his head, his body draped in a white blanket, a giant crucifix round his neck. He carried an aluminium brush handle as a staff and glided regally up the ward in his chair handing out fragments of sliced white bread to the occupant of every bed. In Glasgow, a city riven by religious divide, the comedy was especially edgy, of course, because he was a Protestant; a Rangers football team supporter.

'Bless you my child,' he said at every bedside.

And to the women and the female nurses, his eyes dancing sardonically: 'Kiss my ring.'

Several years have passed, but I can still remember the sustained gale of laughter following him up the corridor that day. People laughed and then kept on laughing and then laughed some more. You simply don't hear that in hospital. He provoked a similar outbreak of mirth in the gym when, bored and restless as he often was, he wheeled around asking all the women present how much they would charge to lap-dance for him.

The physios gathered their professional dignity and tried not to join in.

'Get lost, Snafu.'

'Go away! Aren't you supposed to be on the triceps press?'

He was utterly persistent. 'No, you have to tell me. How much?'

Eventually, casting their eyes around to make sure no NHS suits with clipboards were lurking, the physios played his game.

'Four million,' said one.

'At least. Because my career would be finished if I was found out.'

'Six million.'

'I wouldn't do it.' A humourless junior physiotherapist on rotation in spinal.

His eyes lighted wickedly on me, purple-faced, toppled helplessly over my own knees. 'Hey Mel, what would *you* charge?'

I was flattered to be asked. He tolerated me, just about, as a mate, although his banter was brutal – I was as old as his granny, plus he'd decided I was officer class. I'd been a horse rider, after all, and he'd found out my house had an orchard – so in the gym he loudly dubbed me a caviar-eating snob. In private, when he found me in tears, he was kindness itself. He was a year younger than my own son.

'Half a million,' I said. 'Because my freak value doesn't outweigh the fact I'm too old.'

'Nah,' he agreed.

Snafu got particularly bored at weekends, when there was no gym. One Sunday evening, the place packed with visitors, his terrible screams echoed down the ward: 'Aaaaargh!! Nurse!!!! Come quick!!!! I can't feel my legs!!!' For amusement, he regularly soaked the auxiliaries when they helped him shower, or when the fire alarm went off, as it did often, he sped up the ward screaming, 'Fire! Everyone out! This one's for real.' It was Snafu who yelled triumphantly across the gym, 'Susaaaaan! Ah've pished masel'!' when his catheter tube became disconnected from his leg bag; who invented wheelbarrow races for the paralysed; who decided to practise commando crawl across the gym, dragging his legs behind him, and of course wriggled straight out of his tracksuit bottoms, exposing himself to the world, and leaving the physiotherapists initially too helpless with laughter to cover him up; and it was Snafu who, despite his impaired hands, beat everyone in the target-shooting competition one Wednesday afternoon, part of our weekly games session. As a flourish, to demonstrate he was in the company of amateurs, he also shot the clock on the gym wall: the holes remain in the glass to this day. He had wanted to be a soldier since he was four and before he was paralysed he'd been in line for specialist sniper training and promotion. A man-child: incorrigible, charismatic, vulgar, cynical, careless, self-destructive, heroic, vulnerable, shrewd. Of all the people I encountered in the tiny, little-understood world of spinal injury, he was the one that made me the most sad.

*   *   *

Approaching bedtime on the rehab ward was the worst. The conveyor-belt sequence kicked in again, in reverse, and we sat by our beds, queueing for the team of two nurses to come and hoist us out of our chairs onto the sheets and attach our overnight urine bags. Then we waited for the final drugs trolley. Long-term incarceration in hospital teaches you tolerance, patience and the knowledge that we are all very, very human. Even now, years later, when I close my eyes I can hear the banter of Rosebud in the distance and the squeak and rattle of the night-time trolley she is pushing. And around me I can sense some of my fellow patients starting to flutter and jangle. Respectable middle-aged women, with husbands and flowerbeds and Vauxhall Astras, but now hungry for whatever opiate or benzodiazepine they needed to soothe the mental anguish of their state, their personal paradise lost. They hungered, bodies paralysed but writhing inside for medication, just as mine had writhed in the high-dependency ward. When was the trolley coming? One woman would press her buzzer anxiously and then others would follow. The drone of multiple alarms would sound down the long ward.

'What kept you?' Mrs Bennett would cry.

Rosebud, ever insouciant, was having none of it.

'What do you think this is? BUPA?' she cried. 'I tell you, you're lucky it isn't. I've worked in private hospitals and they bill you for every single pill you take. Even a paracetamol. Youse are lucky youse are here and not there.'

Apart from when the staff came to turn us onto the other hip on a four-hourly rota, we were then undisturbed until the morning. That was the theory. Nights change when you are in hospital. In fact, as I was to learn, nights change forever when you are paralysed. Any joy went. Your favourite sleeping positions ceased to exist, partly because you could not feel them and partly because you could not achieve them on your own. You adopted the protocol position you were put into – on one hip or the other, pillow wedged into your back, another under the upper knee, more pillows stuffed into the bottom of the bed blocking your feet from going into a flexor spasm downwards. Thus comfort was outsourced: someone else arranged your limbs and your torso in a way which was safe for your skin and for your tubes to survive unblocked. Your frozen hands were put into customised splints, the fingers strapped flat against the formed plastic so they could not contract, and all autonomy was removed. You could no longer scratch your nose, let alone pick it. The private geometry of your night, your ability to cuddle into shapes practised from childhood, was gone for ever: a very personal autonomy to lose. Meanwhile, the hour hands stuck, as if glued, to the face of the clock – T.S. Eliot's 'Only through time time is conquered.' Peace was as lost as paradise. The nurses' station on night shift was notoriously noisy; there were a handful of the staff who seemed unable, or disinclined, to lower their voices as they sat chatting. When buzzers rang, they would push back their chairs, the metal legs screeching on the floor. Weirdly, my paralysed bladder used to spasm at that noise: a peculiar sensation – somewhere deep inside an insensate body, in a dormant vital organ which contained a foreign body, a catheter, there was a horrid jump of indignation at the discordant pitch. Imagine. I could hear with my bladder! Was it transmitted via my ears, down some remaining nerve pathways, or was it a vibration in the air that affected my bladder alone, its catheter acting as a misplaced aerial?

In between interruptions, we learnt to endure the passive tyranny of those long hours, where no limbs stirred, no sheets rustled. These were not normal wards. You have no idea how eerily morgue-like paralysed patients are in bed when they cannot move. Nurses are notoriously superstitious; there are rich stories of ghostly scares on night-time wards with darkened corridors. Delphinium, one of the regular night shift, told me of the fright she had when a patient, paralysed from the neck down and normally as still as a corpse, sat bolt upright as she passed, the result of a sudden, unexpected spasm. Muscle spasms could happen, but rarely as extreme as that.

'I was like, waaaaaaah. Nearly crapped myself,' she said. 'He didn't even wake up.'

Night time. Even if our bodies were by necessity quiet, our minds were their own torture chambers, forever churning the random nature of the accidents, the screaming bad luck which had damned us to stillness. Why us? Why me? And often, if we did dream, our dreams tormented us by putting us back on our feet again. Dreams so vivid that when we woke, it was especially desolate to rediscover reality. One night I dreamt that Vitamin D tablets were a miracle cure for spinal injury, and because I already took them as supplements I was able to walk again. There I was up on my feet, walking unsteadily round the ward helping my fellow patients reach things from their bedside tables, and waiting for the doctors to arrive so I could tell them the good news. I woke up, convinced it wasn't a dream, fighting a sickening lurch of hope and then disappointment before cold logic kicked in. I remember one night I even said to myself in my subconscious, now don't be fooled, this is a dream, you can't really walk again, and then I dreamt that to test it, I had woken up, and it was true – I could actually walk again. Double-dip dreaming. A plot within a plot. But of course everything remained within the parameters of the dream. Waking that morning for real was particularly cruel.

Always in the night there were the needy patients, the ones who became queasy or overcome with pain, or indeed were just desperate for human contact to break their desolation. We had call buzzers on wires; paraplegics had theirs on the bedside table, because they could reach. Tetraplegics with some arm function had them draped across their bedclothes, as in my case. Those who could move only their heads and shoulders had them by their cheek, so they could turn their head and press them. I hated using mine, but many people didn't have the same hang-up. There were also the confused souls who couldn't locate their buzzers, and they would just cry out, 'Nurse … nurse …' Of course the nurses couldn't hear, but the rest of us in the room would be woken, and someone in a nearby bed would press their buzzer instead.

Doobie had a habit of rushing in, crying theatrically: 'Who's buzzing *NOW*?' and striding crossly towards the patient with the flashing call button above their beds.

'It's Elsie,' the buzzer-ringer would stammer, defensively. 'She can't press her buzzer.'

And we lay awake and listened to poor wee Elsie being administered to, because we had no choice. One night, when I was on a further course of antibiotics for a lung infection, I woke with an overwhelming need to vomit. I pressed my buzzer and heard for the first time the distinctive slap, slap of a footfall I would come to dread.

'What is it?' she said. Not kindly.

'I'm sorry but I feel really sick,' I gasped. I was panicking inside. This had never happened before. I didn't even know if I could be sick.

She said nothing, but turned on her heel and disappeared. Soon she returned with a papier-mâché NHS sick bowl, the grey bowler hat of despair. Her body language was contemptuous. She thrust, almost threw, it at me, and walked away, leaving me to be sick alone. She didn't say a word.

It was my first introduction to Nettles.

CHAPTER FOUR

THE ANGELS OF MONS

I think one's feelings waste themselves in words; they
ought to be distilled into actions which bring results.
FLORENCE NIGHTINGALE

A catastrophe delivers you into an alien landscape, in which
you must learn to survive. Paralysis takes you hostage. On the
ward, interred long-term, you learn your territory, the space
defined by the square of curtain rail suspended from the ceiling,
delineating your tiny world of bed and bedside table. You lie
and watch and familiarise, as must men behind bars, or animals
in a zoo. Unbeknowst to you, you are already practising your
next career as one of life's observers, your useless fingers brushing the raised cot sides of the bed, rhythmically, plaintively,
because you are not yet able to hold a book in your hands to
amuse yourself. Maybe you will never be able to hold a book.
You do not know yet.

As in a prisoner of war camp, your relationship with your
guards becomes primary. To achieve this, you first try to grasp
their names – hard in the beginning, because most ward staff
do not wear name badges, nor do they introduce themselves.
They are too busy, plus there is an assumption of automatic
familiarity, as most of the patients are there for a long time.
Then you must learn to distinguish their uniforms, and work

out the caste system so that you can tell nurses from auxiliaries – the nursing assistants. And then the cleaners, in green, typically big powerful women blessed with an extraordinary capacity for hard work. The nurses are bogged down with form-filling and drug administering; the auxiliaries, the ones near enough on a minimum wage, do most of the physical work with patients. They are the ones who clean you up when your bowels burst, who bring you a bowl of cereal in the morning and your milky tea, who roll you and dress you and truss you into back brace and collar, then hoist you into your chair, ready for the day. In the beginning, before you get to know them well, you badge them only as noisy or quiet, kindly or less kind. You judge them intuitively: do they enter your bed space with the body language which says, 'What can I do to make you as comfortable as possible?'; or do they approach with the clear intention of escaping as swiftly as they can? Soon you can read them by the way they walk, their faces, the tilt of their heads, the readiness of their smile.

Most of the auxiliaries were the biggest-hearted people on the planet; those with least tended to give the most, both in time and emotional warmth. The canteen staff were the same. Many were extroverts, performers, who saw it as their role to entertain us. In Glasgow, everyone's got a few Billy Connolly genes: they delighted in telling funny stories, often in competition, as they gathered over our still bodies to wash us. I'd lived in Scotland for decades, but I struggled with their rapier-fast Glaswegian. It was like tuning in to snatches of soap opera on foreign TV.

'And she goes, like, "You never!" And ah goes: "Ah did so. No way he was gonnae get away with that!"'

'How no?'

'Have she shown you her latest tattoo?'

'Who's she no' shown it to?'

'I wouldnae have one down there. I'm, like, "Nice! Not!"'

'You know me, half daft!!'

'Bodrum. Half board £49.99.'

'Ma Jamie he's went the same. Boggin. I'm, like, waaaaaaaah no-way!'

Defined as logs by a log-roll, we behaved accordingly, not that we had much choice; we lay and listened to the domestic dramas unfolding over our bodies, and as we gained in confidence might start to join in. I preferred that, because listening to them talk among themselves, as if I was unconscious, made me feel staggeringly isolated and lonely. With hindsight, I realise their chat, showboating, exaggerated stories, made a hard job more bearable for them. It was timeless gossip, the conversation of bedsides and parish pumps and public wash-houses for centuries, and I much preferred the colourful stuff to listening to them moan about their shifts and the weather.

They told me about the time one of the auxiliaries had answered the phone. It was someone famous asking to speak to a patient she knew.

'Aye, fine. Who's calling?'

'It's Sarah, Duchess of York … but you probably know me as Fergie.'

'Fergie, how *are* you? It's Lily here.'

Glasgow's like that.

*   *   *

There was Marigold, an exuberant, friendly single mother with a loud voice and a huge heart, who often sang to us and hugged us generously when she saw we were miserable. Begonia worked nights – a cryptic former rock-chick, introverted but humorous. So many were divorced single women who had raised their families alone. Chrysanthemum worked nights too – you got paid more – and spent most of the day caring for her grandchildren so her single daughter could hold down a job. 'Men? Useless Bs, the lot of them,' she'd say. No one ever swore in front of patients. Elm was an interesting man who kept a Komodo fighting dragon as a pet. Amaryllis, the wonderful Amaryllis, for whom no request was too much trouble, lived in a council house near the unit and had ongoing problems with a helpless alcoholic who lived upstairs and kept flooding her flat. Clematis, a fearless blonde twenty-one-year-old with generous hips, loved to talk about how she put down men. She'd give Doobie a hard time. 'Jesus Christ,' she'd hiss as they rearranged my body, 'you stink. Do something about it.' Periwinkle, an indomitably good-hearted woman with her hair pinned in an elaborate beehive, was saving up for her and her husband's fourth holiday of the year. Turkey, it was always Turkey. She was so sweet. On her days off she often went into the city centre for the young paralysed men in the ward, to buy the fashionable T-shirts they wanted. They adored her.

Crocus was an older woman, a gentle soul who astonished me by telling me she didn't know how to use a tampon. Candytuft had the build of a marathon runner and was always in a hurry, as if anxious to get to her next cigarette break. Like many of the staff, she had tattoos running the inside of her arm and extending down the outside of her palm. At first, prissily, I found it ugly; it looked as if her hands were dirty. Soon, tattoos ceased to stir me to value judgement: all that mattered, I learnt, was that someone had a kind heart, hands that worked and the time to help me. Helplessness is a great leveller and I became fond of the vast majority of the staff. It was a crappy job and they did it as best they could. They personified the essence of the NHS's immense soft power – that world-famous humanitarian ethos of unquestioning free care, of embracing whatever sickness or disaster or disease is cast by the tide upon the doorstep. It's a kind of warm, fuzzy feeling, a mixture of pride, altruism, generosity and compassion, and it's the NHS's most persistent asset. It's what makes staff walk miles through the snow to get to work, or extend their shifts if no cover is available. It's the ethos that says: *It's what we do. It's what we're good at. We might have little, personally, but we are professionals welcoming anyone. Our jobs, working for the NHS, give us importance and status. We belong to something great.* As a result, kings and commoners alike get treated, mostly, with courtesy and kindness. A form of unwritten morality. The public have the same sense of ownership. Their warm, fuzzy feeling tells them, *It's free because it's ours.* You notice, after a while, that for some this brings an unrealistic sense of entitlement – to the best of treatment, to decent meals, to shorter waiting times. Which also means an entitlement to moan when these things are not delivered. Just as you notice the many who remain humbly grateful for the care they receive, however compromised it is by lack of resources.

There was, of course, the occasional member of staff like Nettles, whose ignorance made you dread interaction with them, especially in your helpless state. Nettles was small but heavy-footed, blonde and calculating, a woman who, as the old saying goes, you wouldn't take a broken pay packet home to on a Friday night. I had taken a dislike to her for her lack of compassion over the sick bowl. The feeling was clearly mutual. The next time I spoke to her I could tell, just from the expression on her face, that my English accent jarred. I had lived long enough in Scotland to be sensitive to this. I was, in her eyes, judged simply a snob.

Hospital, in some ways, is like life on steroids, highly coloured. There were all the human emotions you could recognise, hyper-inflated. But it also contained another world of unfamiliar rituals and undercurrents, of strange protocols and jargon. Infection control was an essential but self-perpetuating hospital industry, and when you were learning independence with a constrained body, it often made life as difficult for you as it did for the germs. Every morning, after the cleaners had done the floors, the auxiliary nurses were tasked with sterilising the meagre surfaces in our personal areas: the over-bed table must be cleared and wiped; everything on top of the locker must be put away in the drawer to allow it to be wiped to prevent dust. Only our personal box of straws, a flag of long-term helplessness, could remain out. Every day, trying to become independent, I would place things where I could just about grip them with my feeble right hand. On the table, my glasses, my transistor radio, which I had developed enough finger power to turn on, my headphones, my laptop, my picnic mug with an open handle. With these small totems of normality within reach, I could retreat into my own world and pretend. On the bedside table, there was toothpaste and a toothbrush, which I was just learning to hold, spitting into a plastic beaker.

I was fiercely protective of these things. They represented gains, hard-won goals.

And every day, after their break and before lunch, the auxiliaries would descend, like Valkyries, and sweep everything aside, moving, rearranging, pushing the table out of reach, smashing the precious little pretence of privacy. And of them all, the most thoughtless by far was Nettles. I watched her on days when I couldn't go to the gym, a master of hiding from work she didn't want to do, but Queen Jobsworth of wiping and cleaning, as she placed my table beyond my reach, swept my possessions into drawers I was too weak to open, unplugged my laptop, and pushed my mug to the back wall. Tidying, always tidying, wiping, intruding, controlling. When I pleaded weakly with her to leave my things out, she gave me a death stare and told me it was against the rules. She was hard and cold and unkind. I started to hate her; I fantasised about shooting her with an AK-47; I learnt to recognise the distinctive drag of her footsteps at night and cowered low.

All totally irrational, of course, and I feel guilt now, but at the time it was hard to describe the daily frustration of seeing stuff inches away, and being unable to reach it. The only way to get hold of it, to be empowered again, was either to use the buzzer to call another hard-pressed member of staff, which I hated doing when it wasn't urgent, or to wait until a friendlier auxiliary was passing. Like prisoners we learnt which guards to ask favours of. A ward needs a Nettles: she served the purpose of making the rest of the staff look as if they were bathed in a warm light of kindness and compassion.

In her own insensitive way, I suspect, she thought she was just following orders, because the ethos of the rehabilitation ward was teaching patients independence. We were to learn self-help, so that when we were released to our old lives we would be able to cope with as much as possible. New staff recruits were actively taught that they must stand back and let patients struggle to do things for themselves, for only that way would we become accustomed to what life was going to be like at home. Patients weren't sick, as such, they were disabled and could be lazy; staff mustn't be too compassionate. Their job was training people for freedom. Re-enablement. Intelligent staff grasped the subtlety of this; they could judge when to hang back and when to weigh in; the less thoughtful, let's say, weren't quite so nuanced.

Euphorbia, a senior nurse, was in charge, with Candytuft as her auxiliary, the day she decreed that I would get on a shower chair in the morning and be washed like everyone else. By now, I must have been on the rehabilitation ward for five or six weeks. Euphorbia was impatient with my slow progress conquering low blood pressure, one of the most pervasive side-effects of spinal injury. When you damage your core, you enter profound spinal shock: it is as if your body retreats into itself and makes its final stand deep inside. Military analogies seem apt. The territory you lose is vast. Your whole system falters, stutters, nearly collapses. Whole battalions put down their weapons, hoist the white flag. You lose your limbs, your motor function and your autonomic nervous system, which automatically regulates both your blood pressure and your temperature when you are healthy. Your intestines lose their peristalsis, the process of food through the gut, and your sphincter muscles are knocked out.

Without temperature regulation, you feel permanently cold – that is, until you feel unbelievably hot. And without any controls over blood-pressure regulation, especially if you are as tall as I am, whenever you are raised into a sitting or standing position, your blood rushes into your feet and you pass out. There were times when my bradycardia, low heartbeat, was down to thirty-four beats per minute, enough to call a crash team for a normal person. In the spinal unit such things were unremarked. But fainting was a new discovery for me, a horrid one. It awakened memories of school, where it was always the pretty, delicate girls who used to faint in assembly. As predictable as Victorian heroines, they would fold to the floor with a little sigh during prayers, to general commotion, and lots of attention from the boys, while us roughtie toughtie hockey types in the back row would mutter cynically, 'That's Pauline off games' or 'I suppose it's her periods *again.*' Of sympathy from us, there was none.

Only now, decades later, I can understand just what those poor girls went through, because I'd turned into the same wan, pathetic creature, turning sheet white and swooning at the slightest provocation. Fainting felt as if death was ripping you out of life and you could feel it happening but could do absolutely nothing about it. There was a dreadful inevitability after I was hoisted out of bed and into a sitting position – visual disturbance, flashing lights, waves of nausea – and then rapidly everything went black with dark green blotches. Voices dimmed and retreated into the distance; I grew hot and claustrophobic; and if no one could tip my wheelchair back in time, and elevate my legs in front of me, I would start moaning involuntarily, flail my arms in distress a bit, and then vomit, mournfully and quite helplessly, into my surgical collar. This was possibly the nastiest side-effect of all, for as the faint normally happened in the morning after my branflakes, the smell of sour milk haunted me thereafter, as if the collar wasn't enough of an instrument of torture already. Fainting was debilitating and I was so prone to it that in those initial weeks any attempt to get me into a shower chair was ruled out. When they did try, I was a time-consuming failure, fainting and vomiting and fit only to be hoisted back into bed to recover. Shower chairs are minimalist plastic-seated wheelchairs, designed by the devil in a bad mood. I came to hate them with a terrible intensity, for the effort and suffering they brought me. And I still do.

Always, the pressure to keep moving people through the system was acute and from somewhere on the ward Euphorbia found an electric shower chair which reclined, tipping you back and pre-empting faints, but still facilitating a proper wash. It was a large, elaborate throne which I viewed warily, dreading the trauma. Use it I must though, because my body had to be trained to adjust to its new state. 'Your blood pressure will stabilise after a while,' they kept telling me, but it didn't. I still came close to fainting every morning, and so eventually I was prescribed ephedrine, a fast-acting stimulant, a cousin of amphetamine, which raised my heart rate. Fifteen minutes before my shower, I swallowed the little pill. It worked. The fainting receded. I was to take the drug many times over the next few months – indeed, years later, I still rely on it to stop me fainting after I've eaten and the blood rushes from my head to my intestines and I mewl and swoon. Very useful to avoid embarrassment in restaurants, it is. In fact I'm eternally grateful to ephedrine because it was in the shower, by chance, when I tipped forward in the chair to let the nurse wash my back, that I studied my right foot. It was lurid purple and white, engorged with fluid, the nails sunk into the flesh. The feet of paralysed people are frequently swollen, but this looked ghastly.

My nurse that day was Gillian, one of the seniors and my named nurse on the rehabilitation ward. She was one who really would qualify as an Angel of Mons, perceptive, giving, hard-working, modest to the point of shyness. Just by being on duty, she made me feel happy and safe. She was a great hugger too. Many a time I wept on her shoulder and perhaps she was too self-effacing to realise it, but she was largely responsible for holding me together mentally. She was also a brilliant professional.

'Yuck, look how disgusting that foot is,' I said, not sensing anything was wrong, more to make mordant conversation than anything else.

She looked hard, then looked again. 'Oh,' she said. 'Not good.'

As soon as she could, she had me back in bed and measured my legs with a tape, which showed that my right ankle, calf and thigh were up to five centimetres thicker than my left. Events moved swiftly. Doctors came, felt the heat and thickness of the leg, gave me an anti-clotting injection, told me to stay in bed and then sent me for a Doppler ultrasound scan, which measures blood flow. The technician started in my groin, laying a snail's trail of gel all the way down to my knee. Almost as soon as she had started, right at the top of my inside thigh, she said: 'I can stop already,' she said. 'There is indeed a clot there.'

I managed not to burst into tears, but it was hard. A deep-vein thrombosis was a dangerous thing, with the risk that it could move to the lungs and cause a stroke or a heart attack. The doctors told me to avoid lower body exercise for a week until the warfarin was thoroughly into my system; they were fairly sang-froid. Used to it. For me, it weakened my strategy of denial. There could be no kidology. Every night I pushed down my bedclothes and watched as the nurse injected the anticoagulant into my tummy, wishing that I could feel the big needle going in. My right leg was hot and as thick as a tree trunk and I was back wearing thigh-length white anti-embolism stockings. Now, on top of everything else, I had a timebomb inside me. It was a complication I really didn't deserve, I thought bitterly – but that was an illogical thought, so I banished it. Between the bouts of crying, I was getting tougher with myself.

I cried even harder when one consultant – auxiliaries had no monopoly on insensitivity – told me one leg would probably always be thicker than the other. Later, a comment like that wouldn't matter a damn. Then, it was devastating.

Along with the ephedrine must be added the warfarin, which came in different-coloured tablets depending on what dose you were getting, like menacing Smarties. The dose depended on how thin your blood was, and that depended on the vampires taking it from your veins several times a week to be measured. The vampires were the team of specialist blood-takers who toured the hospital. Maybe it was the nature of the job but they were as grim-faced as the Gullet Controllers, no small talk or smiles: just Formula One pitstop stuff again – elastic band to squeeze the vein, needle in, vials filled, wipe of spirit, tiny plaster, and away.

Four times a day in hospital, for my entire stay, I was swallowing large quantities of pills from little plastic tubs handed to me by a nurse. Years later, when I cleared out the drugs I had come home with, I was astounded by all the things I no longer needed to take. There was one, though, which I could never discard – nifedipine for autonomic dysreflexia. The nifedipine came in ten-milligram capsules. 'Bite into ONE and retain the liquid in the mouth if required for dysreflexia max 4 caps in an hour,' said the instructions coolly. 'Do not eat grapefruit or drink grapefruit juice.' Those pills were dated Feb 2011 and had a sinister backstory. If you were a tetraplegic you were supposed to take them everywhere you went and carry an emergency information card with you, because without them you might die.

Autonomic dysreflexia. The name took on such an apocalyptic resonance it became a source of dark humour. At our weekly education session it was drummed into us how susceptible tetraplegics were to autonomic dysreflexia and how alert we must be. Basically, when you're paralysed in any way, you can't feel if you've fractured a leg, blocked your bladder or got an ingrowing toenail, which is bad enough for paraplegics, but if your injury is at cervical level things are far worse, because your autonomic nervous system can massively overreact to the pain stimuli. Your body goes dysreflexic – which translates as haywire. This means sky-high blood pressure, a pounding headache and flushed skin from the level of your neck break up – if untreated, strokes, heart attacks and death are likely to follow. Nifedipine was the antidote – a fast-acting blood-pressure-lowering drug; if smitten, we were to take one and head straight for the nearest A&E. Do not tarry. Do not pass Go, do not collect £200. You are a medical emergency. Around that time, I went on my first outing from the spinal unit unaccompanied by any medical staff. My friends were entrusted with nifedipine to administer in such circumstances – with those same instructions, as in the corniest spy movies, that I must first bite into the capsule and swallow the contents.

One of the young, super-efficient staff nurses, Begonia, gave a quick briefing on autonomic dysreflexia as our taxi waited. It put the fear of God into my friend Susan.

'She'll flush and get a pounding headache.'

'But how can we tell?' Susan asked. 'How will we recognise how bad a headache it might be?'

'They say,' said Begonia grimly, 'it's like a sense of impending doom. You can't mistake it.'

Every now and again, going round the art gallery, I caught Susan and Alex peering anxiously at me, checking.

'No sign of impending doom?' they asked. 'Are you absolutely sure?'

I have never yet, touch wood, had an attack, but when I crowed about this once to a spinal unit nurse, she smacked me down, telling me it can start at any time. I confess I have stopped carrying the drug, though. The one time I did have to rush to A&E with a blocked catheter, some years later, I was not suffering from dysreflexia, but was terrified it might occur. I told the registrar this, as I sought to explain the urgency of my visit. She looked blank; she had never heard of it. Some of my contemporaries from the unit were a lot less lucky than me. For one poor man, dysreflexia meant an almost nightly emergency after he went home, requiring numerous trips to A&E. While still in hospital some of the bad boys learnt to self-induce it in order to cause chaos. Joker, bored by lights out, worked out how to kink the tube of his catheter between his frozen fists, and would deliberately stop his urine draining to induce the symptoms. Then he'd press his buzzer and shriek, 'Nurse! Help!

I'm dysreflexic!' knowing it would mean lots of fuss and attention and form-filling. The nurses cottoned on to him, but there
was little they could do. The condition, interestingly, is also said
to be utilised by Paralympic athletes. They've discovered that if
they make themselves marginally dysreflexic before they
compete, it can improve their performance. Does that consti-
tute cheating? It is a hard one to call.

My bed had been moved into the bay nearest the window,
and I spent a lot of time gazing at the shabby shrubs, the fence,
and the ceaseless motion of the dual carriageway behind it. One
lunchtime I watched an urban fox picking its way along the
fence line. It wasn't like the country foxes at home, big, strong
and healthy: this was a tiny, mangy-looking vixen limping on
three legs; its fourth, a hind, suspended from the ground,
looked distorted, grey and bloodily matted. Even from a
distance, the wound looked gangrenous. My immediate
impulse was that of a country person, and unambiguous – I
wanted someone to shoot it to save it from a slow, lingering
death. Then, as if someone had stopped time, the vixen paused
and lifted her head to stare at me. We gazed at one other
through the glass, about ten feet apart, for several long seconds.
She was unafraid, coolly appraising. And it occurred to me that
she was looking at a creature just as injured and doomed as she
was, and just as incapable of fending for itself or having a
future. Maybe, I wondered wryly, she's thinking the very same
thing as me: put that pathetic paralysed creature out of its
misery. And which of us has the greater moral heft, I wondered.
I watched her limp away.

My physical plight, I was learning, was the equivalent of
being sent to university to do a degree in humility. I don't think

I had been particularly arrogant before, and I had always tried very hard not to be snobbish, but I was certainly guilty of complacency. Now, with fresh eyes, in a situation from which no amount of qualifications, salary and good taste would ever be able to extract me, I was learning to reassess everything. Passing judgement of any kind was suddenly a dangerous thing to do. The spinal unit was linked to the rest of the hospital by a corridor, and at the end of it, the main entrance for various medical departments, there was in those days a coffee bar. I would escape there sometimes, after gym, pushing myself very slowly and determinedly, and would sit gazing out of the window at the world. Outside, patients would go to smoke, and one day I watched a living cadaver of a man, in a thin dressing gown and bare legs, with a feeding tube dangling from his cheek and bumping on his chest like a hangman's noose. He was grey in colour and looked about ninety years old, though he was probably about my age. A cannula for intravenous fluids projected from the back of the hand with which he raised his cigarette to his mouth. He was joined by a younger woman, also in nightclothes, who had a tracheotomy on her throat but was also smoking. Apparently, if the mechanism of the tracheotomy is uncuffed, it allows some smoke to reach the lungs. Such was the power of nicotine. The sense these people were so evidently dying from their addiction made them uncomfortable viewing.

But who was I to judge? The moral question of how far a public health service should go to treat addicted or self-destructive people is a gnarly one. But it is funny how the middle classes are the ones that agonise over this the most, and see no equivalence in their own behaviours. Poor people who smoke – bad. Rich people who ski off a mountain – unlucky. I was aware my own addiction to a risky, expensive sport was now costing the NHS thousands of pounds a month, if not a week. I figured I wasn't in a position to criticise any dangerous lifestyle choices. To be human is to possess weaknesses.

By then, in terms of humility studies, I was getting considerably wiser. Lunch in the spinal unit was at a rigorously enforced twelve noon – they had a system of protected mealtimes – and we, the patients, made our way, snail-like, towards the canteen from the gym. When my arms got tired wheeling my chair across the carpet in reception, I would stop and scan the noticeboard until the muscles stopped burning and I could continue.

On the board there was an action plan. One of the hospital's goals, it stated, was: 'We aim for respect and dignity be 100% positive (sic)'. Underneath, in the space for 'Actions', it said: 'As a result of your feedback we are working with the person centred collaborative in identifying and addressing real time areas of concern.' It made me smile every time I saw it. Because the average member of the public in this neck of the woods, your tough, pungent Glaswegian, would have one, absolutely correct, response.

'Whit the fuck does that mean?'

Whit the fuck *did* it mean? Translated, I think, it meant that some people had complained about the way they or their families had been treated by staff – that 'person centred collaborative', a euphemism so majestic that if you had spent a week trying, you couldn't have come up with it. 'Real time areas of concern' meant people's moans. At some point a nurse or a doctor or administrator had been perceived to be inattentive.

At some point a patient had been left wanting. Complaints had been submitted, arrows fired, fury vented – where there is catastrophe, there is always anger – and in response the NHS had mounted an impenetrable fire blanket of opaque words.

It was to become an endless source of amusement, watching a feisty Glaswegian workforce function within this maze of inane, pompous directives, protocols and management-speak, about everything from hand-washing to career development. Language-induced paralysis. *Oh for fuck's sake! Just do it!* Daily, the NHS survives because staff at the sharp end thwart the unwieldiness and incompetence centrally imposed upon them. At its most darkly comic, hospital life is a daily battle by good people against the system; and our health service is, when you are unlucky enough to observe it long-term, as close to a benign communist state as it is possible to get in Britain, a flawed monolith, a magnificent, dysfunctional, revered, anachronistic, socially binding but bankrupt, life-saving institution.

Within the structure of what is one of the five biggest employers in the world, there is a job for everyone. Into the whole spectrum of skill, education and ability fits all of human life, from porters and car park attendants to cleaners to nurses, clerks, researchers, administrators, therapists and surgeons. The 'person centred collaborative' is actually the cast list of a perpetual soap opera: a vivid, ever-renewing list of heroes, villains, victims and all the ordinary characters in between. Here the professional, the idle, the dedicated, the lovely and the utterly unremarkable toil shoulder to shoulder. There are staff who skive effortlessly; and there are grafters who do the work of three or four people. Little is done either to punish or reward anyone. Because that's not the way the system works, comrades. It's easy to mock. But what I loved about the communist ethos was that the NHS could fit you in, however lowly you were, and give you a chance. Some of the porters I met were rough, scarred, inarticulate men who would scare you if you met them on a dark night. But it was just great when you approached a reception desk and behind it sat a similar tough-guy with full-sleeve tattoos who confounded all expectations and turned out to be the sweetest, most helpful person you'd meet all day.

I came to revere the quiet, conscientious members of staff, those who would do their work twice over and slip away at the end of their poorly paid shifts. The porters who warned you there was a bump coming, the auxiliaries who made a special journey to fetch chilled water for you. The nurses with their omni-job, saving lives, clearing up body fluids, juggling bureaucratic targets, counselling the bereaved, fixing radiators, TVs, window catches and gluing legs on reading glasses. (And we, the public, expected them to be charming, compassionate and smiley as well, at all times.)

Swiftly, I learnt to find humour in everything and avoid anyone, patient or staff member, who was a professional moaner. Moaning, especially about hospital food, was a black, energy-sapping hole. The canteen staff were gems, often the funniest and sweetest people of all – 'Brekkie darlings!' – and the food, for the most part, was edible. And if it was gruesome, then that was also a bit of a laugh. I took the view that I had not gone into hospital to eat gourmet meals. It was fuel: get on with it.

And where humour was concerned, bureaucracy was the gift that kept on giving.

One night Kuba, who'd had his accident snowboarding, decided he wanted to transfer from wheelchair into bed without assistance.

'See you,' threatened Lupin. 'You're just making trouble when I'm on duty. Have the physios said you can start this?'

'Yeh yeh, c'mon.' He was flirting with her. She was wonderfully flirtable with.

'Just make sure you don't fall on the floor.'

'I'll be fine.'

'I'm not worried about you, sunshine. It's the form-filling that would kill me.'

And it did kill them. One night, carelessly, I slid onto the floor, in slow motion, while being helped into bed. I felt OK, but the nurses flapped, frightened by repercussions. Blame was institutionalised in the system, a game of pass-the-parcel that every employee was forced to play every minute of the day, and they were all terrified of being the one holding the package when the music stopped. After a fall, protocol decreed that a duty doctor from another part of the general hospital must come and examine me, I presume lest I sue. Eventually, well after midnight, an overworked junior doctor, ruled by the tyranny of her bleeper, arrived. She leant over my bed, ticking boxes on the lengthy fall form, poor girl.

'Does anything feel broken?'

'Er ...'

'Can you move your leg? Any pain?'

'Er ... no ... you see I'm paraly—'

But the bleeper distracted her and she was called away to some other distant emergency. They were a lost, overworked tribe, those junior doctors, inexperienced dogsbodies learning on the job. In the middle of another night, a couple of years later, on a medical ward elsewhere in the hospital, I witnessed a distressed elderly lady who had been admitted to the bed opposite me. She came via A&E. Her husband, terminally ill with cancer, was near the end, and she was his carer. Under the strain, her body had betrayed her: she had collapsed in a melt-down of her own faeces and vomit and a neighbour had called an ambulance. She didn't want to be there, utterly distraught about leaving her husband behind. The A&E staff had cleaned her up and decided to keep her in for tests; now a junior doctor had been sent to get a blood sample. Please let me go home, she pleaded. I have to go home.

He tried his best to reassure her. We just need to check you out. But he simply could not find a vein, and the longer he took the more nervous he got and the more she suffered – one of the myriad lonely little scenes that hospital creates, night after night. He spent the best part of twenty minutes puncturing first one arm, then the other, to find a vein. I lay in the dark listening to the harrowing soundtrack from behind the curtains, his incom-petence, her distress, and I writhed inside with pity and embar-rassment for both of them. It shouldn't be like this. Getting old and ill should be tidier than this. But it isn't. Learning to be a doctor should be easier than this. But it isn't. He desperately needed the expertise of those charmless vampire blood collec-tors. She needed some kind nurse with the time to phone a neighbour or family member and set her mind at rest. But these are the sad deficits and these the messy truths of the small hours; this the reality of ill health none of us wants to know.

The NHS estates department was the funniest. There are no crash teams for resuscitation of buildings, just small communist cells who moved – slowly, comrades, slowly – from one planned job to the next. One Friday night, the spinal unit central heating had packed in. The ward was freezing and the heating ducts were emitting a screeching noise. Everyone was calling for extra blankets. At about 11 p.m., three hours after they were alerted, the NHS in-house maintenance men arrived. There were four of them: wearing boiler suits and slightly superior expressions. They ignored the patients completely. After a long pause, someone got a ladder and one of them climbed into the roof space through a ceiling panel. Like a comedy sketch, the other three stood self-importantly at the foot of the ladder, looking up.

'Try the back,' one of them called up.

'Nah, no' working.' Muffled.

'Switch the other yin aff.'

'No' working either.'

The man in the ceiling popped his head back down.

'It'll need to wait until Monday.'

They all nodded. 'Monday.'

And so it did.

Heating worked both ways. In late spring of my stay, there was a sudden warm spell: the temperature inside the unit jumped to thirty-two degrees. Radiators valiantly pumped hundreds of pounds' worth of kilowatts out of open windows and fire exits. Sickening, stifling heat. Our families brought in fans to allow us to sleep at night. We wilted, fainted, puked. Days passed. I wanted to lead a walk-out, except none of us could walk.

I remember, in exasperation, asking one of the doctors:

'Why on earth can't someone *do* something?'

'Ah,' he said, 'a good question. What you learn in the NHS is that only the man who's authorised to turn down the heating is allowed to turn it down; and he will only do it when he's been told to do so by the man who's authorised to tell him. I suspect they can't locate that second man.'

He paused, then added reassuringly: 'It's only been four days. That's not bad.'

In the gym of the spinal unit, a relatively modern building, the roof leaked. In our chairs, we negotiated our way around buckets on the floor. It leaked when I arrived; it still leaked a year later. Then there was the spinal unit's hydrotherapy pool – closed because the showers had been unsuccessfully refurbished by the NHS plumbers and now the drains didn't work properly, allowing water to build up in the cubicles. One of the more militant auxiliary nurses, I think it was the unlovable Hellebore, the queen of union grievance against the management, had complained to the union about the risk of slipping in the standing water as she showered us after hydrotherapy. As a result health and safety shut the pool down. The patients, for once, made a fuss – Dave, Kindle's mum, and others. There was a groundswell of grumbling, like angry bees that couldn't fly. We complained to the person centred collaborative about a real time area of concern, because we loved our swimming, the chance to be free and float, paralysed limbs let loose from hard surfaces. We loved it more than we cared about the staff getting their trainers a bit wet. Very reluctantly, because of our protest, management agreed to buy the nurses wellies. Pool duty became voluntary: only those staff who were prepared to take the risks of injury.

During my time in high dependency, my physio Susan asked to fill in a form with me. It was standard, apparently. Just a depression score. Accordingly, while I lay in bed, and she tried to keep a straight face, we went through several A4 pages of questions. In fact the Hospital Anxiety and Depression Scale (HADS) soared beyond irony to some higher field of parody. Only in the darkest of comedies would you be tasked to approach a person, newly paralysed from the neck down, and ask them such internationally standardised multiple choice questions as:

'I still enjoy the things I used to enjoy – a) definitely as much, b) not quite so much, c) only a little or d) hardly at all'.

'I feel as if I am slowed down – a) nearly all the time b) very often, c) sometimes and d) not at all'.

My personal favourite was the fabulous: 'I get a sort of frightened feeling as if something awful is about to happen – a) very definitely and quite badly, b) yes, but not too badly, c) a little, but it doesn't worry me and d) not at all'.

Who would have thought health service bureaucrats all over the world had such a fantastic sense of irony? Sadly, there was no question about 'a sense of impending doom' on the HADS.

Neuropathic sensation is like owning a body invaded by ghosts and embers and flickers of flame, St Elmo's fire running rampant. By turns hot, cold, sharp – or worst of all, droning constant pain. During the day, you can to some extent tune out, distract yourself with other things. At night, though, your legs get noisy: the ruined misfiring nerves come out to play. In the beginning, post-accident, my legs were as dead as could be. After a few weeks, though, I became aware of the vaguest sensation, like pins and needles, when the nurses handled them as they washed and dressed me. And pretty soon, lying in the dark, I could feel buzzing and hammering and stuttering inside my frozen limbs. Was it blood vessels? Was it nerves? Strange analogies came to me: when they thumped particularly hard it was like someone trying to restart a lawnmower which had been laid up all winter. Coughing, choking. Or a computer whirring despondently, attempting to reboot itself but failing. I was reminded of a hired minibus I once saw in the Alps, refuelled with petrol instead of diesel, kangarooing a metre at a time up the hill from Bourg St Maurice, belching smoke. These were times when the thumping was so strong that I would raise the head of the bed so I could see if my legs were physically jumping. They were as still as in the grave.

Sitting in my chair one day, six or seven weeks after my accident, I convinced myself that my left thigh, the non-DVT leg, had twitched sideways on command. I stared at it, willing it to move inwards towards the other knee. I was sure there was a flicker. Well, maybe. I told Susan, my physiotherapist, and she gave me her classic Oh-yeah-who-are-you-kidding look, because part of her job was to stop people like me destroying ourselves with false expectations.

'Show me,' she said.

I tried. Two grown women bent over, gazing intently at a set of knees.

'See! It flickered.'

She didn't say anything. She put my feet up on the bench, took off my trainers and liberated my toes from the dreaded elastic stockings. She flexed the left foot a little up towards the calf.

'Try and move your toes.'

I tried. I called on all the chasing phantoms inside. And as I watched, willing them to move, the middle and fourth toe went up and down. Susan looked intrigued; I couldn't believe what I had seen.

'Do it again,' she said.

And they moved again. It was the faintest of weak flickers.

'Try the big toe.'

Astonishingly, on demand, it too jerked slightly upwards.

'Move it down again.'

But I couldn't. Nor, when we tried, could I move the toes on the other foot at all. The miracle was over. The left-foot toes were exhausted with the massive effort, but we had witnessed their stirring with our own eyes. It meant, surely, there was some connection. That signals were still getting through. I was too excited to say anything. My mouth had fallen open into a big 'O' and my brain was boiling with joy, excitement, amazement. Susan was very quiet. She put my socks and shoes back on and I saw her looking at my body quizzically, coolly, a professional appraising a lump of meat that had come to life when it had been signed off as dead.

By now, gym had finished and I was late, pushing back to the ward as fast as I was able. My nephew Lucas, who lived in France, had just arrived. I caught up with him in the corridor. The instant he turned and our eyes met, I burst into tears, sobbing and laughing simultaneously, a controlled woman very close to being out of control.

'Lucas,' I cried. 'I can wiggle my toes!'

CHAPTER FIVE

POLLYANNA SYNDROME

'And I can be glad there isn't any looking glass here,
'cause where there isn't any glass I can't see my freckles.'
ELEANOR H. PORTER, *POLLYANNA*

Everyone knew what a toe wiggle meant, didn't they? Even lay people. If you could wiggle your toes, it meant you weren't really paralysed. You were going to be all right. Wiggling toes were the sign. I had a flashback to a Saturday morning perhaps two years previously, in another city A&E, and my long, lanky son in muddy rugby kit lying there, head and neck fixed between orange pads, rushed from the playing field with a suspected neck injury. Me, my heart pounding so hard it was making me stagger, my face a mask of calm, and him breaking into a cheery greeting: 'It's OK, Mum, I can wiggle my toes. Look.' And I looked and the size 14s, studs and all, sticking long off the end of the bed, wiggled away obediently. He'd pinged his trapezium muscle, that was all. Another more recent memory – in high dependency, the young snowboard instructor in the opposite bed to me, lying in a state of shock, trussed in a body brace. But his toes were poking out from under the blankets towards me, and they were wiggling. He would be all right. Now mine were wiggling. Maybe, if I just waited long enough, the fairytale would end happily.

* * *

For everyone with a catastrophic injury there comes a point, as the powerful drugs are slowly withdrawn from your system, when you grasp the enormity of what's happened. When you say to yourself: OK, this is actually not a dream. This is your new state of being. Face it.

In the very early days after my accident, in the loneliness of a night-time ward, I found myself contemplating my situation with sudden forensic coolness. There were no tears trickling into my ears, no self-pity; I put away the inner child and appraised as an adult. Yes, it appeared that things were bad, very bad. So bad that I couldn't cope. I was paralysed. It was unbearable. Then, out of nowhere, came the epiphany. With the utmost clarity, I realised that actually, *things could be worse.* What mattered most of all? Not me. Us. Them. My DIY family, created by me from two marriages and held together by love and determination. Our happy, often dysfunctional little unit, our laughter, our independent hobbies, our loving madness, our group hugs, when we shouted and pogoed to the words of the Sister Sledge song 'We Are Family' – three different surnames under one roof, me and my maiden name, my son from my first marriage and my comedian of a second husband. My two adored ones, who I stitched together and kept apart and defended against each other and who sometimes, in my moments of total exasperation with the friction, forced me to cry out that I felt like a half-eaten antelope carcass being fought over by an old lion at one end and his rival, the young lion, at the other.

I would never forgive myself for the trauma I had inflicted on them, but – and on the back of my eyelids I sketched out options like a management consultant – now was the time to consider just how bad it could have been. What if I had a) been killed; b) suffered serious brain damage, with all the monstrous loss of personality that would entail, or b) broken my neck higher up, rendering myself dependent on a respirator to breathe for me, and potentially bed-bound? I envisaged the boys coping with the three possibilities. If a) ... well, Doug was only twenty, losing his mother would be just too tough, his whole life could be thrown off course, his degree unfinished, his future made so much more difficult without me around as backstop. Plus, he might have become effectively homeless, as his incorrigible stepfather, at sixty-four, would initially have fallen apart without me but would have soon found – men do, men do – some available sexy woman, especially one who cooked good mince, and would then have wanted the young lion out of the house. If options b) or c), I had a painful vision of the two of them sacrificing their lives either to care for me at home or, night after night, traipsing dutifully to visit me in a residential home, to sit by my bedside making falsely bright conversation; or to face the certainty of perpetual guilt if they didn't come. No, no, no. With absolute finality, I knew that would destroy their lives.

While on the other hand, if they had someone who was in a wheelchair but could still feed herself, and who was still *herself*, and who regained as much movement and independence as she could and pretended to be as cheerful as normal ... well, that was a much better possibility, wasn't it? Thus, cornered in the rattiest of corners, in the place where living creatures turn on each other or failing that upon themselves, eating their own limbs, I rationalised tough choices. Decided that I was, in the grand scheme of things, lucky.

I remember smiling into the dark, and experiencing a great sense of a burden lifting. It sounds frightfully stiff-upper-lipped and very British. Sort of, 'Gosh, darling, just noticed my right leg's been shot orf, but never mind, not to worry, still got the other one, haven't I?' But I wasn't really that type. Nor was I some graceful martyr. All I sought, at that moment of inner crisis, was a mental lifebelt, a way to survive. And I'd found a good one.

There was another striking moment of insight when I saw families coming to visit their sons and brothers on the ward. Those young males, mere boys, coltish and silly, raw and fermenting with risk, desperate for kicks and speed and prowess, who'd got in cars driven by drunks, who'd ridden motorbikes or mountain bikes too fast, skied too hard, jumped walls with sheer drops on the other side, tried pills they'd never tried before and dived into shallow swimming pools. And the tragedies were carved on their mothers' faces: gaunt, distracted expressions, ravaged by the knowledge that nothing at all within the doctors' power could repair their beloved, perfect sons. Nothing. Nothing that their love could do either, to protect or mend or save or restore normal life. That unfathomable, bottomless love of mother for son rendered impotent. You would kill to save your son; but too late. Now no sacrifice could spare him his own living death. He still lived, but you mourned the loss of all you had projected onto him in your dreams – power, strength, success, happiness, lovers, children. And I would lie and watch them through the internal glass as they walked down the corridor, those broken women with crumpled faces, and imagine I was them. Understanding their visceral grief.

There was one woman; I remember her hair achingly pretty down her back, blonde against a perfect shade of pink top, her face a mask of anger and despair. She was young. Her teenage son, a promising athlete, had broken his neck in a car accident; one of those to have taken a lift from the wrong person on the wrong day. And it was her face that broke me and also mended me, for she made me realise, yet again, *things could have been worse*. Out of her tragedy, I took perspective. It might have been my son lying here, his neck broken, and I might be her, stumbling in, heart in fragments, trying to smile and utter meaningless comforting words about a body ruined before it had grown. No, it was a million times preferable that it was me paralysed, after a life lived, fifty-two good years, while he was still healthy with his life in front of him. And while I wasn't remotely superstitious, or fanciful, I found myself hoping that in a way I had taken the hit for him. If there had to be a hit. If

My four warriors: from left to right, Dougie, Dave,
my brother Andrew and nephew Lucas.

bad luck had to smite the family, if the spinning randomness of physics, of trillions of atoms interacting, meant that dreadful collisions had to happen at some point, then maybe it had happened to me and I'd lengthened the odds of it happening to the others.

From then on, doggedly, and to a large extent unconsciously, I played the glad game. When those toes wiggled, a flame had ignited inside me. There was a chance that I was going to regain movement. For the sake of my boys, I was going to tackle this injury with every resource I could.

Had early events in my life shaped me into an optimist or was it in my genes? The writer and broadcaster Andrew Marr, a Scot by birth and inclination, has a motto, 'Temperament is fate'; he believes that the attitude with which we approach life largely determines where we go. Hence the distinction between the classic English melancholic, the pessimist you might best describe as alone and palely loitering in some graveyard or other, and the Scottish Protestant, a kind of enduring optimist, cheerfully bound by work-ethic – *Aye, lassie, the only place where money comes before work is in the dictionary!* – but prepared to enjoy life nevertheless. Of the two national types, like Andrew, I fell into the latter category by both nature and nurture. This is no doubt because, as a child, there had been no such luxury as moodiness; my father had the monopoly on that, his moods ruled the household, setting the tone for the day; often the week. For anyone else to be sulky or depressed would have been too much for our mother to bear. So my brother and sister and I were brought up to regard bad moods as the ultimate indulgence, a truer stamp of a rude, spoilt brat than ponies or parties.

Escapism was through reading. And as a confirmed book-worm, in a time long, long before the internet, my formative years were indoctrinated by literary heroines from a previous age. It's bitter-sweet now to revisit my best friends on the printed page – those feisty, tomboyish, ever-optimistic, old-fashioned little girls who acted impulsively, got into scrapes – and, little did I know it, set a curious template for my life. Re-reading them now – whoa! Have I been acting out some kind of WASP morality tale for fifty years, since first I ventured under the bedclothes with a book and a torch? Was I trapped in the moral fable whereby a nineteenth-century God visited terrible revenge upon disobedient, wilful, lively females? L.M. Montgomery's *Anne of Green Gables*, while ever upbeat and hot-heated, was lucky: she survived unscathed but for a near-drowning and an unfortunate case of dyed green hair. Jo in *Little Women* was an inveterate tomboy although she managed to avoid injury. But look what happened to Katy and Pollyanna. Susan Coolidge's heroine from *What Katy Did*, bless her, was a thoughtless harum-scarum, forever ripping her clothes and being late, who ensured her downfall by being defi-ant and sulky. Banned from going on a swing in the woodshed, she went on it nevertheless. The swing was dangerous, but her aunt hadn't told her this, believing it was sufficient to issue orders to a child without having to explain why. When the rope pulled from the ceiling Katy fell and damaged her spinal cord.

> Her once active limbs hung heavy and lifeless, and she was not able to walk, or even stand alone. 'My legs feel so queer,' she said one morning, 'they are just like the Prince's legs which were turned to black marble in the *Arabian*

Nights. What do you suppose is the reason, Papa? Won't they feel natural soon?'

'Not soon,' answered Dr Carr. Then he said to himself: 'Poor child, she had better know the truth.' So he went on, aloud, 'I am afraid, my darling, that you must make up your mind to stay in bed a long time.'

The saintly Cousin Helen, also unable to walk, cause unspecified, comes to visit a distraught, depressed Katy, and teaches her the lessons of disability. Katy, she told her, must go back to school.

'It is called the School of Pain,' replied Cousin Helen, with her sweetest smile. 'And the place where the lessons are to be learned is this room of yours. The rules of the school are pretty hard, but the good scholars, who keep them best, find out after a while how right and kind they are. And the lessons aren't easy, either, but the more you study the more interesting they become.'

'What are the lessons?' asked Katy, getting interested, and beginning to feel as if Cousin Helen were telling her a story.

'Well, there's the lesson of Patience. That's one of the hardest studies. You can't learn much of it at a time, but every bit you get by heart, makes the next bit easier. And there's the lesson of Cheerfulness. And the lesson of Making the Best of Things.'

And so it goes on, and so I re-read it after fifty years, ensconced in my wheelchair, part of me wanting to laugh very darkly, part of me feeling the hair stirring on the back of my neck. Cousin Helen spoke also of a lesson of Hopefulness and a lesson of Neatness. Katy must 'to Love's high class attain/ And bid a sweet goodbye to pain.' The contemporary me winces at the cloying moral lesson but as a child I cannot remember passing judgement. Almost by osmosis, I absorbed it.

And Eleanor H. Porter's *Pollyanna* joined *Katy* on the book-shelves of spinal disaster, a much more saccharine orphan alto-gether, who went through life teaching unhappy adults how to play the 'glad game' – the premise being that no matter how bad something seemed, there was always a reason to be glad things weren't worse. And hey, guess what, Pollyanna, sunshine on legs, is hit by a car and ends up in bed, unable to walk.

'But, Aunt Polly, I feel so funny, and so bad! My legs feel so – so queer – only they don't *feel* – at all!'

She sobbed wildly for a minute. Suddenly she stopped and looked up. 'Why, if I can't walk, how am I ever going to be glad for *anything*? … Father said there was always something about everything that might be worse; but I reckon he'd just never heard he couldn't ever walk again. I don't see how there *can* be anything about that, that could be worse – do you?'

Pollyanna, who is, to be honest, rather insufferable, soon recov-ers enough to gasp: 'There is something I can be glad about, after all. I can be glad I've *had* my legs.' So pitch-perfectly grue-some was Pollyanna that psychologists coined the term

Pollyanna Syndrome, also called Pollyannaism or positivity bias: defined as an unrealistic optimism; having an excessive (and even harmful) belief that all things will have positive outcomes, no matter what; a tendency to remember pleasant items more accurately than unpleasant ones.

But wasn't it extraordinary? That two classics of children's literature, two of my seed-corn books, were stories in which the feisty heroines met the worst fate short of death, the thing universally regarded as the ultimate catastrophe: paralysis. Oh, how transgressive did a young female circa 1900 have to be to be punished so terribly? Very little, it seemed. And in order to find redemption for offending true femininity, they had to suffer and strive to find a way back to normal healthy life.

In fairness, it wasn't just women trapped in this kind of morality play. As a child I was entranced by an obscure short story by Rudyard Kipling, 'The Strange Ride of Morrowbie Jukes', practically unreadable now because of its inherent racism, but still intensely haunting, the story of a sunken village in the desert where 'the Dead who did not die, but may not live' had established their headquarters. Jukes, feverish, riding his favourite pony full tilt in the night – I think that was the bit I liked – tumbled into a vast sand trap where they incarcerated the Hindus who had apparently died of cholera but who revived just before their bodies were to be burnt. There was no way out of this mythical, bestial place where humans stole, murdered and ate crows to stay alive. 'Morality is blunted by consorting with the Dead who are alive.' Jukes never stopped trying to escape, of course, and finally escapes from living death when his manservant throws down a length of rope and hauls him up the steep sand walls.

So they had lived with me over the years, and so they must have returned to crowd my unconscious during the long nights in hospital, that motley headstrong crew, the ones who found a way out of scary situations, who escaped paralysis and the fate of the Dead who did not die yet may not live. (A pretty fair summation of paralysis.) Anne, Katy, Jo and Pollyanna, Kim and Mowgli and Morrowbie Jukes and Stig of the Dump and Scout Finch and the cast from *Swallows and Amazons*, Nancy, Peggy, Susan, John, Titty and Roger, forever optimistic, always turning adventures into triumphs. Perhaps my psychological battle to refuse to accept a bad diagnosis was half-won on stern, old-fashioned bookshelves, all those years ago.

It's a dangerous game, looking back and granting bits of your life significance in hindsight, making the past fit the present, making links and causations between random events decades ago and reinterpreting them in the light of today's random events. But somewhere along the line, for sure, I was imprinted with the knowledge that it was always best to be positive. Nobody ever gave up in my world. False hope was always better than no hope. You could never be sure how things would turn out. I always believed that my injury, terrible as it was, was just one more challenge I was going to overcome. Sometimes the odds against you are stacked so high that there is nothing left to do but ignore them and fight. Against all the medical evidence, perhaps out of sheer stubbornness, I decided I was going to reclaim myself; I was going to do it because it was my body and nobody was bloody well going to take it away from me. Not without a fight. That for the sake of those who loved me I could come back from this in some shape or form. I knew I was strong, both mentally and physically: a coper, a sceptic. Nobody told me what to do. My job was to test the evidence.

Beneath the bluster, of course, I knew the realities of spinal cord injury – there is no repair, no cure for paralysis – but I convinced myself that it was worth giving it a go. I had nothing more to lose. When Dr Purcell told me, with the mannered professional calmness of the spinal consultant – *how often has she had to say those awful words?* – that I would go home in a wheelchair, I told her that, with respect, I was going to try and prove her wrong. In response, I remember she tilted her head to me, an acknowledgement of … what, mutual respect, yes, but also sadness, weariness even. Hers was a tough gig.

Dr Purcell wasn't the only one giving me wry looks. Susan, the queen of tough love, the creature I called the Hobbit because she was not tall, did it every day. It must have been tedious, trying to manage my expectations. She had had me from the start. Much later, I saw her initial paperwork for me, filled in within seventy-two hours of admission. After the rectum test by doctors had found no response, Susan, according to standard international practice for spinal injury, had carried out a pinprick test to assess how much sensation I had below the break in my neck. The answer was nothing. Seven-eighths of my body was a strange, warm-but-dead thing attached to my head and shoulders. Accordingly – how brutal it looked – she simply scored a thick black diagonal line through the section of the form relating to mobility. My chances of walking again were dismissed. Accordingly, my bleak Asia A classification. She had filled in the form after our first meeting in the high-dependency ward. In the box asking her to comment on the patient's understanding of her injury, she wrote: 'Knows she has broken her neck and back. Understands she is paralysed but says she wants to get better.' The words were cool and objective. Later, we joked about what she should have put in brackets after it to underline the extent of my delusion. 'Doesn't have a clue, poor fool.' Or even: 'What a nutter.'

After my things-could-be-worse moment, but well before the toe wiggle, I had tackled Susan on my prognosis.

'I'll be able to walk on crutches, won't I?'

This tough, cheerful woman, a real no-shit-sheila, shook her head. There was no false hope in spinal units, not on her watch.

'No, because you have no abdominal muscles. Even people with abdominal muscles tend to give up on crutches in the end, because it takes too much effort.'

'But I'll use the crutches that go in your armpits.'

'Nobody uses those any more. They totally wreck your arms.'

Traditional arm crutches, the type we think of from world wars past, are rarely used, in the UK at least. Used for any length of time, they can cause sores in the armpit and induce paralysis in the arms and hands. Saturday night palsy, it used to be called – from when you drink too much and fall asleep, your arm slung over the arm of the sofa. Or, even more quaintly, honeymoon palsy, when you fall asleep with your arm under your partner's neck. Or take away the joy of drink and sex, and it's just called plain crutch palsy, for the halt and lame, when the radial nerve near the axilla is compressed. Any kind of crutches, I was to learn, are of minimal use by the paralysed. Spinal injury is a planet rare and cruel unto itself. Bursting all available balloons, Susan told me that my big goal was to see if I could 'transfer' independently – that is, move myself from wheelchair into bed and back out again, using my arms to lift myself, swinging my bottom across from one seat to another. But this was not guaranteed. It required considerable arm and shoulder strength and my injuries might rule it out. My size was against me, because I was tall and strong and quite heavy, not wiry or petite.

She didn't quite spell it out to me that without the ability to transfer I was probably destined to spend the rest of my life being hoisted in a sling by two carers, but the implication was clear. I could work it out for myself. Daily hoisting was one of the worst experiences of my injury, a humiliating process and a fate which I was utterly determined to escape.

For everyone with a spinal injury, there was an elephant in the room. It was that looming, enormous question – will I ever walk again? – which haunted you in every quiet moment of your day, and at night was answered by your subconscious, when in your dreams you sprang to your feet and danced around, crying yes, yes, yes, I can walk again. Waking, you had a fleeting sense still of the elephant's great grey hide pressing against you; could feel its hot breath on your neck, nagging you. Will you? Won't you? it asked, not unkindly, but persistently. So everyone wondered, but pretty soon sensible patients accepted their diagnosis and the elephant went away. Then you got patients like me. One day I was in the gym on the handbike, sitting in my chair while my arms and shoulders cycled a few kilometres. Next to me, on a similar machine, only his had mechanised foot pedals, was Stoical, my acquaintance from hand therapy, whose feet were strapped onto the pedals, legs revolving.

Equipment-envy was my most recent affliction. Everywhere I looked I saw bits of kit I wanted to utilise to get better. Why wasn't I on a machine which did that? I was a little shy of Stoical; he seemed very sorted, knowledgeable, self-contained. He wasn't hanging around. I wanted to be like him. I plucked up the courage.

'When do you think I'll get to use the leg bike?'

He looked at me, glanced at my legs.

'Are you complete or incomplete?'

'I don't know.' I had never heard the expression.

He was trying, in his own plain-speaking way, to be gentle.

'If you're incomplete, you can get some recovery. If you're complete, you never do. You must be complete.'

Next opportunity I had, I asked Susan about complete or incomplete. Complete spinal injury, she said, is Asia A, when there's nothing below the break. Incomplete means some of the nerves are still connected and you may get fragments of movement and power back.

'What am I?'

'Complete.'

'So I can't go on the leg bike?'

'No.'

In the absence of anything else to comfort me, I processed Susan's words the only way I could – as a challenge. My family told me, as families have told loved ones with broken spines since time immemorial, that if anyone could do it, I could. Mindset was all. Change your attitude and you change your world. Temperament is fate. So I believed them.

Dear Dougie whispered: 'PMA.'

'What does that mean?'

'Positive Mental Attitude,' he said. 'It's what young people say, Mother.' PMA in the face of all the odds.

By then, a very special mentor had adopted me. After my accident, piles of letters and cards had arrived for me, both in hospital and at home. For many months I was not capable of facing them, mentally or physically, and Dave kept them from me. To open them required reserves of manpower, willpower, curiosity, emotional strength. Focused on survival, I had none of those things to spare. Eventually, after several weeks, a friend persuaded me to face a few, and I discovered a clutch all with the same handwriting. Annie Maw, a warm and wonderful stranger, had entered my life. Although she got no acknowledgement until much later, she continued to write to the hospital faithfully once a week for the length of my stay. Soon, although she didn't know it, she became one of my inspirations. Paralysed in a hunting accident eight years before me, she drew upon her own experience to throw me lifelines, solace, dreams, and a deeper sense of understanding. She was a poetry lover and blessed me with John Masefield's 'An Epilogue'.

I have seen flowers come in stony places
And kind things done by men with ugly faces,
And the gold cup won by the worst horse at the races,
So I trust, too.

I did trust. There was no choice. In the beginning, my whole body was as dead. Then came the strange internal sensations in my legs, and after a few weeks the vaguest awareness that my legs were being touched when the nurses washed me. A tiny bit of feeling returned to my perineal area – I could also tell when my bottom was being towelled dry. Wasn't this a hopeful sign? Minimal as the sensation was, it was enough to help in the long dark hours when one seeks, desperately, for something to hold onto. The changes were too small to log day by day, but over a little while I also became aware of sensations in my feet. Around my right heel, I could tell – just – when someone grasped my heel. It wasn't like normal skin sensation; it was clouded, far distant, a faint signal from light years away. My legs began, as it were, to regain some minimal consciousness. Occasionally I managed to convince myself, usually wrongly, that I was getting some feedback from my joints. This feedback, known as proprioception, is an unconscious facility which we take gloriously for granted until it deserts us. If you have a normal spine, your nervous system chatters constantly and happily to your brain, telling you where your limbs are; it advises when the left knee is bent and the right knee must lock to bear weight; it tells you if your ankle is facing outwards, your foot misplaced, your hip is twisted. I kept trying to guess at what angle my legs were lying in bed, only to be disappointed when the nurses threw back the blanket.

There was so much to learn. Fairly early, I came to realise that every single injury is different. If you equate spinal cord damage to a lorry hitting a British Telecom exchange box on the roadside, you understand that no two collisions are going to have exactly the same outcome. In every case there will be subtle but profound differences in how wires and cables are wrenched out, fractured, stretched and torn. Sometimes the whole box will be taken clear out of the ground, leaving only a stump of connections. Other times it gets only a glancing blow, breaking just a few on one side. Think of the big cables as the main nerve conduits, and the wires inside them as the connections for billions of nerve cells, all chattering away, sending messages back to the brain. Only then do you get a sense of the infinite variety of damage that can be inflicted. My right hand allowed me to grip a fork and eat; my neighbour in hand therapy could not, yet we were nominally the same level of injury. The lorry crashes in much the same way, but a millimetre further left or right, and different wires are ripped.

As the weeks passed, and I spent more hours in the gym, building up the strength of my arms, I was able to do more. I could, when seated on a physio plinth, my legs straight out in front of me, lean and reach toward my toes, then return, slowly, effortfully, to the upright. 'Good, Mel, very good!' I can still hear Susan's voice, that suggestion of surprise and extra enthusiasm. Spinal shock, that self-inflicted ice age, is said to last six weeks. It was in that rough timeframe post-accident that the toe wiggle came. Exploding with joy at this, and relishing how it lightened the faces of my family, I began to wonder if my diagnosis had been so accurate after all. My optimism, it seemed, was not so wrongly placed. The progress flooded me with positivity and made me doubly eager to get to the gym but also, conversely, lent me patience. Improvement had started and with that I was content to relax, aware that the timescale was out of my control. Long-game strategy. I would hunker down, stay positive and wait; a philosophy which remains with me still.

In the gym, without me realising it, all the exercises Susan set me, together with the electronic stimulation in hand therapy, were building towards one end. Hours on the triceps machine, building up enough muscle to tilt forward a little over my knees and lift myself fractionally in my chair. Pressure relieving, it was called. The art of lightening one's backside. As my left wrist and hand grew stronger and started to hurt less, I worked steadily on balance and torso strength. I re-learnt the simple art of sitting independently on a hard bench; then, for hours, practised the technique of how to shuffle my bottom sideways, half an inch at a time in the beginning. Extend arm, tilt weight forward a tiny bit, lift, push with other arm. While I wobbled above it, my backside, hesitantly, slowly, would slide. Usually I would go a little bit one way, then back again, but one Friday afternoon, near the end of the session, Susan told me to keep shuffling. So focused on the technique was I, that it was only when I reached the corner of the plinth that I saw she had placed my chair there as an extension of the bench – at the same height, with a short, wooden transfer board bridging the two surfaces.

'Keep coming,' she said. 'Now reach across and put your hand on the far side of your chair, and lift towards it.'

And before I knew it, I had crossed the board and my bottom had slipped into the haven of my wheelchair cushion. Safe. All by myself. No hoist. No helpers. Just me, my arms and a short plank. I gaped at Susan, brain boiling at what she had stealthily engineered.

'It's a Friday miracle!' she announced, beaming. 'Mel's done her first transfer!'

She had of course planned it; she liked to reach a landmark achievement on a Friday, to send her patients coursing on a high through the weekend. I burst into tears, and then I looked at the clock, which said ten to three, and cried even harder, because I realised that exactly three months previously I was in a Royal Navy Sea King being expedited to hospital, facing the end of the world. By every measure, it was a massive achievement, as significant, I realise now, as the things I used to regard as landmarks in my earlier life – exams, new jobs, buying houses, half marathons. If not even bigger than that. Transferring would prove as useful in my new life as learning maths. Being able to transfer from your seat to another without a hoist was, for a tetraplegic, epic, a passport to a kind of independence which might not have been possible. On the list of priorities, it's close behind being able to feed yourself. With an ability to transfer, in theory you can – if conditions are favourable and of course that's a big if – move into car seats, on and off beds, sofas, airline seats, without having two people and a crane in attendance. A world of possibility opens up.

There was a huge amount of technique to transferring. You needed to practise the various tricks that get you from a soft bed, for instance, into which your hands and your bottom sink, decreasing your leverage, to your chair. To get in and out of a car you need an extra-long board and some courage, bridging the looming gap over the door sill, like a nerve-racking gangway ship to shore. To cope with a difference in height, transferring from a lower sofa, say, back to your chair, needs very strong arms and a lot of conviction. You have to master balance, arm power, your transfer board (I was now given my own, and never was a varnished piece of wood with tapered edges valued as such a badge of pride) and the encumbrance of your legs. My Achilles heel was my left hand, on which the finger joints and knuckles are distorted and hypersensitive from nerve damage. Learning how best to manoeuvre the wrist to lever my weight, without causing too much pain, was a constant challenge.

Transferring into a car does not, if you are a tetraplegic, look pretty. Nothing like your average celebrity, swinging

mini-skirted legs sleekly out of a limo. Nothing like a paraplegic even, who has the use of most of their torso, and can look
fleet and graceful swinging on their arms and lifting their own
legs as if they are weightless. Whereas tetraplegics flail and flub-
ber, upper body lurching forward, arms behind them like ski
jumpers in order to push, head facing away from direction of
travel, grunting with effort and red in the face. Like sea lions
stranded too far from the sea, we toil and flounder to the edge
of a flat surface to launch ourselves elsewhere. And transferring
can easily go wrong. Lots of my fellow patients, home on weekend pass, misjudged their transfers and ended up on the floor,
from where they phoned the ward for advice.

Soon I too was told I could start going home for a visit – first
for a day then, when the adaptations on the house were finished,
and care organised, for a whole weekend. Those initial trips
home had a certain dream-like quality; they were almost out-of-
body experiences. The only creature who really enjoyed it was
our dog, Pip, who turned herself inside out with joy to see me.
A gentle little Staffie rescue dog, she had been very confused
when I had disappeared; her delight in seeing me again was overwhelming. Her ferocious jaws parted in a smile from one ear to
the other, a grotesquely happy, funny sight. She was the most
relaxed of all of us. Everyone else – Dave, the district nurses, the
council carers – seemed tense and keen for the responsibility to
be removed from them as soon as possible. It was an ordeal for
me too – I was scared. I only relaxed in the car on the way back
to the spinal unit on Sunday night, which I regarded as home.
Gym on Monday morning was all I could focus on.

After the toe wiggling, the clinical staff took to inquiring,
carefully dispassionate, if I had noticed any further movement.

Ankles? Knees? Feet? When something more appears, we will work with it, they told me, so I lay at night, wiggling my toes, straining to push my heels towards the end of the bed. Everyone was studiously non-committal. Their first diagnosis was safe ground, they seemed reluctant to leave it. These areas are emotional minefields; doctors and therapists tread warily. It frustrated me, but I didn't blame them. They'd seen my X-rays and MRI scan; I hadn't. But I was challenging the diagnosis fairly hard by now. I'd give them bloody Asia A, I vowed.

Once the three-month marker had passed they took off my collar, a landmark day of recovery in itself. Then I was allowed to go to the hydrotherapy pool – the privilege so nearly removed from us by the militancy of Hellebore and her objection to wet trainers. The pool was a turning point. It was initially one of the oddest experiences, where the gap between dreams and reality, between past life and present, was both agonisingly close and yet never wider. The chlorine smelt the same as I had known since childhood, the water promised the same freedom and release, the acoustics were as bad, but I was no longer me. I had convinced myself I would be magically set free in the water, cured almost biblically, and would swim away, set loose by the buoyancy. How harrowing and tantalising those sessions were to begin with. Getting in was an ordeal: wedged in a mean little pool chair, far too short to support my thighs, I was lowered into the water by a hoist. It was, it occurred to me, exactly like dunking a witch. The therapists floated me off the chair, packing buoyancy aids around my neck and shoulders, and I tried to cope with the sudden near-panic, the crashing disappointment of my continuing helplessness. Nothing had changed. Still paralysed, still contemplating the damn ceiling, unable to get upright, unable to control my body. Passive as an iceberg, my useless motionless body lurking under the water.

My attitude changed as soon as I was towed to the poolside and was able to get enough grip on the side with my fists to haul my upper body upright. That was bliss – a wave of glorious normality, holding myself against the pool wall, eyes orientated horizontally. To start with, that was enough. Then, in subsequent sessions, as I floated, the physios started working my leg muscles. They bent my knees up and then, aided by the buoyancy, I could straighten them myself. There was movement. Pretty soon came a momentous session when I was being held upright by one of the physiotherapists, my feet on the pool floor and my body weight held by the water. I peered forward, looking at my own limbs under water.

'Try marching on the spot,' said Willie.

I fixed my eyes on my leg, ordered it to rise, to step. And it started to obey me. I ordered it down, using my eyes, and it went – slowly, floppily, but it went. I tried the other. It tried; it lifted at the knee. Yet again, came that explosion of joy in my head. My legs still worked. They did. They lifted on command, helped by the water. I had seen it. Back at the side of the pool, holding myself upright in shoulder-deep water, my feet on the floor, I managed to sink both knees and then straighten them, locking my knees and hips. Susan manipulated another Friday miracle by shuffling me up the side of the pool into shallower water, so that when I repeated the exercise I raised most of my upper body upright out of the water – buoyed by the water, of course, but bearing some of my own weight. She told me I was working towards verticalisation, a pompous term which made me laugh.

Time then for a reassessment of my injury. Back in the gym, going from lying-to-sitting on a plinth had become easier – Susan put her hands on my tummy and could feel my muscles starting to work. I was re-diagnosed from a 'complete' injury to an 'incomplete'. I moved into Asia category B: in other words, there was now some scope for recovery.

'Can incomplete injuries walk?' I asked her.

'Yes, sometimes. It's not pretty, though.'

'I don't care about that.'

I thought about it a bit.

'Can Asia Bs walk?' I asked her.

'No. Ds can walk.'

The elephant in the room leant on me gently, and asked again. Will you, won't you? But another door had opened and I started ogling other bits of equipment in the gym. I was like a child at Disneyland too small to go on the most exciting rides, who watches others fractionally taller pass through the gates with fierce yearning in their soul. I wanted to park my chair at the end of the parallel bars and practise sit-to-stand, as I saw others do with such ease. It became a game with Susan. That machine? No. Then how about that?

'No,' she kept saying, getting exasperated. 'You couldn't manage it. These are for people who have some leg function, or who can walk. And you don't.'

And at the start, it was true. But as some movement crept back, she allowed me to try some of the things I craved, each one a delicious victory. Soon I was lying on the benches beneath the metal cages, my legs trussed up with slings and hooks, attempting sets of repetitions against the resistance of springs. Now my task was to build up whatever faint muscle fibres were still firing.

A salesman came to the gym exhibiting a leg bike which boasted functional electrical stimulation. You cycled with electrodes stuck to your quads and hamstrings, which fired your legs to turn the pedals and encouraged the regrowth of neural connections. He was a paraplegic himself. While he was wiring me up for a trial, I confided in him, a complete stranger. I wanted him to understand why I was hopeful.

'My legs are showing a bit of movement,' I said.

He nodded, not unsympathetically.

'And my toes are wiggling,' I boasted.

He looked at me, the world-weary to the infant.

'Yeah, that happened to me for a while. Didn't come to anything, sadly.'

There's a man who knows how to close down a conversation, I thought. But the message, unwelcome as it sounded, was not something I had considered. Could there be disappointing conclusions to a toe wiggle? Generally, just as I avoided negative people, I chose not to listen to unwelcome truths. My secret idol in the unit remained Stoical. His progress was proceeding slowly and steadily in the gym; I watched closely from afar. I was going to do that next, I vowed, when I saw him given new exercises to try. Around that time, I met him in the corridor. A meeting, like so many between the spinally injured, brief and deep. He asked me how I was doing.

'I've been diagnosed incomplete,' I told him.

'That's good,' he said.

'How about you?'

He was the opposite of an excitable man, but he was animated. 'Improving. Look at this.' He lifted his knees up, one after the other, taking his feet on and off the footplate of his wheelchair. My mouth fell open at the thrill of it.

I rolled on, even more determined that I was going to follow in his footsteps. I was on a constant mission. The darker side to being a Pollyanna, of course, was the hurt and loneliness that lurked below. Pollyanna used cheerfulness as a blanket to comfort her against disappointments; somehow, if she could make everyone else feel good, her own sadness might be assuaged. If she could perpetuate the fantasy that life would have a happy ending, she could stay as a child, innocent and naïve. But this could be unhealthy.

On the other hand, it might not be. The American psychologist Martin Seligman says optimists view adversity as temporary and external, that is, not entirely their fault, as opposed to pessimists who view adversity as unchangeable and personal. While Pollyanna wasn't wise, she was fairly unstoppable – and her approach brought its own benefits. Optimists persist in the face of setbacks and they cope better with chaos, while pessimists tend to give up. In other words, hope can get you through and keep you going, even if you never quite fulfil your dream.

All this, I'm afraid, rang horribly true for me. Single-minded, determined, if spectacularly unwise, I couldn't help myself. My focus on rehabilitation became more and more intense as the weeks began to turn to months. My gym routine was settled: arm weights and leg bike in the morning session; then in the afternoon working towards standing and weight bearing. Long sessions strapped in static standing frames, trying to accustom my blood pressure to the shock of being upright, and trying to lock my knees. Then I progressed to the end of the parallel bars, where I pulled myself into a standing position, over and over and over again. Each time I tried to make the movement slower and more controlled. Upright, wobbling, I had very little conception of what was happening, attempting to stay balanced over feet I couldn't really feel. An awakening body brought pain, something I had not really suffered before. My lower legs burnt constantly, as if in a deep-fat fryer, my knees and ankles locked with spasm and painfully so, especially at night. The positive interpretation – mine, anyway – was that the pain was down to a return of sensation and the stiffness due to muscle ache.

Susan, returning from holiday, rewarded me with another 'Brilliant, Mel!' when she saw me stand. Either she was getting soft, which was impossible, or I was still making progress. My legs, after months of electrical stimulation and grinding exercise, had become strong enough to bear my weight. In hydrotherapy I had managed to stand, propped between the side of the pool and a physio, and then supported by the water I had swung my legs forward in a few consecutive steps. It was walking, Jim, but not as you'd know it. My spirits continued to soar.

My attention turned to the various peculiar walking machines in the gym, all of which the flinty-hearted Susan had previously bombed out. The doctrine of Pollyanna Must Die was carved on the soul of all spinal physios. In one corner, very rarely used, was the heaviest-of-heavy-duty walking machines, the Arjo – a large blue four-wheeled frame, not dissimilar to a Victorian dockyard crane, with a large padded horseshoe for the user to lean their elbows on, and straps that went under their crotch to catch them if their knees buckled. The Arjo walker required four physiotherapists – one to pull, two to crawl alongside, placing the patient's feet, the fourth to follow with a wheelchair to scoop them up if they collapsed. Scarce resources meant its use had to be carefully planned, which Susan did one afternoon. The scene will forever be seared in my memory – a cluster of blue-uniformed therapists and me, at the centre of it, ratcheted manually into an upright position, propped on the frame. As the wheels were released and it started to move, I was able to go with it, my legs loosening and swinging forward, feet wandering vaguely in the air, criss-crossing like a baby giraffe's, refusing to go where I wanted. The physios placed them for me, and I stepped my weight forwards, first to one, then the next. The strange, poignant little entourage shuffled up and down a distance of about seven metres, not once but twice. Out of bravado I tried to do a third walk, but my body failed me. I could barely get up to start. As I slumped, emotionally and physically wrung out, I realised everyone in the gym had stopped to watch. A fellow inmate, Reiver, neck rebuilt with metal pins, told me later that as he watched, a great bolt of envy surged through him. He so desperately wanted to do what I was doing. Later, happily, he would – and more.

I swung round to look at Susan for guidance. What should I be feeling? What had I achieved? Why did she look so pleased? Where were my usual tears? What on earth was wrong with me?

She peered at me and shook her head in exasperation: 'I really hate that – when the physio gets more excited than the patient,' she said.

But was it really a Thursday miracle or a lesson in how hard, ultimately impossible, it might be to achieve any kind of functional walking again?

'So I should be pleased, then?' I asked her.

Underneath, the real question – was it dangerous to be pleased? If truth be told, I was overwhelmed. Terrified.

Ungrateful. Uncomprehending. Unable to grasp that the one thing I had striven so hard for over such a long time, upon which I had focused so fiercely, had happened – not with a bang but with a whimper. I had 'walked' – in inverted commas – for the first time. I needed to hedge it around with as many conditions and caveats as I could, because I was not strong enough, mentally or physically, to cope with too many expectations, my own or anyone else's. What was so strange was the lack of proprioception – my brain told the legs to move, but unless I looked down, or watched them in the mirror, I couldn't tell whether they had obeyed or not. As is relatively common with incomplete spinal cord injuries, I had some muscle power in my affected limbs, but very little sensation. If I was dispassionate, I'd turned a corner which I had been desperate to reach, only to see how rocky was the new road that lay ahead. I had climbed a hill, gasped my way to the horizon, only to discover the peak was still miles away. The work was going to get harder, not easier, with no guarantees about where it would take me. The fight, in fact, was never going to stop.

Susan's advice was blunt: 'Look, you might never have seen around the corner. And at least there's a road there – it might have been a dead end.'

In other words, just shut up, stop thinking, and get on with it. So I did. One of my happiest evenings in the spinal unit – and that's a sentence very few people ever write – was after that session, texting the good news to Dave and Dougie. 'Today, I walked for the first time.' And already, I could plot where I would go next. Every new stage brought new issues. The next one to sort out was my hyperactive plantar flexion – the strong toe-pointing spasm which made my feet catch on the ground when I tried to lift them, thwarting walking. I was fitted with AFOs – ankle-foot orthoses; big white plastic splints, worn inside trainers, which ran down the back of my calf and under the heel. Then I was able to progress to a tall, airy contraption called a gutter or pulpit frame, and within a week, by looking down at my wavering feet and telling them where to go with my eyes, I managed twenty-two steps across the gym with only two physios in attendance.

Maybe, like Katy, I was on the way to redemption. Because I'd learnt that in childhood, hadn't I? That transgressive little girls got better in the end. After two years in bed, Katy got a wheelchair. Some weeks later, she managed to stand.

Katy knew Papa was right and she was careful, though it was by no means easy to be so with all that new life tingling in every limb. Her progress was slow, as Dr Carr had predicted. At first she only stood on her feet a few seconds, then a minute, then five minutes, holding tightly all the while by the chair. Next she ventured to let go the chair, and stand alone. After that she began to walk a step at a time, pushing a chair before her, as children do when they are learning the use of their feet. Clover and Elsie hovered about her as she moved, like anxious mammas. It was droll, and a little pitiful, to see tall Katy with her feeble, unsteady progress, and the active figures of the little sisters following her protectingly. But Katy did not consider it either droll or pitiful; to her it was simply delightful – the most delightful thing possible. No baby of a year old was ever prouder of his first steps than her.

And Pollyanna. Who after a long time spent in bed, writes to her aunt and uncle:

'Oh, I can – I can – I can walk! I did today all the way from my bed to the window! It was six steps. My, how good it was to be on legs again! ...

'Pretty soon, they say, I shall go home. I wish I could walk all the way there. I do. I don't think I shall ever want to ride anywhere any more. It will be so good just to walk. Oh, I'm so glad! I'm glad for everything. Why, I'm glad now I lost my legs for a while, for you never, never know how perfectly lovely legs are till you haven't got them – that go, I mean. I'm going to walk eight steps tomorrow.'

Glad she lost her legs for a while? Oh, pass the sick bag, Pollyanna.

There remained one other unattainable bit of walking kit in the gym, a vast, expensive high-tech beast in prime position next to the therapists' office. It was called the Lokomat. I had gazed at it in awe and undisguised envy all these months. Now Susan had hinted that I might be tested on it. Perhaps it possessed the strong magic I needed to carry me to the next stage of my new life.

Like Pollyanna, I was determined to be glad about the possibility.

CHAPTER SIX

THIS WAY MADNESS LIES

It's the hope I can't stand.
TITLE OF FORMER FANZINE
OF SUNDERLAND FC

The woman, a previous in-patient, limped slowly up the gym to the physios' office, an unmistakably spine-damaged walk, leaning on a stick. At every stride she groaned and sighed noisily, as if deeply aggrieved with the world. Loud enough, certainly for Reiver and I, working alongside each other on the triceps machines, to stop and stare.

As she passed us on her way back, she was even louder. Although she walked reasonably well, she was determined to broadcast her suffering.

'Oh dearie, dearie me. OOOOOOH. This isnae fair. OOOOOOOO, I cannae do this.'

A surge of anger rose from my guts. I dropped my head to suppress it.

Reiver's response was even more visceral. 'Oi, I'll swap places with you,' he called. Pretending to be humorous, but furious really. Preoccupied with her own self-pity, the woman didn't hear him.

He turned to me, anger compressing his face. 'For fuck's sake. She comes in here moaning, when she can walk like that.'

I nodded grimly, all compassion evaporated. That poor woman with her incomplete injury, whatever her ongoing pain, possessed everything that he and I, also incomplete, were working so obsessively to attain. In truth, by then I had gone a bit mad. The ability to walk had become a compulsion, a quest for the Holy Grail. What the paralysed learn about paralysis, eventually, is that there are many things far worse than not being able to walk, the main one being the inevitable double incontinence, part of a vast layer-cake of physical and psychological horrors. But in the beginning the loss of mobility is the all-consuming priority. I was nowhere near ready to accept immobility. Instead I had found, in my focus to stand and move again, a most effective diversion from all the wider implications of my situation.

They had given me a room to myself, perhaps recognising how hard I was trying and the progress I was making; besides, I was by now an old lag, the longest-serving inmate on the rehab ward. All my fellow patients from the early months had been discharged, and I had little energy to spare on the poor newly injured souls learning their first grievous lessons. I felt like a sixth former who had earned the privilege of a common room. It facilitated my training but later, when the sad tale of Gollum unfurled, and the night-time phone calls started, it also facilitated my capacity for madness and made me vulnerable. But I am getting ahead of myself.

It had been eight months since my accident. Psychologically, I was a mess, avoiding visits from friends, reinforcing the wall of denial. Dave and Doug were the only people I wanted to see; I awaited their visits like a lonely dog, eyes fixed on the corner around which they would first appear. Dougie's hair, an enormous head of student curls on top of his six feet five inches, almost reached to the ceiling, making him an unmistakable fond silhouette against the light from the window at the end of the corridor. Dave's walk I could recognise with my ears alone – steps always firm, jaunty, positive, despite the grief he carried. On alternate nights, for many of those months, those two men loyally appeared, criss-crossing the country, clocking up thousands of miles.

Physically I had made remarkable progress. Shortly before Christmas came that first appointment with the Lokomat, the supercar of the neurophysiotherapy world, designed to teach severely impaired neurological patients to walk again by encouraging neuroplasticity. Neuroplasticity was my new buzz word: it means the brain's ability to reorganise itself by forming fresh neural connections, in response to injury. Basically, your body's ability to rewire itself – to some extent. The machine, which cost as much as a top-of-the-range Ferrari, consisted of a tall hoist with a parachute harness, built over a treadmill and incorporating a robotic exoskeleton to encase your legs and feet. Everything was controlled by elaborate software.

At first the therapists put me in the parachute harness and suspended me on the treadmill, minus the robot legs. With the belt turning on minimum speed, they 'walked' my legs by hand while I dangled, a six-foot, seventy-kilo Tinkerbell, from the ceiling, bearing what weight I could through my feet and hands on the handrails, my urine bag tucked up under my chin to prevent the tubes being snagged by the tight harness. By then I cared about nothing. I had become so fixated on walking that I existed fiercely in the moment, in the gym, in recovery. I had quit the normal world.

Then, with difficulty because of my very long thigh bones, at the outer edges of the machine's capacity, I was strapped into the robot legs and began what I can only describe as a dream sequence: watching myself in the mirror striding purposefully along the treadmill towards my reflection. Head up, shoulders back, hips swinging, knees eager, toes buoyant on springs, heels touching down, just the thing. Swish, swish, swish, went the swish Swiss machine, like an expensive washing machine on a woollens cycle, working my legs in a sedate, sturdy, slightly

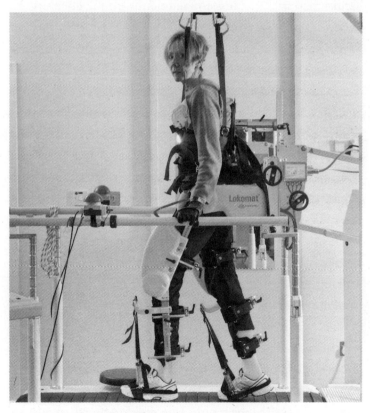

Me on the Lokomat. You can see from my face
that I was going slightly mad.

splay-footed mechanical rhythm. I walked like a wooden puppet in that scene from *The Sound of Music*, 'high on the hill as the lonely goat herd, lay-dee-odl-lay-dee-odl-lay-dee-hay'. And the extraordinary thing was, as I made the movements, and watched the reflection of me making them, I experienced an unmistakable jolt of electricity in my brain – a kind of neural zinger; the mind–body circle being rejoined; the reconnections waking up; the grey matter crying: 'Oh, *that's* what walking was! Hey, I remember how to do this!' It was as if an automatic brain function, lain idle for nine months, had had jump leads applied to it.

My head burnt with joy, excitement, instinctive wariness – *don't build up your hopes, kid, this does not mean you will ever do this by yourself* – as I saw my feet landing gently in front of me and I felt the blood pound in my ears. The first session lasted fifteen minutes, and I felt my buttocks and hamstrings and ankles squealing distantly in surprise, but I woke the next morning with my lower body feeling more mobile. Susan slotted me in for as many sessions a week as she could and soon I was up to thirty minutes a time. Fairly soon I was bearing up to sixty per cent of my own weight and trying to walk with the machine, as Willie advised, as if heading into a stiff wind. And sometimes, when the treadmill stopped and I was unhooked from the robot but still supported by the hoist, my brain could persuade my legs to keep going, to take a couple of tiny shuffles forward and back.

No one was making any promises. The Lokomat might very slowly wake up my legs but in the end it might be of little more therapeutic use than strengthening and loosening muscles. It might speed up what potential there was in my body; it guaranteed nothing. I still couldn't feel what my legs were doing; I could only tell by watching. But I was utterly committed, high on the endorphins the exercise was bringing to long-paralysed limbs.

My steps were taking me into unknown territory. Some people who knew me, from outside the spinal unit, told me they considered my drive to walk again quite heroic, which made me uneasy. The concept of heroism was dangerous ground. I knew I was pretty deranged and being as selfish as a top athlete. Everyone likes to think that if the question was asked of them, they'd respond the right way. They'd be the one to run towards danger, to rise above pain, to snatch the stricken child from the path of the runaway lorry, to make a super-human effort, but as I was discovering, disability complicates that horribly. Research has shown that able-bodied people believe that disabled people, by their intrinsic vulnerability, symbolise imperfection. And disabled people, aware of this, try to transform their disability from a perceived deficit to cultural capital by trying very hard and becoming 'disabled heroes'. So people like me, striving to the point of madness to recover, are also unconsciously reinforcing the pattern. We want to be judged successfully, piously, ill in the eyes of the healthy. The sociologist James Overboe has said that while this behaviour can inspire a few disabled people, it gives the able-bodied the false impression that anyone can overcome a disability – and invalidates the experience of the majority of disabled people because they physically can't. Because sometimes just staying alive with a disabled body constitutes the highest form of heroism, but it's not perceived as such. Disabled people who try very hard, though, are portrayed as more than human, and rarely as ordinary people doing ordinary things. Later, when I calmed down and reflected a bit, I realised that my obsession with walking as the be-all and end-all wasn't doing anybody much good, especially me.

But right then I was a woman on a mission. The physiotherapists increased my work rate. I was getting up earlier in the morning, with the support of the nursing staff, to slot in a session before gym officially started. I was ordered to take my hands off the rails and keep going on the treadmill – plonkety-swish-plonk, plonkety-swish-plonk, toes-turned-out – and the work had become ten times more difficult. Instead of having a modicum of control, I felt like a giant infant bouncing helplessly in a baby walker, Wallace and Gromit and *The Wrong Trousers*. I found myself grunting with the huge effort of moving with the robot legs each stride, willing my hips to flex, my thighs to lift and my knees to bend. Willie told me I sounded like Serena Williams. If I relaxed my concentration even for a second, my feet would drag and the treadmill would swish to a halt, silently rebuking me in a very Swiss sort of way for my inefficiency.

After that first hands-free session, I remember, I transferred onto a plinth in the gym, and collapsed, arms crucifix-fashion, asleep almost before my head hit the pillow. I slept for an hour and twenty minutes while other people's physio sessions went on like a fair around me. You were laid out, said Susan, not entirely unsympathetically when she woke me at 4 p.m., like the prison guard in *The Silence of the Lambs* after Hannibal Lecter ate his face off. Reiver, who had watched me on the machine, desperately yearning to be allowed on it too, had written my name on a brown parcel label and tied it to my foot, as if I was in the morgue. Later, Susan was blunt. 'You're going to

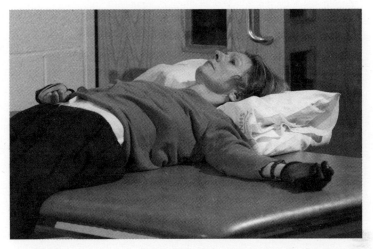

Me asleep in gym. Laid out, said Susan, like the prison guard in
The Silence of the Lambs after Hannibal Lecter ate his face off.

have to man up and stop falling asleep in the gym after you've
been on the Lokomat. Are you eating enough?'

No, I wasn't. I was overdoing it. I wasn't sleeping well, despite
my tiredness, and blood tests showed me to be seriously anae-
mic. The nutrition police were sent in to counsel me, gravely
lecturing me on how to choose high-calorie foods, which, as
someone who had spent her life yo-yo dieting, and knew the
calorific value of everything, I found darkly amusing. Then I
fainted on the Lokomat, because I had not taken my midodrine
tablet, a heart drug, a longer-acting version of ephedrine, which
was artificially sustaining my blood pressure. Everything went
very suddenly white and shut down. When the luminescence
cleared, my head was on Susan's shoulder and Willie was holding my legs up in the air in front of me.

My fragility was showing in other ways, my emotions were
equally unsteady. *The Times* had chosen a spinal charity as one

of their recipients for the Christmas appeal, and I was asked to write something in addition to my usual magazine column. The picture desk in London emailed – could they come and take my picture to go with the article? Although I was a long-in-the-tooth journalist and knew the game, I remember being deeply offended, because I was in hiding from the real world. Until I knew how far my progress was going to take me, I didn't want wheelchair pictures; I wanted to be invisible. Like a remote tribe being discovered by nineteenth-century explorers, I feared that if a photographer captured my image in a chair, they would steal my soul. Revelatory images of me would be far too personal and represented a loss of control.

I emailed back, telling them I didn't want my picture taken. By reply, some callow youth on the desk promptly asked if they could be supplied with an X-ray of my broken neck instead. I had been moved into a single room by then and it was just as well, because my reaction scared even me. I started sobbing hysterically, outraged at his insensitivity, his invasion of my secret kernel of hurt. All the emotional valves opened. It was totally irrational, and out of character, but I was very close to the edge. The poor man's error had been, inadvertently, to request the very thing I was spending my waking hours trying to escape – the reality of my situation, the prognosis I couldn't face, the unavoidable physical evidence of the catastrophe I was carrying around inside myself. During the previous months of dogged recovery, I had deliberately never asked to see an X-ray or an MRI scan of my neck because I knew I wasn't fit to cope with it – and in fact it would be many more months before I did look. Seeing them would have finished me, extinguished all hope. As long as I was improving, I could shut out reality, but his request had shattered the pretence. I missed gym and, for the rest of that day, I wept to the point of exhaustion, and several members of staff were concerned at my distress.

Perhaps it was no coincidence that I received a two-pronged visit from the consultants, Mariel Purcell and David Allan, playing good cop, bad cop. They told me I was over-tired and should cease writing my weekly column. The idea shook me, because writing framed my week, gave me as much purpose as going to the gym. It was something I could *do*. Funnily enough, I learnt later that one of the key things which allow male spinal injured cases to successfully rebuild their lives was getting back to work. For men, employment defines them. Well, maybe I was a bloke, because I felt the same way. I resisted. The doctors and I bargained.

'I could maybe take a couple of weeks off,' I said.

'A month to begin with,' said Dr Allan. 'You can tell them, what is it? – Jeffrey Bernard is unwell.'

'But he was a drunk. There's nothing wrong with me.'

'A month and then we reappraise. No less.'

So a month it was, over Christmas and beyond. That was the winter of 2010/11, when ice and snow blanketed the UK for weeks, closing down road networks and airports. The deep freeze seemed appropriate for me somehow; outside synchronised with inside; a sense of asceticism and suffering, waiting for spring. Like my body, the earth was in a state of suspension, yearning for the thaw. I sat in my room watching the bare branches of the trees, feeling the cold striking through the big panes of glass. They ran out of spare blankets in the unit that winter, and I remember feeling cold even with five piled on top of me and an extra convector heater in my room, for overnight.

For several weeks the ice and snow was so bad that it was impossible for me to go home for the weekend. Wheelchairs and snow are inimical. Some days Dave, even with a four-wheel drive, struggled to get into the city, and I told him to stay at home. That was when, devoid of work, purpose, people, and distractions, I found the loneliness of paralysis became profound. Stillness settled upon me. One Sunday morning, when my curtains had been opened but I was lying passive in bed, because without gym there was nothing to get up for, a magpie came and flattened its black and white belly against the top corner of my window, wings outstretched and flapping against the glass, holding itself there like a hummingbird. I watched, holding my breath, as this big, startling, wild creature pinned itself to my life, plucking and probing at the seals around the window. Then I realised it was removing spiders' white egg sacs from the crevices – perhaps the final stash of emergency rations in a bad winter.

After you damage your spine, or suffer a stroke, there is a doomy word which starts to haunt you – plateau. Plateau means the death of hope; means your body has gone as far as it can. You have reached the level of disability on which you are going to stay for the rest of your life. Although my progress had been considerable, it had also been very slow, and I was now reaching the outer limits of time I could stay in the spinal unit. As a general rule, paraplegics stayed for between three and six months, tetraplegics between six and nine. Unless I could demonstrate that I was continuing to improve in every way – my life skills as well as my walking – my time would soon be up. I knew very well that this would mean an abrupt end to the most dedicated, expert, intensive neurophysiotherapy that I was ever likely to receive. I had been lucky enough to be injured close to the spinal unit considered one of the very best in Europe, and I was terrified of leaving the cocoon of understanding and therapy. Tragically, in my opinion, then or now, spinal and stroke units do not offer physiotherapy to outpatients. To pay a private specialist to supply me with twenty plus hours of therapy a week, as the unit did, was not even a possibility. To begin with, after discharge, I would get one hour a week from a community physiotherapist – for which I was very grateful – but, given my psychological fragility, it seemed that a bleak future loomed.

The only thing to do was maximise my stay. While I drove myself as hard as I could in the gym, I began to joust with the system of bureaucracy dedicated to slowly but surely managing me out of the door. Time in the spinal unit receiving rehabilitation, as in other types of hospital departments, was governed at that time by something called FIM, which once upon a time stood for Functional Independence Measure. I could think of other things the F stood for. FIM was a tool invented by the Americans in the 1980s, and adopted the world over, which was designed to keep long-stay hospital patients moving through the system. It was to keep the accountants happy. You were graded on your ability for self-care, sphincter control, transfers, locomotion, communication, and social cognition. Box-ticking stuff, dehumanising the decision-making. Your FIM score was, in the hands of management, an iron belief system, deployed ruthlessly to keep patients churning. The moment your score started to slow, it meant you were as fully rehabilitated as possible, and it was time to pap you out. It overruled doctors and physiotherapists. My FIM had been stalking me since I arrived;

and, try though I had, it looked like it had finally caught me up.

By nature more anarchist than bureaucrat, I hated it with a vengeance.

Amanda, my occupational therapist, was responsible for teaching me new life skills. Ask a layman what an OT does and they will shrug. What on earth do you need that for? What a non-job. But in the world of the frail and disabled, OTs were gurus, full of golden ideas and practical suggestions to make you as independent as possible. Amanda was a pretty Geordie who looked and sounded like Cheryl Cole, but with short hair, brains and rubber legs from spending so much of her time kneeling on the floor, working with people's frailties. She possessed a great sense of the ridiculous and I loved her. She had showed us how to adapt our house with ramps and in one-to-one sessions in the unit she taught me how to fill a kettle, make a sandwich, put on deodorant. She brought catalogues to reveal dozens of little gadgets which would help me grip kitchen implements and provided me with a grabber, a stick with a trigger finger so that I could reach across work surfaces or pull doors shut. The most challenging stuff for me, though, was dressing, washing, toileting.

One of my spinal friends used the words 'vacuum-packed' to describe the daily curse of waking up with a spinal cord injury: it was true then and it is still true today. Every morning, you are that lump of meat, perfectly shrink-wrapped on a tray. Fat-trimmed, blue-veined, artfully arranged by others, with that wistful emptiness which paralysis brings to limbs, but utterly trapped. No matter how supple and mobile you felt when you fell asleep the night before, every morning you must start all over again, fighting your way out of your prison. On waking, you are invisibly stuck to the bed. There is no giant miracle sharp knife to free you, only sheer willpower: firstly to raise your head and neck from the pillows, then the huge effort to get onto your elbows; then, shoulders and abdomen pinned by a thousand Lilliputian ties, you persuade your elbows to straighten and inch your way to a sitting position. Your hands are set into rigid claws and your spasms rack you from middle finger to big toe. Dressing my bottom half was nigh impossible, but if I wanted my FIM brownie points, I had to do it. My wardrobe had reduced to a minimalist's minimalism – T-shirts with wide necks, no buttons, no zips, no underwear, elasticated-waist trackie bottoms, but the trousers involved a thirty-minute fight on the bed, struggling to hold myself in a sitting position while I heaved up my knees and tried to get the cloth over unbending feet, then rolled, rocking buttock to buttock, to pull them up. My rigid legs actively fought me, defying all my attempts to reach my feet. There were contortions, tears, frustration, exhaustion. Putting on socks and shoes, with hands that could not grip, was almost impossible, but I persevered. After our sessions, Amanda would score me according to whatever progress I had or hadn't made that week.

FIM scores ranged from 18, which meant basically comatose, to 126, which was able-bodied. At your monthly goal-planning meeting, your score was presented to the discharge coordinator, a pleasant but terrier-like woman who enforced FIM rather as the Stasi might. When I came into the unit I was given a predicted LOS (Length Of Stay – the acronyms were like bush-fires, you could never put them out) and by now I had blown my LOS and was screwing up her discharge targets. At the end of every meeting, I held my breath and watched her preparing to set my discharge date. And month after month Susan and Amanda would give reports saying that my physical progress and my FIM score were still improving. She would put down her pen and sigh. Nothing personal, but the slow onset of my recovery and my exceptional but slow progress were buggering the system. It was cat and mouse. She was watching. I was hiding. The minute my FIM score plateaued, she had me. And oh what I put myself through, in my madness, as my recovery headed towards its ninth, tenth, eleventh month. I would exhaust myself struggling to put clothes on, or get my legs on and off the bed by myself. I told Amanda white lies, which she saw through. I pleaded with her to give me 0.5 FIM points, but they didn't do half measures.

'You've got to be able to get shoes on before I can give you another point,' she said.

My score had climbed to 100, but I had reached my limits. It wouldn't climb any higher. And I knew she knew that I knew. The authorities always get you in the end. As a parting shot to FIM, I quoted a major American study on it: 'Each person's potential for recovery should never be limited to a set of numbers.'

Simultaneously, on the life skills front, I was fighting to get myself in and out of a car independently. Being able to drive again when I left hospital had become another goal. In the cut-in-half Fiat Punto in the gym, I had first learnt how to transfer from chair to passenger seat. Now it was into the driver's seat – and it wasn't easy. The Fiat was very low, with flat sills, and my legs were getting lighter as I lost weight. With enough practice I reached the point where on a good day I managed to lift them in to join me. My next challenge was to disassemble my chair and get it in with me, and the cheap and easy protocol was to belt yourself in the seat, lean back out and dismantle the chair and then lift it, piece by piece across your chest to stow on the passenger seat. Watch a strong paraplegic with low-level paralysis doing this, and they will do it in seconds. For me, with rubbish hands and a weak torso, it was as difficult as putting on trousers.

One day, thwarted by the weight and awkwardness of the chair, I left the gym at close of play sobbing with frustration. As I sped up the corridor to the privacy of my bedside, I ran slap bang into two tall men in RAF jumpsuits, brimming with the head-turning swagger of drama, machismo, and adventure that a military uniform brings. The nurses were agog, circling. They loved visits from men in uniform.

'Hallo,' said the bigger, glamorous one. 'I'm Dishy Daz.'

It was my rescuer, the winchman I had last seen when he leant his face close and said urgently: 'Keep breathing for me, girl … Do it for me,' over the clatter of the helicopter. In the intervening months I had daydreamed of this moment. I would be on my feet, on crutches, looking slender, fragile and feminine as I thanked him for saving my life. His eyes would crinkle with tenderness and he'd offer to fly me home. Instead, here I was in my chair, tears streaming down my cheeks, soup stains on my T-shirt and, in the absence of a hanky, hands and wrists smeared with snot trails from wiping my nose.

'I'm really sorry I'm crying,' I sobbed, desperately trying to find a dry bit on my forearm to catch the mucus. 'It's just that I've been trying to get into a Fiat Punto.'

'Oh, don't worry,' said Daz, who routinely dangled on a cable over mountainous seas and cliffs to rescue people. 'Getting into a Fiat Punto would make me want to cry too.'

They had come off their Sea King and left it parked near A&E, as you do if you're RAF Search and Rescue, and they were carrying a framed picture of the aircraft, wrapped up in brown paper, which all the crew had signed for me. They said they'd been carrying it in the chopper for several weeks, hoping it wouldn't get broken, until they got an opportunity to land at the hospital and bring it to me.

Daz, or Darren, told me he owed me one: his nickname used to be Wurzel, but after the article about my rescue was printed in the paper, and after his crewmates had taken the mickey out of him relentlessly, they'd renamed him Dishy Daz. He and the pilot, Al, were lovely men, as you would expect – nonchalant about their dramatic job, humorous, understated, kindly, sexy. Because we project onto such people all that we would wish them to be. I thanked them profusely for rescuing me, and rushing me to hospital when all looked bleak. They must get so used to it; cast in a heroic role. They were not with me for long. Their buzzers went – their helicopter was needed for another emergency – and they said their goodbyes and hurried off back to the helipad. In their wake the nurses swooned and the air swirled; there was that sense of something magical having passed, something thrilling, a glimpse into another world.

By now, Susan had acquired a specialist wide, three-sided Zimmer for me to try walking with. When I stood, bearing my own weight on my feet, leaning now on my hands, it felt as if I was an amputee, propped on two deeply uncomfortable wooden stilts. That discomfort made me want to collapse back into my chair, from where, on the whole, life was much easier. Part of the exhaustion, I realised, came from the intense concentration needed to control my lower body with my eyes, ordering my knees not to buckle. And so we entered the final phase: from shuffling along parallel bars, painfully slowly, awkwardly, I was now onto a small frame and effectively mobile. What should have been a triumph was thwarted by lack of stamina. I might manage two or three steps, then waves of weakness broke over me. There was no fuel in the tank. I could never travel any distance.

There was one memorable afternoon when I set off – lift, lurch, step, drag, gasp, the undead stumbling from its cave – and I managed to do about seven steps before I needed to sit down into the chair that Susan was following me with. It was the closest to independent walking I was ever to do in the unit. And of course I was delirious with joy and optimism. When gym was over, I whizzed back to the ward. At the door of my room I met one of the senior nurses, Laburnum, a woman who believed in saying it like it is.

'I just walked halfway across the gym,' I told her, eyes shining, face alive with happiness.

She looked at me coolly.

'Your walking will never be functional. You know that, don't you?'

She didn't say it in a kindly way.

I had never really warmed to Laburnum. Now I hated her. For my final couple of weeks in the unit I struggled to look her in the face. When you are deranged, you cannot handle too much insensitivity. By now the nurses knew me well and the sensitive ones were aware how hard I was trying. Tansy, a staff nurse, showed me extraordinary kindness after I had what amounted to another emotional meltdown over my hair. Hindsight casts the episode in a ridiculous light, but my distress was absolute. The hairdressers I usually went to, pre-accident, were upstairs in the city centre, ruling out a visit, so I had phoned to ask if a junior could come and do me in hospital. But because, however hard I tried, I had never learnt to speak hairdresser, there was a misunderstanding and she gave me orange hair. Not quite the orange of a see-you-jimmy hat, but not far off. When she had gone, and I saw the extent of the damage, I started crying again and couldn't stop. The only part of me over which I had proper control, my head, had been lost too. So wretched was I that Tansy phoned a nearby hairdresser and volunteered to give up her break in order to push me there.

It was during that same deep winter and few of the pavements were cleared. Great troughs of frozen slush lay in the gutters and at pedestrian crossings. The cold struck into our bones and the front jockey wheels of the chair jammed in the snow. But that wonderful nurse dragged me for about five hundred metres through the worst of it to the hot, raucous haven of a hairdressing shop. This was Govan, so the salon wasn't Charles Worthington, but the stylist was warm, practical and utterly on my side.

'No problem, doll, I'll fix you.'

She toned down the vivid orange to mid-brown, and proceeded to trowel on a few glorious streaks of bleach through the front. No foil or mesh niceties in Govan – here it was slapped straight on with a brush. The end result was great – bold and blonde, a tad footballer's wife, and I was delighted. Who cared if my hair was so burnt it later fell out. That was later. Tansy dragged me back through the snow to the unit, brushing off my thanks. For every bad memory of the staff, I left with twenty good ones like that, of compassionate women who, seeing me in distress, would put themselves out or buy me a coffee with £2.50 they could ill afford, and then sit and hug me while I wept on their shoulders. I guess I spent so long in hospital, observing the demands upon staff and the way some patients treated them, that I went native. While lying very, very still, I nevertheless walked in their shoes. They deserved respect and better pay than they received.

There was no spectacular climax to my time spent in rehab. I left the unit in a wheelchair. To my regret, I did not achieve my dream of walking out of the door. My ability to stagger a few metres, heavily supported, was not enough for any symbolic flourishes; besides, I lacked the stamina to make it as far as the kerb. By now I had accepted that I would always be disabled, but I remained convinced that I was still improving, albeit at a snail's pace, and that if I kept trying I would keep moving forward. In my head, I had not yet plateaued.

The nurses wrote me an 'Ode to Spinal' in biro on the waterproof side of an incontinence pad. I regarded it as a great honour.

The time has come for you to go
And good news for you
But we'll miss you so.
You must see how far you've come
Especially when dealing
With your own bum.

Supps, catheters, the dreaded gym
The nurses at night oh what a din.
Good luck, dear Mel,
For you're a star
Let's meet you downtown
In a wee bar!

Before I left, Susan did my final assessment – the pinprick test for skin sensation and the muscle-function chart. I still lacked sensation over most of my legs, but muscle-wise under the Asia scale I was graded C, knocking on the door of D. My target. Susan's words, *Asia Ds can walk … it's not pretty, but they can walk*, were always in my waking brain, the portal to all my thoughts. To achieve D, the majority of my large muscle groups had to be graded 3 or above. I was at that level, with lots of 4s and even a 5, everywhere but in my hated right leg, which was only 2.

'It's not that I'm competitive or anything, but can't you just say I'm an Asia C/D?' I wheedled. 'Asia D minus?'

'No!' cried the Hobbit, exasperated. 'You've already gone from A to C, which is further than anyone else in our experience.'

As the hours to my departure ticked by, she and I eyed each other warily, like an undemonstrative but devoted married couple about to be separated for the first time in twenty-five years.

'No getting emotional, now,' I warned, with tears pricking my eyes.

'Of course not,' she said. 'It's not like I've devoted hundreds of hours to you or anything.'

In truth she was probably quite relieved when I finally went. It was time.

I left hospital a week before the anniversary of my accident, having survived my first year by optimistic instinct, and the odd bit of Buddhist philosophy. The man I like to call my Zen Master, a former patient at the spinal unit, was someone I met when he came back to join one of the activity days, a sailing session. He had also broken his neck falling off a horse, but his was a completely different injury to mine, and he went on to a remarkable recovery, walking, riding, skiing again. He told me the greatest gift for anyone with physical or brain injury was time. Time is key. Years on from his accident, he was still noticing small improvements. 'We are quite unused to the time required to fix these incredible bodies of ours, more complex than a galaxy.' Don't say, he advised, 'I will always be disabled', but state instead, 'I will always be recovering from my injury.' One was open, the other was closed. And he blessed me with a wonderful image – he got comfort from imagining that inside our bodies battalions of miniature therapists and medics were working night and day doing jobs of mind-boggling complexity, trying to repair the damage. They needed us to do the big stuff: to draw in energy by eating and sleeping well, doing the exercises, while they pressed on with the micro stuff. And, crucially, they needed us to keep faith. The body's default position was to heal.

In hospital, I had tried to exist in the moment, concentrating fiercely on the job in hand and rejecting corrosive thoughts about the future. The tears, the self-pity, the profound inner loneliness, these were the constant enemies, besieging the castle walls. From being diagnosed as completely paralysed, I had confounded the doctors and regained some function, after a fashion. From being totally insensate from the armpits down, I was continuing to recover some feeling. But there had been no miracles. With spinal-cord injuries, the word does not exist. From a strictly medical point, it was probable that my body had been in deep and prolonged spinal shock, which had confused the initial diagnosis. I was in fact a very incomplete injury. I wasn't proof that doctors are wrong; I was proof that every injury is different.

The poignant thing is that my delayed diagnosis gave me the capacity to dream dreams when it was probably unwise to do so. The person who was going to be hurt most was me. Had I had a more serious injury, with no chance of recovery, I might have accepted my fate quicker. As it was, I threw myself, every atom of my body, into trying to walk, to be the old me again. I launched myself at the challenge, happily blinkered, pretending to be a thirty-year-old paraplegic when I was in fact a fifty-year-old tetraplegic. Mankind is hardwired to do so, I guess. And yet I don't regret it.

The legacy of my injury has been to force me to live with the biggest 'if' in the world. If I just tried a little harder. If I could have given it another six months. If I could only bear a tiny bit more weight in my arms. If I could walk further, then maybe one day my bladder function would start to return. If I can do this, then I should be able to do that. If. If, if. It was a game without a finish.

Welcome to my new world, the eternal torture of possibility.

CHAPTER SEVEN

AUNT AVERIL AND
THE HIDDEN ARMY

ESTRAGON: I can't go on like this.
VLADIMIR: That's what you think.
SAMUEL BECKETT, *WAITING FOR GODOT*

When you're healthy, and busy, and things are good, and everyone you know is in much the same position, you think that's what life consists of. You inhabit the upper world. This is where the happy, shiny people live, the ones with white teeth and lithe figures; it's what's you see in TV commercials and glossy features in lifestyle magazines. You have expectations, and yes, of course there are frustrations and disappointments, but you continue to make plans; and yes, of course you're a bit complacent, and unthinking, because life is so busy and you don't have time to think. You're a consumer of good things; you dream of better things. Online, on screen, in every form of media you devour, you see yourself, or someone you aspire to, looking back at you. The upper world is in fact an echo chamber, based upon a presumption of good health. Most of us, at one time or another, have lived there; some of us, the lucky ones, never leave.

What you don't realise, of course, until something happens, is that just below the surface there's another world altogether, a parallel existence, where all the people you never think about live – the sick, the halt, the lame, the chronically ill and the elderly. The imperfect people; those for whom life is a daily struggle. 'Life's a bitch. And then you die,' we used to say, after a hard day in the office. Joking. Down in the parallel world it's not so funny, because it's true. When I fell off my horse, I nose-dived, like Alice down the rabbit hole, from the upper world into the lower one, a place I didn't know about. In an instant, one tribe cast me out and I was forced to join another, a hidden army of people fighting their private battles against ill health, simply trying to keep going the best they could. Here was a reality warp, the secret counterbalance to the media gloss of Western culture. When you fall, you lose so much more than you thought possible: you are stripped of your personality, your confidence, your pretensions – stripped of the carapace of who you think you are. Some of the most intense human fears are of losing your world, your brain, your body, of perpetual suffering – these are elemental phantoms. You thought they only happened to other people. And yet here you are: what you dreaded most has come to pass. *Who are you now?* That's for you to find out. Your job, for the rest of your life, is to fill hospital waiting rooms, to accept, to learn patience, to develop the skills needed to play the bad hand you've been dealt. No longer a participant or a player, you are an observer.

My eyes were opened. I was a raw recruit in a tribe which had novel ways and strange habits; with esoteric shopping catalogues and shops full of bewildering items with huge price tags, manned by over-eager and occasionally creepy salesmen. This lot did things very differently because they had no choice. Above all, they were vast in number, living all around me, hiding in plain sight. Researchers in the US scoured public health records in 2016 and found that more than half of Americans were living with at least one chronic health problem, substance abuse or mental-health condition. Recently in the UK, the King's Fund identified that about fifteen million people in England are smitten by one of the big six chronics – cancer, heart disease, strokes, diabetes, dementia and obesity – but add to that disability, neurological disease, arthritis, COPD, hypertension, mental ill health, epilepsy, asthma and substance abuse, and the number is off the scale and rising steadily. Already my tribe accounts for half of GP appointments, two-thirds of out-patient appointments and almost three-quarters of in-patient bed days, and dealing with us takes up the lion's share of health and social care expenditure. I was now part of a vast constituency of people neither desperately ill nor healthy, just frail, ageing or always chronically needing something, who were fated to haunt hospitals, seeking answers that were never quite definitive.

Hospitals were foreign territory before. The maternity ward, yes, but that was different, or you might have caught the inside of A&E occasionally, when your children hurt themselves, but then you were a mere anthropologist, tiptoeing into the jungle, and you could amuse the kitchen suppers for weeks with what you saw. 'Honestly, Freddie is sitting in his muddy rugby strip, still got his boots on, and there's this guy totally out of his brains, blood everywhere, handcuffed to a cop …'

Now you're a serial hospital lingerer, weary of the dead-eyed receptionists, accustomed to non-spinal nurses asking, 'Can you stand at all?' because your wheelchair inconveniences them. Another of those sarcasm-defying questions to add to the growing list. (You remember the deadpan wit of Chic Murray, the sketch where he was writhing on the ground, unable to get up. 'Are you all right?' asked someone. 'Yes, I'm just trying to break a bar of toffee in my back pocket,' he cried.) You learn that the main entrance to a hospital is like a customs post between two worlds, where the fit scurry through as fast as they can and the unfit create log jams in the manner of fragile grey snails. You seize gratefully upon the staff with kindly faces who offer you brief sanctuary; you become battle-hardened to being patronised.

You study those who sit and wait alongside. Once upon a time, it occurs to you, you were all open-faced children, lined up for school photographs, squinting happy hope and light at the camera lens. Now, unravelled, you know better the hollow promise of life. You are the people who spend your time waiting, always looking for something to let you think you still exist, telling and retelling your sad stories at different desks to different members of staff, the weary slow-motion hospital waltz of those who will never be healthy again.

I should have known better, really I should. Profound and mystery illness had blighted my mother's family; every summer of my childhood had been spent at my grandmother's home, where my disabled aunt lived. Not that the word 'disabled' had currency then. Aunty Averil was referred to as an invalid, an umbrella term for chronic illness of any kind. Not valid. Literally, from the Latin, not strong. Legally, null and void. Worthless. Untrue. A word only suitable these days to describe driving licences or immigration visas, not human beings. You can still be invalided, heroically, out of the Army, but incapacity benefit replaced invalidity benefit in the last century. In the

1960s, however, Aunty Averil had capital letters. Wrapped up in that scary, significant word was supposed to lie both reason and an explanation, but I knew only a puzzle. 'My aunty is An Invalid,' I used to boast in the playground and hope that no one would ask me what it meant.

If Averil's plight was an enduring mystery to us as children, so it was to the rest of the world. Averil was the first-born child of my grandparents, who lived in County Down, a few miles from Belfast. She had three younger sisters and two brothers, a happy gang untouched by war who enjoyed what we would describe as an idyllic Edwardian childhood of picnics and tennis and dressing-up parties. But in 1924, when Averil was twelve, she started to develop strange, debilitating symptoms. Eventually, the doctor gave the family the grim news: he believed she was a victim of the terrible affliction called sleepy sickness. No one knew what caused the illness, where it had come from, or how it was spread, but it had been first identified in the winter of 1916–17 in Vienna, and had reached around the globe in three years. In a world debilitated by the impact of the Great War, followed by the Spanish flu pandemic of 1918, sleepy sickness, later named encephalitis lethargica, slipped unnoticed across oceans and over thresholds. Averil was one of a clutch of victims in Northern Ireland; several people died of it in Belfast. England, Northern Europe and New York were the worst-affected places. For the next eight years, this bizarre, devastating epidemic attacked nearly five million people – many of them, like my aunt, girls under twenty. Forty per cent died in the acute stages; the rest, perhaps even more terribly, went into strange decline and slowly turned into statues, speechless and motionless, often with their brains intact but frozen within useless bodies for the rest of their lives. Doctors were bewildered. Initially the victims were diagnosed with delirium, schizophrenia, Parkinsonism and sclerosis, or as atypical outbreaks of rabies, polio and botulism.

Victims would be conscious and aware, yet not fully awake and unable to speak. Only one part of the body, it seemed, did not succumb – the part of the brain controlling intelligence, imagination, judgement and humour. The victims, imprisoned in frozen, distorted bodies, could understand and remember but couldn't communicate. 'Their fate, so to speak, was to become unique witnesses to a unique catastrophe,' said the neurologist Oliver Sacks, who was later, famously, to reverse some of its ravages briefly in an experiment recorded in his book *Awakenings* and a film in 1990 of the same name.

Alone, alone, all, all alone,
Alone on a wide, wide sea!
And never a saint took pity on
My soul in agony.

That verse, heavily marked with pencil, jumped out at me from the printed page while I was writing this chapter – some deep magic, some random strike of coincidence took me to it. We had had our living room repainted, and the furniture had been moved. As I replaced old family books in the bookcase, I opened a worn, slim, canvas-backed school text, *English Narrative Poems* – and then blinked with wonder. On the inside cover, in a careful, rounded, girlish hand, was written 'Averil Oakman, V Lower'. Tucked inside, there was a page torn from an exercise book ninety years previously, marking Coleridge's

Rime of the Ancient Mariner, that immense expression of desolation. On the scrap of paper she had listed the reasons for the
ancient mariner's suffering: '1 lonliness [*sic*] 2 dead men 3
rotting deck 4 slimy things 5 thirst 6 the curse which had never
passed away 7 not being able to pray 8 the fever.' On the last
page of the printed text, she had underlined 'till my ghastly tale
is told/This heart within me burns.' And then, as if to cheer
herself up, on the page of the textbook she had drawn and
coloured in a picture of a fat flower fairy sitting on a branch.
Inside she was a little girl like any other.

The onset of Averil's encephalitis lethargica was less acute
than some. She remained at home, part of the family, even
attending school, and normal life went on around her as she
declined. There is a picture of them all, taken about 1930, and
Averil would have been nineteen or twenty. She is on her feet
but her tall, wasted body is plainly propped up by my grandmother. Averil's right hand is clenched into a spastic fist, while
the other hangs limp. Quite the most poignant thing is the fact
she is smiling brightly; the expressions of the rest of the family,
by contrast, seem a little subdued. Studying that photograph
again, as I write, I experience a bolt of connection. I'm familiar
with that defiant smile, just as I am with the faces of loved ones
shaded with sadness. They're mirrored in pictures of my family
today.

Averil's illness cast a permanent shadow on the family, creating worry and survivors' guilt. My grandmother devoted her
life to looking after her. It is no coincidence that Averil's next
two sisters, Harriet, her junior by two years, and my mother, by
four years, in turn devoted their adult lives to caring for others.
Of course those girls read books like *Pollyanna* and *What Katy*

Did – they were defined by the message of determined optimism, of forbearance and resilience in the face of disaster. Of course those same books were passed to my sister Lindsay and me in childhood, and in turn helped shape us. Because of Averil, everyone in the family was brought up to be stoics, even if they didn't always understand why. It is human nature to find patterns. It is human nature to make patterns. And then fail to escape them.

Among my earliest memories are summer holidays spent at the family home, and of Averil in her chair, propped in pillows, swathed in old crocheted blankets and picnic rugs, her head bent rigidly towards her chest. Her arms stirred like twigs. She would jerk sometimes, and spasm. She was then about fifty years old. During the day, she was placed in the sunshine at the front door, Mitzi, her dachshund, asleep under the blankets at her feet. Her eyelids drooped, her face had a mask-like quality – characteristic of the disease – but she had a lovely smile and the intelligence shone out of her eyes. Somehow, perhaps

Granny and Averil at Tyrella beach in the 1950s.

because I knew how important she was to my mother, I felt I should greet her when we arrived; I have a clear recollection of reaching out a hand, and she moved her tight, scrawny fist as much as she could towards me, so I could touch her knuckles. It felt awkward; she was a little frightening, this Invalid-with-a-capital-I. Our eyes met and in hers, even then, I could see empathy, understanding, a desire for connection. Then, to my shame, we grandchildren simply ignored her, running around playing. But if I looked up, I would sometimes spot her watching us, straining to see from under those lowered brows, with that shy, wistful, amused expression. I wish now, so much, that I had tried to talk to her.

She spent a lot of time reading: the Bible, mostly. Granny was a god-fearing Anglican in a Northern Ireland riven by religious divide. Averil would turn the thin pages by rubbing repeatedly across them with her clenched fist, her good arm. Her right one. Like mine. Mostly, she would spend her days copying out passages from the Bible into her diary. I remember seeing her write, the pages wedged on her lap under her face, the pen jammed between her rigid fingers, her right arm, wrist fixed, tracing faint, spidery lines on the page. She could not feed herself, and Granny would spend long hours spooning gruel into her mouth, followed by giant cups of weak tea. Occasionally, there were scenes when she became distressed, crying out incoherently, and I remember witnessing small, awful melodramas when her frustration would overwhelm her – and God knows she had reason – and she would put her fist to her nostrils and try to suffocate herself. We had to run inside, then, and tell Granny. As I write these words, I am filled with a profound sense of sorrow.

Here again, time wrinkles a little; the gap between then and now grows thin.

Averil died in 1966, just before her fifty-fourth birthday. By chance, on the centenary of her birth, 21 April 2012, a piece of music that I had co-written with the composer Sally Beamish, 'Spinal Chords', was broadcast on BBC Radio 3. The music was to express the challenge of paralysis. My sister, who also had a great affection for Averil, remarked that it was a beautiful coincidence to commemorate someone so utterly forgotten. Three years after Averil died, in 1969, some sufferers of encephalitis lethargica in a chronic hospital in New York were treated by Oliver Sacks with a new drug called Levodopa – L-dopa. A number of patients made a brief, almost miraculous recovery from the encephalitis, and started to walk and talk again as functioning human beings. Some bore witness to the horrors that had happened to them over decades of incarceration; some were convinced it was still 1920 and they were the age they had been when they fell ill. Sadly the effects of the drug did not last and mostly the patients relapsed into their frozen or catatonic state.

Paralysis is a universal human terror. In the twenty-first century, engineers across the world – in the US, New Zealand and Israel – began to work on the idea of an exoskeleton for paralysed bodies: an external robot body you would strap on and walk again. It was not quite the magic bullet that L-dopa delivered, however fleetingly, but it offered the same sense of the curse being lifted from the afflicted. The fear of petrification – imprisonment inside ourselves – goes right back to fairytales, with a magical release for the good and worthy. The prince awakens the sleeping beauty; the stone statue returns to life;

King Midas, through personal redemption, rescues his daughter from being frozen in gold.

Everywhere, people in wheelchairs pricked up their ears and dreamt about wearing magic robot legs, even just for one day. My friend Annie wrote to me, reminding me of the Hans Christian Andersen tale of the eleven princes, brothers, who are turned into swans by their evil stepmother. Only for a few hours of darkness every night were they allowed to be human again, because their solitary sister was battling the spell by knitting stinging nettles into shirts for them. Princess Eliza gathered the nettles in graveyards and knitted away, under a vow of silence, her hands permanently blistered from the stings, for if she finished by a certain day her brothers would be permanently released from the spell. What we would give to be normal again, Annie said wistfully, wishing she could knit nettles, even just for a few hours of darkness.

I tried an exoskeleton once, when a set of New Zealand-built Rex legs were brought to the spinal unit. They were vast, bulky things, a children's toy Transformer brought to life, which held me upright and allowed me, whirring and clunking, to take a few steps until low blood pressure made me ask to be released and allowed to sit down. Disconcertingly, my brain tricked me; although I was safe, I felt as if I was toppling to the right with every step. I wish I could say it was mind-blowing and inspirational, but it just felt very scary. It would be interesting to try electric legs again, now my mobility has improved, but I doubt that for me they would ever be functional.

We may all dream. It is only human to do so. When you are in a damaged body, or have a chronic condition, you never quite cease to tease yourself with that 'if only' and the 'what if'.

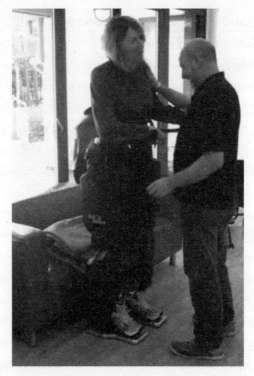

Trying the exoskeleton called Rex.

The universal fantasy of being allowed to re-enter one's old body, however briefly, and experience life again. Maybe this is not just for disabled people; maybe everyone, growing old and weak, yearns to re-enter the kingdom of their youth for a while. I have discussed this with sufferers of Parkinson's disease, who fantasise about knocking back some magic potion and then half an hour later springing to their feet to walk, talk and move – 'just like,' one woman quoted her granddaughter, 'a normal walking talking granny'.

And what, I wonder, in our fantasy hour of freedom, or our week, or month, what would any of us want to do? It is a powerful thing, to open the prison doors to dreams. Would you want to play with your grandchildren? Or spend it making love one more time to your beloved partner? What seems certain is that you would turn towards contact with the human world; to people; to warmth, and touch and talk and the reassurance that you are a functioning human being, loved and connected. To escape severe physical disability's hardest element of all, isolation.

I think of Averil often. There are times when I catch glimpses of my twisted hands or hunched shoulders and it awakens deep childhood memories of her, but I appreciate how enormously lucky I am by comparison. She was a human being, a woman, with an identity and a vivid personality lost behind the mask. As Oliver Sacks wrote, how hard must it be human, to *stay* human, in the face of such unimaginable adversities and threats. Can we ever begin to understand the stillness and darkness of that arrested, frozen life, and the courage and humour? I remember those amused blue eyes watching me play.

As all damaged people discover, spectating on life is scant compensation but it can be wryly entertaining. Think of us as your audience, you normals, think of us as a minority tribe of little people with big eyes, who sit very still in the shadows, watching you on the upper stage – you, the healthy, dominant tribe at its asinine best, squawking and fighting about stuff which you think matters and which we know doesn't, always in a frantic dash to get somewhere as quickly as possible. Gathering our painful wisdom around us for warmth, and laughing at things which really shouldn't be laughed at.

CHAPTER EIGHT

HOME

The eyes of others our prisons;
their thoughs our cages.
VIRGINIA WOOLF

You are lucky indeed in life if you find where you want to be. Some people spend their whole lives searching for the place and never find it. Nearly thirty years ago we found home – those intangible warm arms, that beating heart – in a higgledy-piggledy old cottage, perched in the foothills of the Trossachs mountains in Scotland. There, in a hidden valley, up a long rough track, in a place where people would choose to go on holiday to get away from everything, we found happiness. Quite simply, after we moved there we never wanted to be anywhere else. It was, and still is, a primitive dwelling in the rural Scottish vernacular, metre-thick walls and only one room deep. Over the centuries, it seemed, whenever an extra farmworker was hired, or a son needed a home for a new wife, or a cow a byre, or someone required an outhouse, an extra room was tacked onto the gable end. By the time we came, the property stretched for eighty yards across the side of the hill and boasted traces of about six front doors. It had low ceilings, zero insulation and tiny rooms linked in a chain, and records showed that people had been living there for at least three hundred years. What the place possessed above all else was an intensely good feeling: it looked to the sun; its face was open, kind and welcoming. The people we bought it from, who qualified as authentic 1960s hippies, had brought in a water diviner. He had found a ley line, one of those mystical energy highways apparently emanating from the Highland Boundary Fault, running through the kitchen: this was why the cottage was so special, the reasoning went, and had remained inhabited long after other similarly remote ones nearby had fallen into dereliction. Dave and I, cynical about mysticism, wondered privately if the diviner might not merely have traced a water drain, but refrained from scoffing: we might not believe in ley lines, but we were not about to question any harmless blessings. And certainly time showed how much people loved sitting in that kitchen, rocking with laughter and friendship.

I adopted the same attitude towards the rowan trees which had been planted outside the front doors, a traditional act to placate the fairies. They were supposed to bring good luck and although I wasn't remotely superstitious it seemed a little churlish and insensitive to cut them down. Respect old magic. Best of all, for me, a rough hill came with the smallholding, marginal land between us and the forest which the farmers did not want, but it sufficed for my horses, and there was a tumbledown old stable where the Clydesdale working horses once lived. Dates from the early 1800s were carved in the stone. It was a budget paradise. We hiked and rode and reclaimed bits of the hill from the gorse; and then rebuilt bits of the moss-laden farmsteading as we could afford it, relishing the unlimited space and freedom. Dougie had perhaps one of the most idyllic childhoods

Dave learnt the art of dry stone dyking.

possible, running wild from morning to night with his friends from the nearby village.

Late one night, the phone rang.

'Is that V—?' said the voice, fey, smoky, asking for the previous owner.

'No,' I said. 'Sorry. She's moved. We live here now.'

'Oh, you lucky, lucky people. Don't you know, man, that place is the centre of the earth?'

I laughed.

'No, really. Take it from me, man.' He drew deeply on a smoke. 'Listen, I'm phoning from Germany. I'm an old friend of V—'s. You're living in the centre of the earth. That place is just … special.'

And perhaps it just is. We were never happier. In the beginning, fresh from two broken marriages, we had stretched ourselves to the limit to buy the house, and were totally broke. After a couple of years, living more or less on lentil soup and porridge, we remortgaged and had enough to put a new roof on the bones of the old stone barn. Inside we created a budget holiday house, furnished it from quirky hand-me-downs and unwanted second-hand furniture, and advertised with what was then staidly named the Scottish Tourist Board.

The whole set-up was fairly eccentric but our holidaymakers seemed to love it. Seared in my memory is one conversation I had with a mother of two children, part of a family from London. We were leaning on the gate chatting while Dougie, who was about seven, played with the woman's children in the stream at the bottom of the hill. They were about two hundred yards away, paddling, building dams. We could see their heads bobbing around busily, hear the occasional snatch of voices.

'You know, that's the furthest away my children have ever been from me,' she said. 'I don't let them out of my sight. Don't you ever worry here?'

I tried hard not to gulp. 'No,' I said.

I didn't like to tell her that some days Doug went out to play anywhere within two square miles and I didn't see hide nor hair of him for hours. She might have reported me for child neglect.

If our home was special, it was also exceedingly hands-on. In such a remote, rough and ready place, you needed to be fit and active. Somehow, living there, you were almost part of nature itself; the distance between the 1700s and the twenty-first century was a very slim one. After my accident, the idea of going back full-time in a wheelchair to these beloved, primitive surroundings, to reinhabiting my old life, was terrifying. I had returned briefly on weekend passes while I was in hospital, but they had the feel of camping trips, away days from the place which was my real home. My awareness of my own disability, the acuteness of my handicap, depended very much on where I was and who I was with. In the spinal unit, with its smooth wide corridors, with wheelchairs more numerous than people, my paralysis was unexceptional. There was a safety blanket in the company of your own kind, and tacit reassurance in the fact that somebody else was always worse off than you, which guaranteed the presence of experts around to help. Besides, life in hospital was organised on our terms: the staff served us, the rhythm of the day, crude though it could seem, was designed around our needs. It was a secure place. We fitted in. We didn't really notice each other's wheelchairs; we saw ourselves as inmates serving time in the penitentiary. There was nothing usual or strange about paralysis, because that was all we saw around us, a landscape of normality.

My old environment, though, was an altogether more fearsome place and there I felt my disability a thousand times more intensely. In this place, so well known to me but now so foreign, of course I wanted to be the same person as I used to be. I wanted magically to have my life restored, as if the walls of home, embracing me, could somehow do this. Home, beloved home – home would surely cure me, wouldn't it? While deep down of course I knew it couldn't. As a practical person, the gap I experienced between what I could now do and what I used to be able to do was ferocious. The process of coming to terms with this involved much frustration and grief. I was neutered; I wasn't me any longer, not a can-doer, not a participant. Now I was irrevocably changed to an observer. The consequences of my accident started to become real to me and it was more difficult to pretend I was enduring the short-term hardship of a bush tucker trial. It was also scary, because I had full responsibility for my own care. Now I was the only expert in the building.

There were many things I could not fight, in this world designed for upright human beings, and especially human beings with working hands. When I was on my own they tipped me over into self-pity and hysterical sobbing fits, when I would bend over my knees and cry uncontrollably until my thighs were sopping wet and my leggings covered in snails' trails of shiny snotters. 'Fucking hell,' I would scream when I was alone, and I couldn't reach a book, or had smashed a jug, or was unable to unlock a door. 'Fucking, fucking, *fucking* hell.' I wasn't as accomplished as Grunt at swearing, back in high dependency, but cursing was great therapy, easing physical pain and reducing violence – perhaps, in my case, against myself. My wrists had strengthened to the extent that I could turn my hands towards my mouth and bite my nails – I did that ferociously as a kind of release. I remember the first time I was at home on my own after I came out of hospital: just me, no one within earshot, no neighbours, or passers-by, no nurses or patients. And it was as if a year's worth of despair, dammed up inside me – it was as if in the solitude the dam burst. I started wailing, ululating and throwing the top half of my body around in grief, the way you see Middle-Eastern or African women behaving when they have lost their sons to terrorism. An absolute removal of inhibition, a primal expression, casting off the cloak of emotional control. I guess it was good for me. The dog, in distress at my distress, jumped in my lap and quivered; stroking her, I managed to calm down.

The cottage, which was on six different levels, every room descending a step downhill, had been comprehensively ramped. It was like a skateboard track, downhill all the way from the living room to my bathroom … wheeeeee. It was sufficient; I could get around; I could exist here. Slow pushing up to the top of the house in the morning, fast downhill to bed at night. Just don't forget anything and have to go back down to the bedroom too often. Good physio for the arms, I Pollyanna-ed it. Dave and I had been too long apart. He needed my practical eye. He'd taken a whim to prune what he thought were apple trees, but had instead massacred the flowering cherry. The paperwork was in chaos; he was burning heating oil like five-pound notes.

In the night, I woke to hear a nurse in my room, only without the usual torch.

'Who's that?' I called, thinking I was in hospital.

There was an audible gasp from my sleepy husband, returning from a night-time pee.

'You startled me,' he said. 'I'm so used to being alone.'

Dave and I spoke briefly about whether we should sell up and move to the suburbs, to a place all on one level, with a flat tarmac drive for the car, and a smooth pavement all the way to the local shops, handy for carers' and doctors' visits and independent movement. We did not linger long on the idea: for us it constituted a kind of spiritual death. We could not contemplate leaving this quirky, wild place; impractical though it was, our hearts were here. Houses hold power over you. Owning property, as E.M. Forster said, and Lionel Shriver has riffed into twenty-first-century literature, makes you feel heavy. Houses pin you down and can oppress you. For all its unsuitability, our cottage was light to own: it was happy to have us; we knew that, like the landscape, it would endure long after us. For sure, if we remained I would be more hermit-like, and we would have to try much harder to find carers willing to brave the track, but it was somehow an imperative. Here we could remake life, such as it was going to be. For me too, there was the added awareness that Dave had already had enough sacrifices thrust upon him without having to leave his beloved domain. He loved his space. The laird, we used to call him. Mr Territorial. If he saw a strange car coming up the track, or walkers, his hackles would rise, he'd reach for the binoculars.

'Shooters to the tower,' Doug would yell. 'It's young people! Wearing hoodies! Plainly drug dealing! Prepare to fire!'

Dave took it in good part.

Recreating life as a tetraplegic, though, was brave talk. Perhaps it would have been the same anywhere, because really it was less about space and surfaces than the psychological process of learning my limitations in an able-bodied world, of finding a different role to the one I had before. Practical frustrations tortured me, the little ones often more so than the big ones. It was one thing to know that I could not dash down to the barn and grab a spanner to fix a wonky light; it was another to realise I couldn't actually grip the spanner hard enough to turn the nut. With one hand that worked not at all, and the other with minimal grip, life was extraordinarily curtailed, deliberate and slow. Slow! The word was not adequate. From being someone who could achieve twenty things in five minutes, I now struggled to make a cup of coffee in the same timeframe. And once made, I couldn't carry it anywhere; I had to sit and drink it where I made it. If you want to immobilise someone in a wheelchair, you pass them a hot drink, or indeed anything they cannot either balance on their lap, wedge between their thighs or grip with their teeth. All around me I saw things that needed to be done – to be picked up, or adjusted, or tidied, or fixed or opened, instinctive stuff … and I could do none of them. I could only look. It was a very real torture.

Until you live in a wheelchair, you never realise just how little you can do with your hands if you want to move at the same time. Both hands are needed to propel and steer using the push rims on the wheels; and those rims are only an inch off the floor and half an inch from the outside wall of the tyre. Your hands are only ever as clean as the rims. And if you are cursed, and your push rims get mucky – on the yuck scale, dog turds are the worst, closely followed by syrup or cooking oil – your hands are immediately contaminated too. Then, if you can't call on anyone for help, you must maneouvre into a position at the sink where you can wash – first your hands, then, very laboriously, leaning out as if in a racing dinghy, the rims. You will think they're clean, but they won't be, for there will be some on the spokes, or you will surely have missed a bit. So you must wipe them again. Only then can you move again. On a good day this can take up to forty-five minutes. And it is deeply tedious.

Your hands, in effect, replace your feet: the palms grow thick and calloused from pushing, mimicking the skin on your heels. Your shoulders hunch with the lifting, leaning and pushing, and after a while your neck bows and thickens, your upper body dowager-humps, adapting to a job it was not designed to do. Role-reversed, the top half of your body becomes the propulsion, the engine, rather than the decorative bit that used to float along admiring the view. Meanwhile, your world shrinks indescribably, as if overnight you have been released onto the pages of *The Borrowers*. The only things in easy reach are those at shoulder height or lower, and no more than half an arm's length away, for your chair will not allow you any closer. If you work at able-bodied heights – the kitchen worktop, for instance – you are always operating your arms above shoulder height, which is exhausting even for the able-bodied. Cooking was a clumsy process, chin resting on the bar of the Aga, watching from close up the chemical reaction of heat and food in the frying pan, elbow high above my head as I stirred blind, dropping and clattering and breaking dishes. I tried, several times, to get Dave to sit in a wheelchair and see how difficult it was to perform the most simple tasks. He refused. There is only so much reality a man can take. He did not want to experience my struggle. I have heard of professional three-day event riders who are equally averse to sampling life in a wheelchair. Perhaps it is superstition. Or perhaps they just don't want to know, to dwell on the consequences of the dangers of their sport.

Independent, mostly, during the day, I needed help at both ends of it. I could not get up, dress or wash myself, nor, at night, could I lift my lower legs onto the bed. I battled the need for night-time assistance for a long time: and there were a few brief months when I managed, by dint of a transfer board, a sliding sheet, and a horrendous amount of strain on my shoulders, to get into bed by myself. I would use a transfer board topped with a sliding sheet – a loop of slippy nylon – to move my backside from my chair to the end of the mattress and then lean backwards, hauling myself up the bed towards the pillow on my elbows. It always felt precarious, transferring alone, and the strain on my arms was too much, as was the further rolling and pushing required to take off a pair of leggings while I was lying on them. I timed myself: from leaving the chair to pulling over the duvet took an hour. Within two years, as my shoulders wore out, I gave up the ordeal and always sought help from someone. There were certain elements to my life where it was foolish to persist in being independent – it gobbled valuable time and energy better devoted to other things.

At night, it became Dave's chore to throw my lower legs onto the bed and pull off my leggings for me, the least sensual of operations. We both would much rather have it that way than be visited by carers coming in the evening. Mornings were bad enough: we were learning the reality of loss of privacy which serious disability brings. Privacy, like health, was another thing you took utterly for granted until it was taken away from you. Now, every day, a succession of entirely pleasant semi-strangers trooped into the house. First the district nurse, to do my bowels, then the council carers to shower me. It was essential, but it felt like an invasion.

When you are very disabled, a real tension exists between dependence and a loss of privacy. The two needs tug against each other; flourish alongside each other; you suffer both simul-taneously. The loss of privacy is often the more profound. I had grown accustomed to being reliant on people I hardly knew to wash, dress and roll me. I could, without any embarrassment, ask these women to peer at my genitals and tell me if they looked sore, because I couldn't feel anything, and question whether they had dried between my toes as well as I would have done. Our bedroom, once a private place, was now a func-tional, public space, shelves stacked with medical supplies. For

Dave, Mr Territorial, someone who didn't like to be organised, the sacrifice of his home was considerable and difficult. Not only did it impose set times for him to get up, but it imposed outside expectations on him. Spontaneity was cancelled. Our house was not big enough to allow him to retreat. Privacy denied is wearying, draining, like loss of freedom. Later I heard about the case of a young ex-serviceman, dreadfully disabled in Afghanistan, who needed someone with him twenty-four hours a day. The fact he could never have private time, on top of every other indignity, depressed him. The charity Canine Partners paired him up with a dog which was trained, on his command, to press a button and summon help. It may seem nothing to an able-bodied person, but it was huge for him: it meant he could spend time alone in a room every day with his thoughts. Just him and his dog. Dave and I understood that so well now.

My old domain had slipped out of my control, because of my physical incapacity. The stables, barn, fields, garden – all outside territory became impassable. Inside I pursued the same small, well-wheeled track from bathroom to bed to kettle to kitchen table. At the bottom of the tiny, narrow stairs I would look up and find my memories of the rooms upstairs fading, floating away to join childhood memories of places I had loved. Daily, I tormented myself, trying to push back the boundaries, to find home again, that place where everything would be all right and all would end well. Home: that sanctuary which existed for me, forever framed in the lovely lullaby 'Morningtown Ride' by The Seekers, which my sister had sung to me when I was a little girl on the back seat of the family car, where we rocked and rode with each other, bound for that elusive safe haven out along the bay.

Music of any kind still had the capacity to disarm me emotionally. But that tune, on the achingly rare times I caught it on the radio, made me sob. It expressed the search for somewhere exquisitely, intangibly, irreplaceably, precious. You always knew Morningtown was a fantasy place – but now you knew, with crushing certainty, that you were never going to find it.

Like a wounded animal, I created a lair mentality. I existed in the rooms of the house which I could negotiate, and fed upon the view from the windows, leaning from my chair to try and see more. From the living room I inspected the uneaten grass in the field behind the house, fantasising that one day I'd see the big handsome chestnut gelding idling by, giraffe-necked, stealing the odd tasty shrub branch from the garden with prehensile lips, like he used to do. And in his shadow the pony, eyes bulging with guile, muzzled to prevent death from over-eating, reaching through the fence to tease at even tastier morsels. If I could just catch a glimpse of them, even in my peripheral vision, maybe it would be proof this was all a bad dream and I'd wake up and everything would be all right again. Maybe they were there, Terry and the pony, maybe they were just a little further along the fence and I couldn't see them.

The whimsy reminded me of a time when I was very small and fascinated by mirrors. My siblings Andrew and Lindsay, thirteen and eleven years my senior, told me that that mirrors were magic windows. A family of magic people lived behind the glass, and when we came along they jumped out, dressed as us, and imitated us. 'If you stand at the edge of the mirror, and you pop your head round very, very quickly,' said my tormentors, 'you'll catch them unawares. They'll be doing something else.'

Thus I would flatten myself against the wall beside the huge gilt-framed mirror in the hall, darting my head round the frame periodically, to try and outsmart the child who was pretending to be me. Andrew and Lindsay loved the game; it stopped their baby sister pestering them. Now I was playing magic mirrors again, just a different version – I peeked through windows for the pictures they had framed eighteen months ago. They were never there. Or maybe, just as when I was four, I simply wasn't fast enough.

Emotionally, I felt as if I had been born without skin. Belongings assumed a loaded significance. About a year before my accident I had bought my first dressage saddle, a gorgeous thing, elegant and slim, evolved from centuries of the art of high equitation and the interface between rider and horse's body. Dressage saddles are timeless classics of haute ecole – as achingly well designed and gracious as any haute couture from Chanel or Balenciaga; I had always wanted one but never been able to afford it. It was the equivalent for another woman of buying a Gucci coat or a Dolce & Gabbana handbag; a totem of desire and self-reward. There comes the tipping point where every girl says to herself, I'm getting old, I deserve one. In the end, I bought a beautiful second-hand saddle, using my credit card. When I was in hospital Dave, God love him, paid it off in instalments and lectured me like a Presbyterian minister every time he sent off a cheque.

It took months at home before I was strong enough to venture down to the barn where I had kept the horses – largely untouched, but now with the feel of the *Mary Celeste*. Dave came with me; we were both pinched with tension. The night rug which I had slung off my horse before I went off that fateful morning was still doubled neatly over a loose-box door, but now thick with dust. I couldn't bear to go near my tack room: I knew the smell would, like hearing music, strip away my defences, but the urge to see and hold my saddle, to mourn a little, was too strong. I asked Dave to bring the saddle out to me and put it on my lap: an act of masochism, I suppose, but also an acknowledgement that I would have to start toughening up if I was to continue living here with the ghosts. When you've been around horses and their tack all your life – indeed, around anything: babies, dogs, tools – you handle those items with inner sight, an unconscious understanding and familiarity. Bridles assemble and disassemble in your hands in the same way as you plait hair or a craftswoman does her knitting. Saddles fit in your hands and arms, balance happily against your crooked hip. But my arms, of course, could no longer hold the weighty, unwieldy thing, my hands could no longer stroke its curves. Only my eyes could feast on the familiar and they were blind with tears. We retreated back inside and I yearned for that skin thickening to speed up.

If my relationship with house and possessions had changed, then an even bigger revolution had taken place in my relationships with people. 'The fidelity of our bodies is so basic that we never think of it – it is the certain grounds of our daily experience. Chronic illness is a betrayal of that fundamental trust,' wrote Arthur Kleinman. That word 'betrayal' was key. I felt like a general whose soldiers had deserted en masse and left him naked on the hillside. Betrayed, I was discovering that a normally functioning mind and body are central to the reciprocity of everyday life. We look after ourselves, don't we? We interact, we transact with each other, from positions of strength.

From being a mistress of my universe, a giver of energy and assistance, now I was dependent, vulnerable to rejection; and I had to spend my days calculating the appropriateness of my demands on others when I could offer precisely nothing in return. I could offer only love, or friendship, or wages. How to get by without being a nag or a burden? If I expected too much, demanded too much, they might dislike me. This was an entirely new landscape to negotiate. Every time I opened my mouth a stream of supplication emerged. *Could you ... Would you ... Please pass me ... Sorry but I can't reach ... Help me ... Oh, I've dropped ...* Continually, I assessed the size of my good-will overdraft, drawing on other people's kindness. I can't ask Dave to do that *as well* ... I'm not too uncomfortable, I won't wake him to get him to move my legs – I'll wait till the alarm goes off ... Will my carer be upset if I ask her to ... I wonder if my cleaner would mind ...

When the reciprocity of everyday life is unbalanced, especially in a culture which emphasises independence – and my family's did, especially – then you feel insecure. It felt like a particularly cruel redundancy, taking away my self-worth. The most frustrating thing was my inability to slot back into my domestic role as the powerhouse, the doer of practical things for others. The mother lode; the family services industry. Don't most women, even the most feminist of us, still fulfil this? One Sunday morning Dougie, stressed to his limits by exams but nevertheless taking time to visit me, dashed back to university on the other side of the country leaving his flat keys behind him; and Dave, also stressed or maybe just more blond, put £70 worth of petrol in a diesel car and was stranded elsewhere. Once, I would have solved their problems by teatime, jumping in a car to hand-deliver the keys, rescuing Dave on the way home. Miserably, I could only sit at home, take the phone calls and commiserate; I wasn't even capable of posting the keys next-day delivery, because my hands weren't good enough to tape up the package, were I even capable of getting to the post office.

Later the same week poor Doug phoned me the evening before an exam, exhausted, cracking, with a blinding headache and no food in the flat but breakfast cereal. Poor guy had been through so much grief, and was trying so hard to catch up with his studies and do well. He needed Migraleve and a hot meal and never mind how far away he was, I needed to go to him. Any mother, bound by those universal tramlines of responsibility and indispensability, would have sprung into action. Because mothers don't get sick. Dougie was by then twenty-one years old, but it didn't change anything. Whatever I was doing, there was always a space reserved just for him. I was still his mum and he needed me. The accident did not take away the purity of that, but it limited its practicalities.

He had written this poem about me when he was about eight.

My mum is fun
She rides her horse through bogs
She runs up rivers and climbs through bushes
She's very messy
And she's SUCH a fussy speller
But my mum is fun.

After my accident, this big, sweet, happy-go-lucky young man had become a Trojan, lifting and maneouvring me as if I was a baby, trying to be uber-cheerful for my sake. Now, as he broke under the strain of all he carried, I could do so little in return. As a mother, your deepest fear is not being there for your child. There was no possible way for me to jump in a car and drive a mercy mission to him. Nothing to do except suppress my own emotion and parent him by phone, both of us torn pitifully between our old identities and the new. But my inability to fulfil my role filled me with melancholy. Later, when the inner Pollyanna had had the chance to reassert herself, it occurred to me that in fact things could have been worse: he might not have phoned; or I might have become tearful talking to him. Sometimes hearing a voice is enough.

He scraped through the exam.

Before my accident our house was a fairly blokey, low-main-tenance one. Dave, Doug – by then, a student, on and off – and me. *Band of Brothers* stuff. They bonded over *Platoon*, *Jarhead*, *The Guns of Navarone*; from the next room I learnt the dialogue off by heart. Sometimes, to get their attention during a war film, I would dive onto my front through the living-room door, shouting *Daka-daka-daka-daka-boom!* and pretending to machine-gun them. I enjoyed the company of men. We took each other for granted and were secure, happy and busy doing our own thing. Women, however, will under-stand when I say that while I knew they adored me, it was only occasionally either of them really noticed that I was there. 'Is there something different about you, Mum?' after I wore a dress for the first time in years. 'Are you upset about something, darling?' after I wept for an hour at a sad film.

And 'Ew, that smells like fly spray' (both of them) after I got a new perfume. However, in our new, post-nuclear-bomb world, we had to reconstruct roles and relationships afresh. From being a key member of the platoon, unifying them, pulling my weight, I became the desperately wounded, needy comrade the boys had to carry on their backs for the rest of their lives. Roles were thrown into reverse so quickly that you could hear the cogs crunching. At home, they took up watch over me. It took me a while to understand that when something terrible happens to you, it is often much more shattering for others to deal with. This is certainly so in the early stages when you are focused on survival while they must deal with the wider picture – without their main emotional prop to support them.

Both practically and emotionally, Dave and Doug had stepped up to the plate heroically. They hid their distress and put their lives on hold. Terrible injury, unavoidably, destroyed the natural order of things and neutralised me as a mother to the extent that the most I could do for Doug was not to weep too much. I had to detach somewhat. Hide my distress from him. Hide it from everyone, even myself. If there was a pattern established, it was that we all acted like brave soldiers, camouflaging the very worst of our raw emotions from one another. I'm not sure that *Band of Brothers* stuff is to be recommended, post family trauma, and with hindsight I have often wondered if I should have taken the lead and handled it differently, encouraging more discussion and disclosure between us. But somehow at the time, in war, in crisis, the horror was all too immediately apparent and understood, and we adopted a less-than-contemplative survival strategy. On the occasions when I tried to get them to open up, they shrugged and squirmed and said, 'Just got to get on with it.' Expressing their feelings through practical action was much easier. *Doing* stuff to try and make it better. For Doug, it was a crash course in determination and maturity; through gritted teeth he managed to keep his studies going. Many would have given up. One day he came home as a surprise, lifted me into his beat-up little car and drove into the forest, where he put me in my chair and pushed me miles down the tracks, deep among the trees.

'I just thought you might be missing the places where you used to ride,' he said.

As another surprise, he managed to reserve me much-sought-after tickets to the final phase of the eventing at the London Olympics, and offered to take me. He didn't over-complicate things. He wanted to make me happy again.

Dave, his easy home life utterly derailed, took on responsibilities he'd always successfully avoided. There was an earned nobility in accepting that your wife, once someone who needed nothing done for her, was now a dependent who needed constant support. By family tradition, we also tried to find humour to fend off the worst of it. Overall, my casting on this new stage darkly amused me. It made me feel as if I had morphed into some decrepit old duchess who must be waited on hand and foot. Plus, there were some old purgatories that, no matter my new physical handicap, I could not avoid. Tax returns were one such, a job always left to me and now very pressing but far more daunting, for eighteen months' worth of mail teetered in multiple trays and overstuffed cardboard envelopes. And my hands no longer worked.

Dave, to whom paperwork is akin to anthrax, adopted a peculiar, pivot-eyed, facial twitch whenever I asked him where his P60 was.

'That's why I married you – so I'd never have to answer a question like that ever again,' he said.

The paperwork was piled so high it had started to cut off the light coming in the windows. Reaching the files was one thing, lifting them another, separating the sheets maddening, and finding space to make new piles another challenge. My fingers were still not strong enough to open an envelope. In terms of dexterity, I was a secretary trying to do her job while wearing a pair of leather boxing gloves.

I tried very hard to persuade the kitchen to become mine again. In it I felt very strongly the dislocation with the past. Memories of the old days were everywhere, of those wonderful summer mornings when the house was full of visiting family or friends. I'd be first in the kitchen, leaning against the sink, nursing a huge mug of coffee, waiting for the beloved sleepy faces to come tumbling through the door – young and old, in nightwear, totally relaxed, sharing that blissful no-stress, can't-give-a-stuff holiday feeling. And we'd laze around, catching up on the news, family gossip, intimacies, making toast, teasing Dave when he emerged, and he would reduce us to hysterics with his surreal insults and stories. Years of laughter hung in the air around our kitchen table; I couldn't bottle it, but everyone present knew it was the best place in the world to be. In the same room, at the tail end of the day, I used to enjoy brief time alone, the part of tonight devoted to creating order for tomorrow: housewifing, clearing the table for the next day, loading the dishwasher, switching off the lights. The gentle ceremony of the night watch, slipping into bed after everyone had gone to sleep.

But so much of that had gone. Now there was no slipping out of bed first for me; no longer the thrill of claiming the morning, filling the kettle, waiting for everyone to congregate. Now I had to lie and wait in bed for my carer to get me up, and I was invariably last to reach the kitchen. I would listen to the distant fun, smell the toast, hear the hum of chat and yearn to be part of it. Often, by the time I toiled up the ramp into the kitchen to join the party, they were loading the dishwasher, news exchanged. I'd missed the best bits – or at least it felt that way. At night, perversely, it was solitude that was denied. I had to be put to bed; I could never enjoy the peace and satisfaction of the final check. The modern acronym is FOMO – Fear Of Missing Out – used to express the fear that all your friends were having more fun and excitement than you are. FOMO is just a re-tread of age-old human angst – the door we never opened into the rose garden, the hidden laughter of children in the foliage, the fun we missed. The games we were excluded from. Regret and exclusion.

Gradually, I came to understand that FOMO was probably my long-term fate. Like a bereavement, it was something that I was going to have to learn to accommodate. It has got easier but in those early days it was hard. Because looking after myself was so time-consuming, and I moved at a snail's pace, I could not keep up with the world. There was little or no time to watch things, meet people, go places. I missed the fun and urgency and buzz of being around newspaper people, picking up information almost by osmosis. Wildly over-optimistic at first, I had hoped I might return to my desk and pick up my old worklife: the realisation that this was physically impossible came slowly but painfully. And then there were the lunches and get-togethers I couldn't attend because they were up a set of stairs, or too far away; and after a while, once you'd said no a few times, people stopped asking you. Friends came to accept your perspective – that the venue wasn't easy and there would be a fuss. Your rational brain knew that you were far better staying at home, but it didn't stop the yearning inside. At first, the insecurity of not being in-the-know gnawed at you, then you resigned yourself to being an outsider. There would always be gatherings, loved ones, laughter, but they couldn't be spontaneous, and you would never surprise, or be unobtrusive. FOMO does fade. Gently, like a liner moving off her berth, you start to slip away from your old life.

Chronic illness encourages the sick to adopt a social set piece: the sick role. The traditional one, which Aunt Averil was cast in, the passive victim of an epidemic, gave her a certain settled status in the twentieth century. Nobody asked her whether she was humiliated by her situation; I doubt she was ever asked how she felt emotionally. She was someone to be done unto. The traditional sick role assumes we should behave, cooperate, should want to get well – I think of little fictional Katy, laid up in bed with her bruised spine, unable to walk, dutifully learning patience and the love of God. She accepted the moral duty to be a 'good patient'. In those same days of ultra-conformity, there was poor Averil, occasionally so desperate she tried to break out, refusing to read the Bible and becoming a bad patient – inconsiderate, protesting, fighting, trying to block her own breathing.

The established code of medical sociology reflects the belief of the majority of the public, who regard sickness as a form of deviance. Deep down, unconsciously if not consciously, the healthy world rather wishes we didn't exist. But if we have to be sick, they'd like us to be good patients and accept the rights and obligations of the sick role. There's an expectation that everyone should fit into this morality tale; it's what the whole welfare system is based on. If the sick show a positive personality and a creative response to their plight, then they're a triumph; they're being successfully ill, finding solutions, treatments and therapies, 'fighting' their symptoms, 'battling' their diagnosis. The healthy approve of them. That culture was instilled in me: I was a shining light, always in pursuit of virtue in my accomplishments post-accident, hence, maybe, the popularity of my newspaper column. Hence, perhaps, the way a whole lexicon of war language is applied approvingly to illness, and especially to cancer. Nobody dies of cancer these days without it being said of them that *They put up such a great fight.* These kinds of semantics are being challenged increasingly in the twenty-first century, especially by a new generation of physically disabled people, pushing back the physical, rejecting the belief that there's something wrong with them – and, accordingly, rejecting moral judgements. Over the last century Averil, The Invalid, has evolved first into a patient, then into a health-care user and now, via identity politics, into the militant for whom the body is a basis for political action. The problem is that wider culture hasn't caught up and remains traditional: politicians still strive to lower the benefits bill and the qualifications for disability payments continue to be a battleground. Able-bodied taxpayers – and not, I suspect, just the reactionary ones – retain old-fashioned moral expectations of the sick.

For me, though, it was a quandary. I felt the weight of that moral duty to recover, but paralysis was not recoverable from. It was a dead end. A no return. What was I do? Even though I knew – and science knows; Christ, *everyone* knows – there is no existing cure for broken and crushed spines, not to *try* to get better at the very least seemed improper. Hence the need to resist disability, the failure to accept. As a hopeless neurological case, perhaps one reason you employ warlike talk is on behalf of your family. Because no matter how grimly rational you are, you continue to fight your ill health to demonstrate to the people you love how much you love them and want to remain around them. Perhaps it's the wrong thing to do. You never stop hoping you will improve, in some tiny way, for them. You never give up.

Today, wearied, battle-scarred as it were, I'm not sure it is helpful to use such imagery. In the beginning, newly disabled, I found myself facing the huge task of coping with the emotional and practical consequences, while aware that I felt both reduced from the inside and also perceived as such from the outside. A lesser person. If I was to display my suffering, show anger, self-pity, frustration, guilt, all perceived negative emotions, I might alienate people. And I needed people. And they expected me to conform. They said things to Dave like: 'If anyone can cope with this, Mel can.' My moral duty was to get well again, or at least to pretend that I was fine. I smiled brightly. I'd survived, hadn't I? I felt bound to put on a brave face and say, 'I'm fine', so that everyone would be much more comfortable. This, I found, was a stereotype I fitted quite naturally.

There was huge solace, also, in work. Continuing to write as much as I was able fitted the approved code. I was fascinated by

how disabled people had coped in centuries past, long before
the welfare state. There was no special treatment. The damaged
were expected to work to survive; and in turn they themselves
expected to do so. The idea that disabled people could only do
certain jobs is a modern construct. Work was the only passport
to life, so they just got on with it, frailties, bowed bones, pain
and all, and did lowly jobs on behalf of the more fit: they
cleaned, they swept, they became street vendors, they laid out
the dead, they did cooking and washing for others, and they
nursed other sick people – once, on BBC Radio 4, I heard that
sixty per cent of those who performed nursing duties in the
eighteenth and nineteenth century had disabilities themselves.
Interestingly, these people continued to define themselves by
work. I could understand that, and as I toiled long, sore hours
hunched over a computer, I was amused to think I was following a template laid down hundreds of years ago. My ancestors
would have been proud of me.

Reacquainting myself with people was difficult. They only
knew the old me and this new, short creature folded in a chair
was unfamiliar to them. Some people cried. I found it flattering
that they should care so much. Others were very cool and studiously normal; they'd obviously schooled themselves. Sheryl
Sandberg said after she lost her husband that old acquaintances
'looked at me as if I was a ghost'. I reassured my old friends, as
expected, that I was fine and then taught myself to relearn them
as people with newly working bodies; I noticed as if for the first
time how they walked, and sat, and carried themselves. I decon-
structed their ease of movement, their power, with envy.
Hungry eyes. I went on my first trip to the city centre shops.

Wow, how fast people moved. I was transfixed by how beautifully their legs worked, how easily their hips flexed, their buttocks swayed. In the bank it was so difficult to talk to the teller over the eye-level counter; and I felt buffeted and pressured by the lunchtime queue behind me. I used to be one of you, I want to turn and tell them: forever in a rush, groaning inwardly when a person in the wheelchair held me up. The bank teller was pleasant but I was trembling with exhaustion by the time I left. One day, three girlfriends, riding pals, came for a cup of tea together. I studied them greedily, those smart women, in sassy jeans and boots and nice jackets. We had a laugh and a chat, and then they left, and I watched them from the door as they swung their legs into their cars and sped off, and I knew that even by the time they reached the farm gates they were re-entering their busy lives, they'd be on their mobile phones, catching up on texts, calling people back, planning the rest of their hectic week. Long after they left I sat very still by the window, feeling cheated and jealous. The reasons to develop hermit tendencies were starting to mount up.

Meeting strangers, as opposed to friends, was something else again. These people did not know me, the real me. How could they? They only saw a person stuck in a chair, not me properly – *me*, tall, strong and dynamic. They could have no sense of what I was like, inside or outside. They did not know how I moved, or looked, or achieved. And I felt differently towards them. They were superficial; I almost felt I was wasting my time with them. How could they ever be as close to me as old friends? This person you see, I wanted to explain, isn't me. This – tapping my breast bone – isn't actually the real me, it's someone else. Annie says she often feels she is hovering a foot or so above her own head, looking down on herself, thinking, 'Who is that person?' Strangers, you noted, treated you differently to the way strangers would have treated you before injury. Either you were invisible, or they were often too attentive, even patronising. It was amusing sometimes, how extraordinarily, cloyingly nice some people were, when they wouldn't have looked at you twice if you'd been standing up. I didn't like it but I tried my best to make it easy for everyone. In a way, you start to pretend you're standing in for the real but absent you, a representative for a missing person. It seemed to be the only etiquette possible.

No relationship with home could be properly rebuilt without learning to drive again. The remoteness of the cottage was both its glory and its challenge. When you are paralysed, you must learn to drive with your hands: for paraplegics, with fully functioning upper limbs, this is less difficult. For tetraplegics, with limited arm and hand ability, it is more problematic. My determination to get back behind the wheel was absolute – cars had always symbolised freedom for me – but because I was still living in my head, rather than my head and body, I had little idea how scary it would be. As residents of the spinal unit, tetraplegics had been gently dissuaded from applying for the compulsory NHS driving assessment for as long as possible. Staff wanted our arms and hands to get stronger. And our heads. As I was to find out, it's fairly traumatic to be faced with the fact that on top of everything else, you've lost such an intrinsic skill. This was not about refamiliarisation with old powers; rather it was radical surgery on your psyche.

There was a long waiting list, but eventually I was called to a mobile test centre, a lorry parked in the grounds of a semi-disused psychiatric institution on the outskirts of the city. It seemed an appropriate setting for what was possibly one of the most stressful days I've ever spent. I began it as someone convinced she was still a bold, experienced driver, unfazed by horse lorries, towing, and farm vehicles, and ended it as a humbled wreck, capable only of creeping along at ten miles an hour with a long line of exasperated motorists behind her – people she could see and hear in her mirror muttering: 'For Christ's sake, who let THAT out on the road?'

My assessor was a totally charming woman called Janet, who by the end of the afternoon I just wanted to hug and call Mummy. Best of all, she had dual controls. My most serious problem was gripping on the knob on the steering wheel with my left claw, to turn the wheel. At right-hand junctions, the feeling was that of a small child trying to stir a giant raw Christmas cake – the arm just wasn't strong enough to grip the wooden spoon, let alone turn it. My right hand was operating a lever – push to brake, pull to accelerate. Every bit of auto-matic, unconscious driving experience from the past was rendered obsolete: I was starting from scratch. How indignant I was. Driving forced me to the core of my humility studies. Me, who had, at one point in my career, when terminally bored, been a part-time motoring correspondent, paid to drive flash cars? Nothing could prepare me for the infant-like help-lessness. The human condition means, I think, that we all possess hidden pockets of arrogance, even the most self-deprecating among us. Deep inside, we nurture little kernels of pride, buried treasure. That day, mine were stolen.

The assessment took three hours, by which time I was so mentally shot that I almost didn't care whether I'd passed or failed.

'Well?' I said to the sublimely encouraging Janet.

She beamed at me. 'Oh, you're going to drive,' she said. 'Of course you are. We just need to make sure you get the right car for you, adapted so you can steer with your right hand.'

It was a painfully slow process building up confidence. For weeks my first Motability car, complete with hand controls, sat on its delivery mileage outside the house, taunting me. Preoccupied with other health issues, I found excuse after excuse why I couldn't begin. When I did, forced by an exasperated Dave, it was on our mile-long farm track, up and down, dodging the potholes, going so slowly that dear Pip, our beloved dog, who was trotting beside, kept stopping and looking back at me. Gradually, as I persisted, my fingers softened and the car stopped surging and jumping.

At first Dave came with me, then left me on my own, another milestone of progress. Hard to describe how ridiculously momentous that felt, feeling so vulnerable and isolated on my own in charge of the car, yet also how free, mobile and independent. If you aren't compromised in some way by health or disability, it's probably hard to understand this; or to appreciate how insignificant things can represent huge landmarks. That afternoon I went up and down the track five times, then, the last time I reached the public road, took a deep breath and set off for the village. I went up the main street, successfully avoiding all cars, round the war memorial and back home. Left-hand turns all the way. A friend told me about her elderly aunt, who would only ever turn left at junctions – sometimes it took her days to get to her destination.

Later, after my first long drive – fifteen miles – I texted Dougie. 'Maws a pure cruiser!' he texted in fluent Glaswegian. It reminded me why I could neither stop fighting, nor labelling it fighting.

But fighting implies casualties.

One day I got an email.

My name is —. I took early retirement in order to pursue my hobbies of horse-riding, hiking and tennis. I had a riding accident in Oct 20 – and am now a C3/C4 [*damage at a high level to cervical vertebra in the neck*] incomplete tetra. I have read many of your articles and my experience and thoughts mirror yours in an uncanny way. However, I am now thinking of calling it a day and treating myself to a final holiday in Switzerland. I have finally accepted that a f***ed spine does not always respect intensive physio and exercise. In fact, the more I do, the worse my horrific sensations and hypertonia become. I now know that this disgusting life will never be acceptable – 100 metres hobbling on a frame held by useless hands is point-less to someone who used to ride 4 or 5 times a week and walk 12 or more miles twice a week.

Sorry to be so depressing but just wondered if you ever feel this way. If so, I would love to hear from you. I hope for your sake that you find a way to cope but I just want out now.

Good luck

Dear —

If it helps, right now I'd like to book a flight to come with you. I'm really struggling just now … the pain and the fact everything gets harder instead of easier. And I'm in a trap of my own making, writing 'inspirational' columns. It is my family which keep me alive – I couldn't do it to them.

But here's what I'd say to dissuade you (and I speak as someone who used to be *The Times*'s unofficial pro-euthanasia correspondent, cos my mother took her own life very bravely when she got dementia). 1) it's not even 3 years yet and look where you started from. 3 years is nothing, in terms of nerve regeneration. I get so many letters from people still improving after 5, 10 years. 2) 100 metres is a bloody long way. I'd kill to do 100 metres 3) hands do improve … i've heard of amazing accounts of recovery 4) Switzerland's too grotty for me.

So I join you in the depression. I understand. But try and ride it out and things could improve

Good luck

Dear Melanie I so feel for you. I was so independent, arrogant really and so proud of being fit and healthy. I only took painkillers for injuries due to riding accidents, I loved my life and had no time for moaners. I cannot believe this has happened to me. Now I am so bitter – I see fat slobs waddling around – people I would have despised before and now I actually envy them because they can walk. I glare at people who smile at me and make way for me – and mutter, 'Yes go on, make way for the cripple.' I cannot accept this life – my muscle rigidity and pain have increased – my bike and standing frame are gathering dust and most of my carers leave more depressed than me. Anyway, I am going to Switzerland next Saturday – I can' t believe this is happening – I had such a wonderful retirement planned, I know I can back out till the last minute but I don't think I will.

I really, really know how you feel and wish I could have met you. I wish you all the best for the future.

Lots of love

Dear —

I replied, torn between empathy and a feeling of intense obligation. I respected her decision but could she delay her trip until she was less depressed? Could getting an assistance dog help? Or phoning the Samaritans? I told her that there had been a suicide in the extended family recently and I had seen the distress it left behind; there had been so many people who loved the person, but in his depressed state he didn't realise. Although I totally respected her decision, I said, I hoped that she would keep fighting for a bit longer until the sun came up again – because I thought it might. And I sent her my love and told her I cared. I never heard from her again.

The correspondence affected me deeply. Guilt flooded in and wouldn't drain away – should I have asked for her phone number? Probably. Had I done enough? Probably not. Had I said the wrong thing? Probably yes. I felt I had let her down. Given her clichés as answers. Guilt, but yes, if I'm honest there was also a sliver of self-pity. How could I cope, on top of everything else I was dealing with? Following the recent tragedy in Dougie's step-family, involving someone he was very close to, I was still deeply worried about his mental health. How, in these circumstances, could I do anything but support life? Gareth Williams, a medical sociologist, identified what he called the routine of narrative reconstruction – how someone after chronic illness can 'realign past and present and self and society'; in other words, a way to make sense of events in our lives. Unconsciously, I suppose, without planning or strategy, I had begun, quite literally, a narrative reconstruction soon after I hit the ground. Writing about what was happening to me became a way of processing the trauma. I tried to be honest in my writing, but for the sake of those who loved me, it was inevitably forged as a narrative which was positive enough to sustain us all. I pulled my punches. I was my own spin doctor. Writing became a liferaft of sorts for the dark days, a way of processing and rationalising grief, during which I had made several mordant quips about escaping to Switzerland. Indeed, had I been without family, as this woman appeared to be, I might have done the same as her. Access to a humane way to end your life was to me as primal as the right of women to decide the fate of their own bodies with regard to fertility. Indeed it struck me that it was no coincidence that it tended to be the same small minority of predominantly white, religious, able-bodied men who wanted to pass laws about both issues. Why should anyone exert control over disabled or suffering people? Only those of us who day-in day-out gazed upon our own paralysed or neurologically impaired bodies and endured the pain and weakness and frustration had the remotest idea what it actually meant to inhabit those bodies. To us was automatically granted the absolute moral right to know what was best for us; we just needed the law to catch up. And so I had every sympathy with my correspondent but nevertheless felt culturally and morally obliged to encourage her to delay, to be certain. Perhaps I should have been more honest. Either way, those two suicides, close together, altered the way I discussed the right to die. I remained fervently in favour of a person's right to a good death at a time and place of their choosing, and with assistance if necessary, but I could no longer be flippant.

During that first year at home, I tried to put my situation into some kind of perspective. Things might have been so much worse, as I had long ago decided. How could I of all people complain? Being able to drive again, and to continue to earn a living, undoubtedly made life easier, both practically and psychologically. I was not good, though, at living in the moment and blocking off consideration of my future with an incurable disability. Introspection was toxic and I found myself in tears more and more. In an email, Zen Master tried to help. Imagine the future is like skiing, he said. As you approach an awkward turn, worried about the difficulties approaching, the mental apprehension feeds back and affects your physical ability to succeed in the turn. Similarly, if you play a musical instrument, the anticipation of a tricky bar coming in the tune affects the bars before it, which would otherwise have been effortless. The secret was not to fear what was coming, but to try and enjoy the present. When things got very tough in hospital he shrank his focus to a pinprick in time and visualised himself in the foothills of a peak he had climbed a couple of times. The approaches were hard, loose scree and boulders. He tried not to look up and think, 'Oh my God, look how far it is.' Instead, he would attend to his footfall, stop every now and then, catch his breath and look down and think, 'I've come all this way already.'

Best, he said, to try and live more lightly. He wrote, in a letter I cherish: 'Rupert Sheldrake the philosopher writes of the "privilege of consciousness" – how we are probably the only species that knows that we exist. An elephant knows how exactly to be an elephant – but we don't know how to be just a human being. We think outside the box. And maybe that's the trouble. So, with that privilege comes immense responsibility. That consciousness we have, it soars far beyond us, anticipating, judging. It is unfettered and in the situation you and I have found ourselves in, we need to live more lightly; deliberately and consciously we need to come back to just being, like our beautiful horses munching hay in the stable. Not have an opinion about ourselves, our appearance, our pain, the awkwardness of movement, the indignities ... It's simple, but it's definitely not easy.'

I tried to allow the smells and sights of home, denied to me during my lost year in hospital, to take possession of me, tried to relax and wait, just *be*, instead of striving, striving, striving all the time, tight with effort. The sun warmed the front of the house. Pip, wriggling with life, went around smelling of fresh earth and dew, her nose covered in soil where she had been digging. There was so much simple delight to be had in her company. Staffies are comic, vocal little dogs, they converse in squeaks and burps, and mini-whines, or they rumble around scratching, upside down on the grass or the carpet, snorting like a pig. They're also very loving.

Pip.

She was a constant low-key, undemanding presence in the house and there were intense, fleeting fondnesses, moments you should remember and cherish but never do. One Sunday morning, I spilt her biscuits all over the floor as I tried, over-ambitiously, to refill a big container. (I was always spilling stuff, especially food; Pip would follow me like a seagull after a trawler.) Dave turfed her outside while he cleared it up, which of course made her think she'd been banished for doing something wrong, and she sat outside the door trembling, gazing at us through the glass. Oscar-winning pathetic. The floor was swept. He let her in, her demonic jaws wide with joy like a Cheshire Cat.

'Smile,' he said. He adored her.

And she smiled so hard her lips met over the top of her nose. Her tail whirring like a rotor.

'It's all Melly's fault,' he told her.

And the clock stopped for a couple of seconds while the three of us grinned at each other.

About then, there occurred a vivid coincidence. The acting books editor at *The Times* had asked me to review *A Crown of Thistles* by Linda Porter, about Mary, Queen of Scots, and I sat outside in the sunshine reading it, facing the hillside which rose just to the east of our cottage. The chapter was about James IV of Scotland, who in the late thirteenth century lived at Stirling castle, not that far from here. James had decided to fight the troublesome Earl of Lennox, based at Dumbarton castle, and thus in October 1489 the two armies marched 'and met in the remote foothills of the Trossachs, where a little known battle raged for several days around the Field of Gartloaning'.

The hairs on the back of my neck stirred, the book fell into my lap, and I raised my eyes in astonishment – because the field facing me, in our little hidden valley, was no less than the field of Gartloaning. Despite living here so long, I had never heard even a whisper of battle. I was living that famous quote from *Casablanca*: 'Of all the gin joints, in all the towns, in all the world, she walks into mine ...' What chance, I mused, led to me to be sitting outside reading one precise page in one precise book, of the thousands published every week, which revealed a long-lost secret about a remote field – just as I was facing that very field?

I checked with our local village heritage society – none of them had heard of the battle. I did what research I could on the internet, which confirmed both the battle and how little known it was. What felt thrilling was that we had evidence pointing to its veracity. Some years earlier, the boys had unearthed a two-pound cannonball from under a gorse bush on the hill behind the house. Up until then, its provenance had been an unsolved mystery.

Some months later the warm arms of the house tapped me on the shoulder again, half-murmuring further ancient secrets. We had recently had a drainage ditch dug at the end of the house because the nearby well, marked on the earliest maps from two hundred and fifty years ago, had suddenly started to overflow and was causing a swamp. Things subterranean must have shifted in some way: perhaps a tree root had disturbed things; whatever, the ditch was dug. And one day Dave and his son Steve, standing chatting beside it, chanced to knock a boot against something solid in the discarded earth. When they explored, they uncovered another cannonball, a five-pounder this time, a beast of a thing. Such a relic, the wet clay still clinging to it, sang with history. It occurred to Dave that the last man before him to hold its weight in his hands was the soldier who loaded it into one of the first cannons, nearly five hundred years ago. Discussing it in the pub that night, a friend told Dave that a ball that size would never have been fired at an individual; it would have been aimed at a structure sheltering many enemies, in order to implode the wall inwards, hurting as many as possible. Following the logic, some kind of dwelling or structure must have existed on the site of our house since the late 1400s. I found that idea very heady magic, much stronger than any ley lines. I was deeply affected by the feeling of human continuity, stretching over so many centuries, bound up in the footprint of the place we called home. What had these walls witnessed, over so many years? What was absorbed in the stone, built and then rebuilt, from the many generations of people

Who touched them last? Some poor terrified
soldier 500 years ago.

who had lived their brief lives here, scrabbling an existence
from the tough land? Could I feed off that sense of place; the
message that said although our time was brief, we were part of
something bigger?

A lot of laughter and kindness, I decided, had happened
here, more so than strife. The place was still the centre of the
earth, man. Whatever kind of quantum mechanics had
funnelled time and the chaos of existence and brought me here,
I was lucky.

Some sacrifices, though, were harder than others. As I was to
find out.

CHAPTER NINE

A LOST BODY

*Much more of the brain is devoted to movement than
to language. Language is only a little thing sitting on
top of this huge ocean of movement.*

OLIVER SACKS

It was time, unavoidably, for reflection. I was two people now,
not one. There was me – that was my head and brain, and my
shoulders and arms; the bits where I resided. The small bit. And
there was other me, the big heavy useless bit which didn't work
any more but which had to come too wherever I wanted to go.
We were like conjoined twins, resentful, bickering, pulling in
different directions, refusing to cooperate. Actually, the cognitive me hated the broken-engined rest of me, with a vengeance,
but there was nothing that could be done. Fait accompli. We
were utterly trapped, dependent on each other to survive.

Because my spinal cord was not totally severed, I was never
entirely alone. Being attached to an appendage that used to be
a body was a bit like being haunted. I heard echoes and whis-
pers of suggestion from the past. I happened upon the occasional sensation inside of muscles or tendons tugging,
stretching, trying to fire. My ruined nerves tricked me – was
that flicker real, or just the electricity of hope? – and tortured
me with phantom pain. Sometimes, there was muscle memory

when I tried to move, and it was as if I asked and my body remembered and instinctively tried to obey: deep, deep inside, I felt a flicker and a tensing of muscle … and then nothing more. There were many strange add-ons to paralysis. Because my natural thermostats were bust, I needed the temperature at least three degrees hotter than ordinary people. Often, my feet and legs felt boiling hot, but to touch were ice-cold. Some nights, when Dave swung my legs onto the bed and took off my shoes and socks, one foot was warm, the other icy. As the months passed, I began to grasp the intricacy and intensity of my condition – and the enormity of the damage. I have a friend who chopped off an index finger trying to clear a grass blockage in his lawnmower. The operation to sew it back on failed and he learnt, over a couple of years, to use his middle finger in its place. Now, he notices a strange phenomenon: when he moves to extinguish a candle, for instance, and the flame burns in the space where his index finger would have been, he finds his body recoiling. He is alerted to a burn on flesh that no longer exists; his eye–brain–hand feedback reacts to a void; the air alone is singed. Paralysis is the opposite of this; the inversion of amputation, less spooky, more gruesome. The flesh remains but feels nothing, and can be badly broken, burnt or scraped without its owner realising. Newly paralysed patients, pushed in a chair, unaware that their foot has slipped off the footplate and is dragging on the floor, have scraped their flesh to the bone. Friends in wheelchairs, perhaps a little osteoporotic from loss of weight bearing, have broken bones in their legs and not realised. Boiling water, splashed across the thighs, was not felt, but sent other parts of the body into spasm in sympathy. Skin lifted into blisters, suppurated and was slow to heal, but there was no pain at the site – a deranged nervous system expresses its upset in more general and obscure ways.

When your flesh is dead to you, feeling little or nothing, increasingly, you are dismantled inside. Without motor function, you become devoid of physical presence. Who are you any more? This must be what identity theft feels like. Remember how, when you were small, just you and the pavement in the sunshine, you would try and escape your shadow? Jumping to surprise it, hiding to shake it off. But you never succeeded. Well, now I really had lost my shadow and it wasn't fun at all. Try as I might, I still didn't quite believe it was for real; that I was a statistic, one of the poor sods who every eight hours in the UK suffers a spinal injury.

What made it especially difficult was that my injuries had not merely taken away my control of my body, they'd made my body positively hostile towards me. My appendage went out of its way to be as inconvenient and obstructive as possible. This was not just an absence of controlled movement; it was the arrival of a horrible side-effect in its place: spasticity. There's a common misconception about paralysis. People think your legs go soft and floppy and cooperative, and indeed many complete injuries do that – hence the paraplegic wheelchair racers, who fold their legs into an impossibly small space under them in their racing machines, diddy little limbs they can package temporarily away. But a lot of incomplete injuries don't. I was the opposite of soft and floppy. Soft and floppy would have been wonderful. Instead, I had rigid, spasming limbs which refused to cooperate. The muscles in my torso and legs, reacting to the incoherent messages coming down my damaged spine, would either make me jerk and jack-knife, chest to knees, or go into a violent plantor flexor spasm, my legs straight out like telegraph poles, knees grinding together, toes straining down, back arching as if – as in the movie *Alien* – the monster was about to burst from my abdomen. I reminded myself of an old horse which has been shot in the head and then goes down, brain dead but its limbs still jerking. This uncontrollable power was called 'tone', used in a technical sense, and I took large doses of a drug called baclofen to subdue it. The body, in an undamaged state, works in a kind of antagonistic harmony – muscles work in pairs, opposing pulleys that straighten and bend each other. With incomplete paralysis, one set of pulleys gets disconnected so the opposing set becomes dominant, and the limbs bend only one way. The plantor flexor spasm, the ballerina with rabies pose, should be countermanded by dorsi-flexion, when your tendons and muscles pull up your toes – but dorsiflexion is often the first casualty of neurological injury. In your hands, the classic symptom of spasticity is the fingers clenched into a fist, because the extensor tendons, the ones responsible for straightening, which run from the forearm bones over the wrist and down the top of the fingers, are inca-pacitated. Unchecked, therefore, the flexor tendons lock your fingertips into your palm.

The baclofen could only do so much to deaden the misfiring nerves. On big muscle groups, doctors have found that a site-specific injection of botulinum toxin, Botox, can help make limbs more malleable. Typically, with paralysis, the abductor muscle on the outside of the thigh, which pulls your legs apart, gets knocked out, which meant that the adductor muscle on the inside, responsible for closing your legs, goes haywire. (Damage to the adductor is what's called a groin strain.) My adductors were so overridingly powerful, so out of balance, that my knees locked tight together and my right leg took on an unwelcome life of its own, scissoring across the left when I was upright. In the out-patients' clinic when Dr Purcell injected my right adductor, it was as hard and tense as stone and the needle gave a horrid groan as it went in. Once or twice she gave me Botox injections in my wrists and forearm to try and relieve the jack-knifing of my knuckles. My fingers had progressed from weak and straight to strong and clenched. They were those of a puppet with over-tightened strings. The small dose of Botox would poison the nerve temporarily. We took grim amusement from the fact that beauty-obsessed people with normal bodies had this done to stop their frowns; we had it done so that our hands might be remotely functional. Ill health in these instances could feel like inhabiting a Presbyterian sermon on the theme of the fortunate and flippant who never know how lucky they are. Frankly, you'd give anything to rejoin the world of the flippant. The moral high ground brought sparse compensation.

The concept of struggling with lost identity is a relatively recent one. Since the 1950s medicine has evolved from the point where it regarded the patient merely as a body in possession of a problem – like Averil – to an interest in the patient's emotional experience. One of the turning points was Mike Bury's description of chronic illness as biographical disruption in the early 1980s. He suggested that falling ill shatters our self-image: it forces us to recognise pain and suffering, normally only seen as a distant possibility or as the plight of others, and it shifts our expectations of a normal future 'to one fundamentally abnormal and inwardly damaging'. Chronic conditions disrupted everything – structures of meaning, relationships, material and practical affairs.

Kathy Charmaz's work, equally pivotal in the early 1980s, developed the concept of loss of self to describe the experience of 'former self-images crumbling away without a simultaneous development of equally valued new ones'. Oh boy, I understood that. Various aspects of chronic illness amplified one another, a loss of self in one area often spiralling into a loss within another, with devastating consequences. The prime impact of chronic illness was in a physical day-to-day context – eating, washing and toileting – 'because above all else coping with chronic illness involves coping with bodies'. Oh yes, that damn appendage. My paralysed body, big, hostile and uncooperative, was impossible to circumnavigate. Cognitive-me couldn't dodge around or escape from rest-of-me, because rest-of-me – in Charmaz's wonderful phrase – 'imposed fleshy limits' on any identity reconstruction. Hence the cause and effect I was becoming familiar with. The stigma of my situation was self-fulfilling: it caused low esteem, which made me anti-social, which removed opportunities for self-validation and made me feel more stigmatised. Psychologically, I was like Pip chasing her tail. Only it didn't make me happy.

One of my biggest hurdles was being so tall. Always it kept coming back to that. It's actually quite hard to describe to people of normal height what it's like to have grown up at the very outer percentiles, and then to lose it abruptly. Both my mother and father were very tall for their generation, five feet nine and six feet three respectively. My big brother was six feet five, my sister five feet nine. We were regarded as a family of giants and secretly we all rather liked that. I ended up just over six feet, exceptional at the time for a girl, though much less so now. At school I was routinely taller than everyone except the lankiest of the boys. Growing up, it brought its burdens, especially with adolescence and the shortage of tall boys in sixth form. I was terribly self-conscious of my height and developed futile strategies to try and hide it, slouching, and practising the art of dropping one hip. There were no shops for tall girls in the 1970s and if I wanted fashionable clothes I had to make them. For jeans, I had to shop in the men's section.

Sport was easy though, and as I grew up and became more confident, height slowly became my friend. A reason, in the end, to develop a secret kernel of arrogance. When you're tall, you find you can enjoy live music from the back of a crowd, scan busy rooms to avoid bores, never lose a child in a supermarket, spot when people need their roots touched up, paint ceilings without using a step ladder, walk home at night unintimidated. Above all, being tall is your identity. You take totally for granted the degree of effortlessness and authority it confers. The advantages are huge. Generally, you don't have to try so hard. You can, literally, rise above the majority, stand above conversations which are boring or noisy. Your perspective is a superior one, acknowledged in a cultural way. Tall people are more noticed, successful, respected and command greater natural authority. Men, in particular, are perceived as being more attractive. Tall women are described as striking. Tall politicians win elections and presidencies. It is as if, in primitive memory, we seek a leader who can see further into the distance for danger and smite down the enemy from a greater height. He or she who holds the high ground wins the battle. On a practical front, tall people never have to struggle to reach anything. Life

I came from a family of giants. Milan 1961:
I was four years old and three feet six inches.

is generally made easier by a few extra inches in your arms and legs. As a child, trees are lower to climb into and fences to clamber over. With long limbs, basketballs are simpler to net, hockey balls more powerfully hammered, hurdles less of an obstacle on the running track. You can mount the tallest horses and survey the world from ten feet high. From the saddle, I was accustomed to peer benignly into gardens and bedrooms, could greet people airily from above. You could never be unaware of that height difference, the atavistic essence of horseback, and fail to understand the dangerous haughtiness of peering over tall hedges and down at pedestrians, as lords and kings once looked down at serfs and foot soldiers, silently demanding obeisance beneath the soles of their boots and their horses' flanks. Yes, being tall was a good feeling.

Even better, being a tall woman meant being a bit like a man. There were huge benefits. As a schoolgirl I discovered the feminist delight of antagonising a particular breed of short, thin-skinned men – everyone will know one – who resented you for the extra inches you possessed instead of them. I remember an economics teacher who accused me of dumb insolence simply for looking down at him, and I cherish new generations of women, unabashed in six-inch heels, towering happily above men. I trust these girls still rework the best tall woman put-down of all time – to be deployed when a vertically challenged chap is cheeky enough to suggest he would, well, enjoy a shag: 'Well if you do, and I find out, I will be very angry.'

But gosh, all this meant height was a hard bereavement. From being defined, created and sustained by it for fifty-two years, paralysis had robbed me of most of my personality. I felt emptied of sound, character and movement. My overview, my long limbs, my physical dynamism, my presence – gone. All the subtleties of body language gone too. How do you express who you are when you can't move? Suddenly, you are noticeable in a crowd not for your height or face or clothes, but because you're so small and because you're in a wheelchair. You go from door-lintel height to waist height; your world shrivels exponentially. Not only do you grieve for the abstract sense of being up there, spinning to take in the view, filling your senses with freedom, but you suffer a most unbelievable personal disempowerment. The natural quiet authority which comes from being upright vanishes. You cannot project your wishes without sounding querulous. Shrill. You cannot get cross, or angry, or have the last word, or turn on your heel and stalk away – for you are slow, small and weak and intrinsically vulnerable. Passivity and submission go with being waist-high. You're down there examining the fake tan on women's legs, the scuffed backs of people's shoes. You're fart height. Crotch height. Muffin-top height. Shiny suit-bottom height.

Without my body, I found it very hard to rejoin a world structured on movement and physical reciprocity. It felt like nobody heard me any more, or respected my wishes. Dave, unconsciously, became much more dominant. Unconsciously, his grammar changed. He stopped using the pronoun 'we' and started to say 'I'. 'Our' became 'my'. His house, his plans, his requests, his barn, his furniture, his tractor. (Pronouns are powerful things: even worse was the deployment of 'it' when someone wants to belittle someone or something. Men and women in unhappy marriages deploy it to describe their spouse. I had always hated it when horse or dog trainers, faced with a defiant animal, would suddenly drop the 'he' or 'she' and start using 'it'.) For Dave and I, the balance in our relationship subtly shifted. He was nearly four inches shorter than I had been, a happy joke which we never equated with power but weirdly, since my giant-toppling accident, since I had become the smallest and most helpless in the family, authority had transferred away from me. Down the plughole drained confidence, personality, power, decisiveness. And that private thrill of physical arrogance.

When unfamiliar community therapists came to help me, and I hoisted myself upright, teetering above them, there was always that moment when they exclaimed: 'God you are tall, Mel.' Yeah, I was, wasn't I? The emptiest boast of all. Shame I lost that advantage. Shame that now, when I do stand for a few brief minutes, it feels like I'm in a cherry picker. The perspective had changed.

What happened to me was a premature assault on self, decades before I could have anticipated it – perhaps something akin to how it must feel to be diagnosed with cancer in your forties. I was catapulted into old age and infirmity, a transgression of natural rules. My healthy body, like everyone else's healthy body, had been what's called an 'absent presence', only noticed when dysfunction or illness set in. But good health, in the twenty-first century, was more than absence of illness; it was sport and leisure and hedonism, adventure holidays, charity challenges, Ironman competitions, spin classes and boot camp and Pilates. Health wasn't just my livelihood, it was my social network. And then of course, with that premature assault of chronic health, I had to learn to lower my expectations of the ability of modern medicine to come up with solutions. Our Western culture, focused on beauty and pleasure and the myth of a perfect life, makes it hard for the healthy to accept the reality of illness and the existence of death. People are threatened by the permanence of chronic illness and would like to think there's a cure for everything. They reject scientific dead ends.

Perhaps it felt like this in the early days of cancer treatment, when everyone presumed that it was only a matter of time before Big Pharma came up with the magic bullet. But breakthroughs came and went over the decades; no one cure ever appeared. Instead, it has taken the best part of forty years for the world to realise that, for cancer, it probably never will. That instead of off-the-shelf pills to nuke lungs, bowels or breast, there has emerged a totally different and far more complex perspective on the different diseases: the long-term, laborious task of genetic analysis and the customising of various drugs to target an individual's unique illness. Scientists can improve and prolong life, sometimes hugely successfully, but they still have no fairytale ending.

Because humans need fairytales, however, the same dream of the magic bullet afflicts spinal research. Within a few months of getting home and starting to watch TV again, I found the stories of spinal breakthroughs began arriving. Patients with electrical implants in their spines who could now stand. Paralysed dachshunds that could walk again. Rats with severed spines scampering along treadmills on their hind legs – then, later, a memorable BBC *Panorama* on the operation by the late Professor Geoff Raisman in Poland to regrow a man's severed spine by implanting olfactory cells. As a journalist, I knew what a divisive word 'breakthrough' was: editors demanded it, otherwise it wasn't a story; scientists and doctors hated it, because they knew it probably wasn't; and sufferers, the poor sufferers, of which I was now one, were tortured by it. Asked to comment on television news on the man with the implant empowered to stand, I tried to explain the vast gulf between someone whose lower body could now feebly stir, when surrounded by wires and helpers, and the normal, fluid, unconscious, pain-free mobility enjoyed by the able-bodied. Please don't mistake this for a recovery or a cure, I said. For thousands of spinal-injured people with some lower body movement, electrical implants or not, there would never again be ease of movement, no dancing round the kitchen, or release from incontinence, or skipping upstairs, let alone running marathons. The daily teeth-grinding discomfort of living with paralysis was not going to disappear any time soon. We have many more years to sit in the waiting room.

I remember the evening in the spinal unit when a magician came to entertain us. Come the hour, like a three-line whip for a critical parliamentary vote, all patients who were not in bed were herded to the step-down unit, a wing of the hospital where we were trained for freedom. Families had been invited too – there were little children there, sitting on their fathers' paralysed knees. The magician was a showman, cocky, knowing, full of banter. And we sat mute in our wheelchairs in ragged rows, the broken and dazed, the drugged and the angry, and watched him pull cards out of his sleeve, and lines of flags out of his mouth, and rip up five-pound notes only to have them reappear in the possession of someone in the second row.

'Now I'll really show you some magic,' he boasted, and did the rabbit in the hat trick.

And I saw myself, and I saw the people around me who needed real magic and miracles more than that silly prat would ever know, and I wanted to laugh and cry at the same time.

The problem was, able-bodied people believed in the illusion of the breakthrough, the rabbit in the hat. The healthy saw what they wanted to see. They wanted to know that doctors could now cure paralysis, so they wouldn't have to feel sorry for us any more, or worry about themselves in the future – and if that bloke they saw on telly could stand, well, he'd soon be walking, wouldn't he? And if he could walk, well then, that must be a cure. Job done. It was fascinating to see how paralysed-person-walks held the trump card with the public, just as it did with the newly paralysed like me. There were more horrible side-effects than an inability to walk but healthy people weren't interested in them. For a while at the beginning I wasn't either. Certainly, walking was totemic and dramatic, the sexy, circus-act stuff. Remember those bold people, like the event riders and my husband, who refused to sit in a wheelchair and properly experience its limitations? Call them cowards if you want, but acknowledge their honesty, their need to remain standing and dominant. All this explained much about why the newly injured channel their grief into trying to regain their limbs.

What then of the other side-effects, the all-too grotty and the hidden, the taboo stuff beyond our control to address? Pain, for instance. By chance in the spinal unit I met the daughter of one of my fellow patients, a senior scientist in the pharmaceutical industry. Before her father's accident, she'd had no idea of the impact of neuropathic pain and had been shocked at how little research, and how few drugs, existed to tackle it. To quell the horrid, ever constant jangle in your legs you could either take gabapentin, a powerful drug designed for epilepsy seizures, which sedated many people to semi-vegetable status; or my bête noire tramadol, the opioid so mind-twisting that the comedian Frankie Boyle built a career on it. The payoff for avoiding these drugs and keeping a clear head was that discomfort became your lifelong companion. I was fairly puritanical. I whittled out medicines like oxybutynin (to stop bladder spasm) that were doing nothing for me, and reduced the dose of those that remained essential. This meant reliance on ibuprofen and other common analgesics like aspirin. If they wrecked my stomach in the long run, well, so be it. I could at least think straight. But lots of people preferred a bit of oblivion. They took every powerful drug they could get. Both gabapentin and tramadol, I later noted wryly, were much sought after as illegal street drugs and there were calls for an end to prescribing them. I'm not surprised. I saw what they did to people's heads.

One weekend on the spinal unit the peace was broken by the sound of screeching. My mate Reiver came zooming down the corridor in his chair, glee writ large on his face.

'Catfight in Room 5 – Crazy Daisy and Fruitloop!' he told us.

We clustered in our chairs in the corridor to listen, a jam of nosy metal, leaning as far forward in our seats as we were capable in order to hear. Like schoolchildren spectating in the playground. 'Fight! Fight! Fight!' Fruitloop was an alcoholic who claimed to some that her man had thrown her off a balcony. She was one of those patients who existed in a haze, permanently stoned on tramadol and methadone, plus the onset of alcohol-related dementia, plus of course any drugs she could persuade her visitors to bring her. Crazy Daisy, her face reddened and broken with years of similar heavy drinking, also existed on a parallel universe of opiates, a heroine in her own ever-evolving soap opera. She told different stories to anyone who'd listen to her, or merely those who couldn't get away from her, how she'd fallen over a coffee table when she was pissed one night and damaged her neck on the furniture. She had been only partially paralysed the first time; the second time she'd fallen she'd broken her neck and had a tracheotomy to allow her to breathe. She carried oxygen on her electric wheelchair and had tubes strapped to her face. Her stamina for finding an audience, though, was extraordinary. She glared around her, revolving-eyed, paranoid, scanning for prey. Anyone who would listen to her rambling tales of woe.

There had been tension between the two women for a few days. Now Crazy Daisy thought Fruitloop had been rifling in her bedside drawers and called her out. They were in adjacent beds. Both of them, it might be said, could have started a fight in an empty room.

'You stole my fucking money, you bitch.'

'Didnae touch your money.'

'Aye you did. Ah seen you.'

'Those are my fucking drawers. You have got your own.'

In the tragi-comic slow motion of wheelchair life, Fruitloop turned her back in a huff. Crazy Daisy rammed her electric chair into her back wheels, yelling abuse. Fruitloop reached for her buzzer, trying to escape. Locked together, they tussled impotently, shouting abuse, the darkest of human comedy. That's what happened when you took too many drugs to try and dull the pain. That's what happened when there were no miracles.

The hospital staff could never really spell out to us how much harder life would be at home, with the loss of the ability to breathe fully, to pee, poo and have sex – a rather compelling list. We had to find out for ourselves. You discovered that looking after yourself was now a full-time job. Here lay most of the tension between cerebral-you and the rest-of-you, the recalcitrant bit making constant, high-maintenance demands. Your head regarded the body with resentfulness and weariness, like a non-maternal mother who desperately wants to go back to some high-powered post but is stuck at home with a needy, fretful infant. My body was my prison, my dependency. Much as I hated my useless appendage, I had to care for it. Be kind to it. Hence, I found a constant tug between wanting to neglect it and the self-sabotage of doing so. I had to be stern with myself, order myself to commit to that existentialist, time-consuming grind of pill-popping, bag-emptying, pressure-relieving, pain-dodging, sterilising, all the while smiling gratefully at kind people and repeating, 'I'm fine, thanks.' There was no time for anything creative. I was always busy waiting for the next industrial chore and life was screamingly dull. I missed being dazzled by arguments, acting fast.

Two hours every morning, in that first year out of hospital, were spent on a shower chair poised over the loo, battling with my entire digestive system, reliant on district nurses. The more I lost confidence in the process, the more desperate I became. Every morning was a detective story. Had I pooed enough to get through the day safely without an accident? Why were my feet and ankles so swollen? What, if indeed anything, was going wrong? I developed an even deeper admiration for vets, who had to diagnose problems in creatures which couldn't tell them where they hurt. In the absence of normal sensation, there was so much guesswork. If my body became racked with severe spasm and tone, it was telling me that there was a problem somewhere. Spinal units have a checklist – bladder, bowels, skin lesions, bruises, ingrowing toenails, sprains, broken bones. All these could cause this kind of symptom. But which one? It was a process of elimination. Some causes were easier than others. An ingrowing big toenail, rejecting the ever-swollen flesh surrounding it, had become inflamed. Then the other big toe, in sympathy, started rotting, ingrowing, pus-filled. Or that porridge burn on my thigh, napalm from a tipped bowl, and now behind a see-through waterproof dressing, which had gone gangrenous green.

'Totally healthy. Call me if it goes bright red,' pronounced Helen, my amazing district nurse, briskly, peering at it. She was my substitute mother: I obeyed her.

It took many months to realise that I had developed a serious underlying problem since leaving hospital, of which the spasming and oedema and the swollen toes were a symptom. I looked six months pregnant and struggled to lean forward in my chair; or lift myself from chair to bed. Everything I tried to do, my body fought me. An X-ray showed my paralysed guts – we each possess around twenty-five to twenty-eight feet of those great gloopy essential coils – were constipated right back up into my small intestines. I was readmitted to the spinal unit and my insides were blasted with laxatives. I began to use drain cleaner at home – Laxido. As Dave said, they'd be hardly likely to call it Laxidon't, would they? But the spasms and symptoms of discomfort in my limbs did not diminish.

In the war against cerebral-me, rest-of-me was definitely winning. The semantics of battle again. Then my bladder joined in. Peeing, when your bladder is paralysed, is done in different ways. Paraplegics, with hand function, can transfer onto a lavatory and self-catheterise intermittently when their bladders are full. Tetraplegics have neither the hand function nor the mobility to do this and the only long-term solution is an operation to install a suprapubic catheter. Above my pubic bone, a hole was drilled into my bladder and an indwelling catheter was placed in it to drain into a bag. But piercing the bladder, a vital organ, compromised its natural antibacterial coating and there was no resistance to the ever-present bugs, in particular E. coli.

A pattern of continual infection was established: I finished a course of antibiotics and a week later was dragged down by another bug. I could tell immediately. The spasms redoubled, and my urine developed the unmistakable E. coli whiff – rich, sweet, like rotting vegetables. It disgusted me. But there was no escape.

Some academics (Corbin and Strauss) interpret chronic illness in terms of three types of work. Illness work – managing the practical consequences of your problem; everyday work – living, eating, washing dishes; and biographical work – the reconstruction of the self. That first category, keeping functional a paralysed bladder and bowels, was all-encompassing for me and I accumulated a level of knowledge that allowed me to challenge doctors and nurses. My local GPs, hugely supportive women, readily held out their palms and said – you know more about this than us. Thus I developed a certain fragile independence and detachment from health professionals. With the spectre of sepsis ever hovering, I endured the monthly catheter change, carefully monitoring the nurses' hygiene. And always, always, I weighed the consequences of intervening. Did I remind the nurse to change gloves between removing the old catheter and putting in the new, and risk alienating someone I liked and needed, or did I let her use the same pair of gloves and risk another infection? I took strength from emails from spinal-cord-injured people who said they had, over time, learnt to tell exactly what lay behind the symptoms their body was exhibiting. As one tetraplegic woman advised me, professionals could help to a certain point, but we were essentially on our own. 'It took me a long time to realise that, especially in regard to the day-to-day aspects of living with this condition. There is a clinical versus real-life dissonance: which is all to say, conventional healthcare can keep us alive, but our quality of life is largely up to our own initiative.'

Bladders were something which, as a fit person, I had lived in happy ignorance of. It's a sad fact that urinary infection and incontinence have been the ultimate Cinderella of health. The world of 'smart' technology has bypassed this problem scandalously, even though one in three of us will suffer incontinence in our lives and catheter-associated urinary tract infections (CAUTI) place a huge financial burden on the NHS, estimated to cost up to £99 million per year, or £1,968 per episode. The ubiquitous Foley urinary catheter, a crude tube with an inlet hole and a retaining balloon on one end, remains unchanged in its basic design for ninety years – in medical terms, medieval. Hospital admissions caused by urinary-tract infections have trebled over twenty-five years, and patients who are in hospital for other reasons are increasingly doomed to acquire a UTI when they're there. The implications for the future, in terms of hospital costs and premature death as antibiotics cease to work, are terrifying. Yet nobody – politicians, policymakers, the medical profession itself – will tackle this unsexy, taboo problem. It makes me mad that high-tech implants are already being used to keep eyes, heart valves and joints functioning; we have face transplants, bionic eyes and gene injections, not to mention driverless cars and bendy phones and rockets to Mars; but no one has yet funded the design of a 'smart' sphincter to alleviate one of humankind's most basic miseries.

A continually poisoned paralysed bladder, I was learning, was as frustrating and unfixable as paralysis. Because of repeated infections, I was sent for several cystoscopies, an examination with a camera. The first one I had done privately. I was to cross boundaries into greater self-knowledge.

'Did you know you have a very wide urethra?' asked Miss G, the Greek urologist, when she came to speak to me afterwards. She sounded genuinely enthusiastic.

I shook my head.

'It's about the diameter of a pencil. Very unusual.' She really seemed to be expecting an answer.

What did she expect me to say? Oh yes, I come from a long line of very wide urethras? A stretched urethra wasn't like having a big penis; it wasn't a physical attribute anyone would be pleased about, demonstrating as it did that yet again my body no longer belonged to me. This was part of an intricate body awareness I could frankly do without. Within months I was back in again for another cystoscopy, NHS this time, which almost descended into farce. It was conveyor-belt stuff, like inseminating cows: a long line of people of all shapes and sizes sitting waiting to be taken through to be tubed. There was the protocol of form-filling.

'Do you have discomfort when you urinate?'

'No, because my bladder is paralysed.'

'Oh.' The pen hovered, unable to tick the box.

Then the pre-procedure sample – and the inevitable result.

'Sorry. You've got an infection; we can't do the procedure.'

A rare red mist came over me at that point: I raised myself up on my elbows with as much speed and dignity as I could muster, eyes blazing, and hissed: 'That's precisely why I'm here! That's the whole point! I'm not leaving without one!'

The specialist who did the cystoscopy was very pleasant – 'Your bladder looks fine,' she said. 'Nothing nasty there' – but the staff gave me not a single answer to my questions that I hadn't heard before. Drink more bloody water. Take cranberry juice. La-la-la-la-la-la. I was a frontierswoman, inhabiting territory where there really were no solutions and no experts.

Still the debilitating spasms and stiffness persisted. I felt like screaming at the walls: *Please, somebody, just let me know what's wrong with me. Find a solution.*

Some months after leaving hospital, I was called back for a signing-off appointment with my neck surgeon. This presented an opportunity for me to try and reconcile the two parts of me. I vowed that I would be brave enough to look at my neck X-ray, the point where the two parts had come apart. The fulcrum. The breaking point. Undeniable physical proof of the catastrophe. The unseen image had haunted me for a long time and I had vowed not to face it until I could walk, aware I was not emotionally resilient enough. Jennifer Brown, who had performed the operation to plate my neck, pulled up the before and after X-rays on screen. The before was surprisingly benign-looking, just a slightly exaggerated bend and a widening at the C6 cervical vertebrae at the front of my neck; one bone chip floating away.

'It doesn't look too bad,' I said.

'Though I suspect we didn't see the neck at its worst.'

She said it gently. She meant it bent much further on impact but came back. The fresh X-ray, taken more than a year after injury, she was very pleased with: it showed the small metal plate she inserted had stabilised the joint and there was new bone growth. The image made me feel buoyed and optimistic; it was the opposite of upsetting. Appraising me, she asked if I wanted to see the original MRI scan.

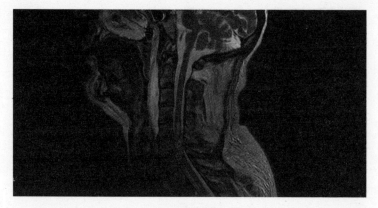

My MRI scan.

'Yes.'

Immediately I knew it was a mistake. Here was darkness. This image was horrid, showing massive collateral inflammation around the cord reaching right up the neck. At the focus of injury, within the boundaries of the spinal column, there was a black, egg-shaped void reaching from one side to the other: a hole of nothingness. My foundations rocked a little. The surgeon leant forward and pointed at the screen.

'Looking at this, with the swelling up at C4 and C5, the outcome could have been so much worse,' she said coolly.

In other words, I was lucky to have kept the use of my arms and hands and lungs, even if they were impaired. I thanked her and wheeled out of her room, trying to chew on that piece of good fortune. This was my body and I had to try and find a way to love it. Being Pollyanna was a tough gig sometimes.

Down the side of that black void in my spinal cord, as seen on the MRI scan, some connections persisted, or were restoring themselves. Neuroplasticity was at work. About eighteen months after my accident, I noticed the intercostal muscles in my chest had recovered enough to let me blow my nose properly again. Now it was time to resume work to encourage the same thing in other parts of my body.

After I left hospital I went from four hours a day of inpatient physiotherapy, or twenty hours a week, to one hour a week with a community neurophysiotherpist called Emma, who came to my home. It was as if someone had pulled the communication cord on an express train and my body seemed to screech to a halt. Committed and skilled as Emma was, in the time she had with me, she could do nothing to combat the trauma I experienced from the abrupt reduction in exercise. It was like reaching the end of the bungee cord – my achingly slow rehabilitation didn't just stall, it regressed. Without the constant help to exercise – I couldn't do it by myself – my body seized up. A private neurophysiotherapist, Kenny, was very good too, but he cost me £60 an hour, plus travelling time, for a home visit, and after a while I was simply unable to sustain the expense. My hospital hand therapist, who had devoted an hour a day to straightening and exercising my damaged fingers, did not have an equivalent in the community. Anger and hopelessness gnawed at me. Unwittingly, I was experiencing yet another of the hidden scandals of modern-day healthcare – the lack of NHS physiotherapy and rehabilitation for neurological conditions and other chronic illness. The sufferers of strokes, brain damage, heart disease, diabetes, obesity, broken bones and other neurological illness collectively number millions, but as soon as they leave hospital they fall into the abyss. The NHS has almost totally given up on a sufficient out-patient physiotherapy, because nobody ever died from being stiff and weak, and misery is not yet a cause of death on any certificate. But physical rehabilitation, done properly, is the key to recovery, quality of life and greatly reduced demand on other NHS services. It is fundamental to a healthier population. The process of recovering faculties, strength and movement, which goes on for years, is halted overnight by the withdrawal of exercise and physiotherapy. I simmered with anger at the lack of preventative work in public health.

Clearly, if I wanted to rejoin the two parts of my body, the rehabilitation journey was my responsibility. Archie the joiner built a hut for me inside the barn, with a small set of parallel bars in it, and when I felt able to impose on two friends at a time to help me, I used it. But it wasn't often enough. At one of my weekly sessions with Emma, when I was weaker than usual, my knees suddenly buckled on the parallel bars and I slid in slow motion to the ground, with her, half my height, unable to hold me. As we rolled on the dusty floor, I burst into sobs of utter despair. At which point, she fixed me with a fearless eye – she was a former rugby player – and surprised me with a question.

'Would you consider anti-depressants?'

'Superwomen don't need them,' I sobbed.

'Superwomen do,' she said gently. 'Sometimes superwomen need them the most.'

And so for once in my life I took some good advice. With hindsight, I realise I had been suffering from smiley depression since my accident. I had fallen into the habit of bursting into tears every time I got into my wheelchair in the morning, after my council carers had left me, at the thought of facing the day. Then I pushed myself up to the kitchen and started crying again as soon as I saw Dave. He found this dreadfully hard to cope with. He didn't do tearful women. Having the sense to accept that I needed some outside help to cope was one of the better things I did in that early period post-hospital. With fluoxetine I still felt like me, but a more mentally resilient and much less tearful me. The peaks and troughs had been subtly smoothed out. Most important of all, I didn't well up with misery every time I saw someone I loved.

An intrinsic problem was not being able to exercise on my own. Rapidly, I realised I could not continue to call upon my friends' goodwill to turn up once a week to do a shift with me. It was far too much of an imposition, especially when there was no end in sight. At that point in my walking I still needed orthotics, a splint upon my right foot to stop the leg dragging, worn inside my trainers. Dave lacked the patience for the fiddly business of putting them on. And both he and several emphysemic girlfriends – too many fags, girls, too many fags – found it hard pushing me back up the rough stony track to the house from the gym. Some physiotherapy students were organised for me but I felt that I was taking advantage and dropped them abruptly, shamefully. My bad manners upset me even more. The sense that I was asking too much of everyone overwhelmed me.

Wonderfully, my own body began to help me. Slowly my leg improved to the point where I no longer needed the splint. My feet would lift on demand and no longer dragged. Another big advance came after we went to a major exhibition of disability aids and Dave, on impulse, tempted by the end-of-show knock-down price, bought me a Norwegian-made machine called a Topro Taurus, a heavy-duty walker which I rested my elbows on. It was a kind of light-weight cousin of the vast Arjo walker

I had used in the spinal gym, only with the added advantage that this had a battery in its stem which helped me rise to a standing position. I could operate the lift with my right thumb. This was a breakthrough. Over the years the Norwegian, as we called it, has become a stalwart friend, a life-changing, brilliant piece of kit. I continue to use it every day to exercise and to get into bed; there is no exaggeration in saying it has saved my sanity and my body. Alone, I can safely use it to stand by myself and stretch my legs. With someone in attendance, I can practise walking. No NHS therapist I spoke to had ever seen or used one, but every therapist who saw mine was seriously impressed. How many other similar superb devices are languishing, unexploited, because they cost too much to contemplate? In a properly funded world, every geriatric and stroke centre would have multiple Topros, or similar.

Snakes and ladders has its origins in an ancient Indian morality game. The lesson being that one climbs up and attains salvation by doing good, but plunges downwards to a lower life by doing evil. There are fewer ladders on the board than snakes; and the snakes tend to be longer than the ladders: a calculated reminder from the spiritual authorities that a path of good is much more difficult to tread than a path of sin. As a metaphor for being paralysed I found it apt; what I disliked was when a certain brand of religious people wrote telling me that 'God puts you where he wants you to be, but the reason is never told; it is for you to discover.' This divine predestination stuff infuriated me. My issue with religion, much as I tried to respect others' faith, was that it failed the ultimate test of humanity. When terrible things happened at random to lovely people, or natural disasters swept away thousands, it belied the existence of a protective loving divinity. Were we to turn scornfully to God or Allah or whoever and say, well, where exactly *were* you? How could this happen on your watch? Wasn't it your job to stop that? Do you take us for fools?

Even as I got angry, though, I felt I betrayed the friends and strangers alike who prayed for my recovery. Their love and kindness brought undoubted positive energy and I gladly accepted support from any quarter. Snakes and ladders weren't just the Christian myth of paradise and the fall; they were a symbol of the unpredictable secular vicissitudes of life; a game of optimism versus frustration; a supreme test of patience; an eternal reminder of Robert the Bruce learning to try, try and try again from the spider spinning his web. They were about biological and psychological survival. When you're recovering from any life-changing illness or injury, you will always land on the snakes more often than you encounter the ladders. You also learn, painfully, that the snakes never go away. Happily, though, neither do the ladders.

Another thing that never went away was the support of people who read my writings in the paper. They were the ultimate kind-hearted strangers, good Samaritans who stopped their own busy lives to drop me words of encouragement. Here was muscular christianity with a small c, Kindness with a big K, the things I very much identified with. Some of them were also delightfully eccentric. They knitted me bedsocks, sent me stuffed hedgehogs, silk pillowcases, sweet pea seeds, hand-made jewellery, offered me shares in racehorses, wanted to take me skiing, carried my picture up mountains, ran marathons with my initials tacked on their headband. Potters potted mugs with lots of handles on them for my crocked fingers. One emeritus professor in his nineties, an Oxbridge scientist, sent me a hand-built prototype of an electrical stimulation invention which he believed, if I connected my fingertips to it, would resolve my issues.

Someone in particular shines a light from that time, someone called Judith from Twickenham. She had very distinctive handwriting. I knew no more of her than that. While I was in hospital, she sent to the spinal unit spectacular boxes of chocolates – I mean truly spectacular, like nothing I or anyone else had seen before. They were Hotel Chocolat extravaganzas, at a time when the brand was young and little known in the UK; display boxes a metre long filled with handmade sweets of a beauty and intricacy akin to an art form. We kept the boxes in the occupational therapy kitchen and they were brought out every day for hand therapy: it became part of the tetraplegic daily goal-setting, to be able to reach, remove and place a chocolate in our mouths.

Over the months, Judith sent three of these monstrous treats. Later, when I had returned home, she located me via head office, and another box arrived, again with no sender's address. Frustrated at being unable to contact her, I put a mention of her gifts in one of my columns. Thank you, I said, to Judith from Twickenham for your mysterious ability to track me down wherever I am. And then filed the memory of her kindness, and the unusual fun and pleasure it had brought, to the back of my brain.

Fast-forward a couple of years, and I was invited to the Cheltenham book festival, where I was interviewed by Libby Purves. Afterwards, a small number of the audience stayed behind to speak to me. As I chatted to the well-wishers in the darkening twilight outside the tent, I was aware of a tall man in a tweed jacket hovering at the back of the group. Eventually, only he remained: a stooped, distinguished, older man, hesitant, shy.

'Hallo,' I said.

'Er, yes,' he said, shaking my hand. 'My wife, such a great fan of yours. Er, you might remember … Judith from Twickenham …'

'Gosh yes,' I cried, with a rush of enthusiasm. 'Of course I remember!' I told him how much the gifts had meant, how much fun we had had with them, how I had longed to get in touch to thank her properly. 'I even tried to find you on the voters' register in Twickenham.'

'We moved to this part of the world.'

'OK, well, I'm so glad you're here. She has been so kind.'

'Ah, but you did mention her in one of your pieces. That meant so much to her. She was thrilled to know they had reached you and been enjoyed.'

It was almost dark under the tent awning. I beamed up at him. Brightly looked around.

'Where? … Is she? … Was she at the event …?'

'Oh no. You see, she died a few months ago. But she would have loved to be here.'

'Oh …' I was silenced. I reached out and took his hand, saw in him the grief and the stoop of loneliness, the unquantifiable yearning. There were tears in his eyes. I didn't know what to say, in that shared moment of intense grief. My companions and the organisers, who had been chatting behind me, were restless to be gone and interrupted our conversation.

'Yes, well, mustn't keep you,' he said. 'It has meant so much to meet you. Goodbye.'

And that is my memory of him, alone and stooped, walking away into the gloom.

'Thank you,' I called after him. 'Thank you for coming to talk to me.' And in that encounter, I realised, lay all the sweetness and sorrow of life.

CHAPTER TEN

JUST LIKE A WOMAN

I tell you, hopeless grief is passionless.
ELIZABETH BARRETT BROWNING

The tale was well rehearsed but unfathomable; a riddle I repeatedly tackled but couldn't solve. The body was lost, but where was the woman inside? Was I a woman any more? I looked for her in the mirror, but this, I soon realised, was the special corner of hell reserved for me and the likes of me. Some days, I would spend a long time there searching. Gripping the hand basin in my bathroom, I pulled myself forward, trying to recognise the folded-up creature with the haunted face, peering over the bottom of the frame. You're still not there, Mel. You're not you. And then the killer question – *Who's gonna love you now, huh?*

I had changed so much. My nose had been broken and the right eye, heavily bruised by the impact, was subtly rearranged, asymmetrical, the eyelid drooped. There was now a macular distortion on the retina; that eye saw a bump in straight lines. On the plus side I didn't need glasses for driving or watching TV any more. There was a permanent white scar on my right upper lip, split when I hit the ground, and on my throat a four-inch red line, a cat's scratch, where they had plated the cervical vertebrae. Trauma ages the face less than subtly: pain accentuates the lines. It was as if while suffering roughens you inside, coarse sandpaper on the soul, it scours you outside just as cruelly. When I cried, baggily and often, I looked like a Shar-Pei puppy, features folding so intensely into themselves that often, as they say in Glasgow, I looked like someone who had been sat on when their face was still hot.

Once, years before, I interviewed a beauty queen, who arrived in tears because she'd bumped her car, and I remember watching, enthralled, as the tears welled up and tipped slowly and sensuously down her peachy cheeks. My God, I thought enviously, what skill, to look gorgeous even when you weep. I was her polar opposite. Besides, my skin felt dry and harsh – I hadn't worn moisturiser since I fell to earth, for the simple reason that it was too frustrating a) to get the lid off the cream and b) to apply it with clawed and crooked fingers. The absence of that ritual felt like the removal of a basic woman's right – soothing cool cream across your face, with supple gentle fingers. My skin yearned and itched when I saw face cream adverts for L'Oréal, Clinique, Clarins, Nivea, but daubing cream on clumsily with my knuckles didn't assuage it.

In the early days, lying in hospital, when all that mattered was survival, I had amused myself satirising the shouty puffs on the front of a typical woman's magazine. The stuff women agonise about. How to lose two stone in two months without trying! Get your man to pay you more attention overnight! Grow long, luscious fingernails! Banish bingo wings for ever! Get a figure like the stars! Slim down those chunky runners' calves! Forget expensive colonic irrigation – try the finger of Rosebud the NHS nurse! Put your femininity to the test! It's easy, girls. All you have to do is break your neck. So much superficial angst, irrelevant before, had become vanishingly trivial. But beneath the flippancy, that dark question lurked, ever-present: *Who's gonna love you now?* And I would get a flash-back to the helicopter, Dishy Daz the winchman leaning over me, and my fleeting certainty of sexual bereavement. The knowledge that no man would ever again lean in desire.

Quite early on, certainly within the first few months, I initi-ated The Conversation with my husband. He was a sexy man; I was to all intents and purposes a dead body. Being best friends suddenly didn't seem to be quite the glue it once was. Besides, if you were going to pick a caregiver, some saintly, practical, selfless, patient man who would devote himself to a terribly disabled wife, you would not pick Dave. In a million years, you wouldn't pick him. Dave was loyal, shrewd and wise and he adored me, but he was also the ultimate entertainer and seducer whose greatest skill was making people laugh; an irresponsible, irresistible, incorrigible, flirtatious, harum-scarum, hard-drinking man's man and ladies' man who shied away from

In happier days. Like Harris Wittels, Dave knew every woman had a twenty per cent crush on him.

sickness, difficult stuff and sacrifice. I'm sure he thought, like the comedian Harris Wittels, that every woman had a twenty per cent crush on him, and he was probably right. He really didn't cope with negative things well. Perhaps I had read Jonathon Livingston Seagull too many times as an impressionable teenager, but I always reckoned that if you loved someone, you set them free. In my particular circumstances – well, it seemed only polite. Courtesy of my mother, I had a certain amount of sacrifice in my DNA.

'Listen,' I said. 'You know what I'm going to say. I think you should leave. I think we should, in the gentlest, most loving way, agree to split. This wasn't in the contract you signed up for. I'm not a woman any more, or a wife. You'll never cope with this.'

'Don't be so bloody stupid.'

'Please. You didn't ask for this. It's only fair you go, find a life with someone else; we can sell up, each buy a house.'

'Don't be ridiculous, you're stuck with me, just as long as you don't mind me going to the pub. I'm going nowhere.'

And he never has, instead evolving in a way nobody who knew him before could ever have imagined.

I found myself in a classic situation. The writer Susan Lonsdale speaks of the common assumption that women with disabilities are asexual, both as viewed by others, and as they regard themselves. Women are haunted by the loss of self-images from the past and concerned about the person they have become. Women are socially identified with their bodies. 'A woman is taught very early on to be conscious of her body shape, body size, body smell, her hair (including where it should be as well as where it shouldn't be) and her facial features – in short, of her physical appearance. The diet and fashion industry reinforces this concern for much of a woman's life, as a teenager and an adult.' This 'norm of attractiveness' is precisely the thing you lose when you become disabled, and the void is filled by negative self-images. Lonsdale identifies four factors which foster this, and unsurprisingly one is the negative perception of the outside world. People look at you in pity, if they look at you at all. Attractive young women get it worst – the sentiment, often thought, embarrassingly often blurted out by the unthinking: 'You're too pretty to be in a wheelchair.' As if, somehow, being disabled equates with ugly. As if only less attractive people aren't wasted when they are disabled.

My unconscious prejudice was the same, even from the disabled side of the divide. When I tried to associate the concept of beauty with disability, it was a dead end. This was a place where my intellectual compass failed. I had many reasons to live, but the secret thrill of looking good, of being admired, of being a player in the great competitive game of physical attraction, with all its hurts and joys, was no longer one of them. I genuinely could not find any beauty in my body in my chair; only loss. When I made an effort with mascara and a pretty scarf, friends would say gamely, 'You look lovely today', because they were kind and wanted to encourage me to feel good. 'You're still you inside.' But they knew and I knew and they knew I knew. When I looked, I saw a shipwreck. A wheelchair first, and then that strange, still person in it, her dowager's hump growing, her middle settling. That wasn't me. But it was. And my appearance and my helplessness combined were so asexy, unsexy, that I cringed.

Personal vanity is a curious thing. In the past, genuinely, I had not spent much time on my appearance. I spent money on horses, not on clothes. Once, I contemplated cosmetic Botox for a deep line between my eyebrows where I'd been scarred by an encounter with a swinging horse's head, but had told myself not to be so silly; now, my face addled with suffering, I received cynicism-free NHS Botox to relax my paralysed fingers and legs. Never burdened by classic beauty, I was always aware that my sexual identity resided in my sense of fun, my dynamism. Movement. Get-up-and-go. I made the best of my appearance by smiling a lot, but most of all by keeping moving. Stand tall, talk with your hands and arms, address tall men eye to eye, drop a hip to speak to smaller men. Don't get trapped by bores. Don't stay too long in one place. Step out one long leg and swing tactfully to another conversation. Let the energy swirl behind me. That poignant old mix of insecurity, insouciance, bravado which, as I grew older, morphed into confidence and independence, a lack of reliance on men.

Gone too was sensuality and sexual movement. Never mind spontaneity; when your limbs do not work and you cannot feel, you can hardly make lunch, let alone love. Sometimes, after my accident, Dave admitted that he would see a couple walking in the street together, hand in hand, laughing, bumping shoulders like mates, and he would feel a terrible pang. Movement was central to everything, repeating circles of cause and effect. Attraction needed movement. Movement needed clothes. Attraction needed the right clothes. Sex needed movement. Clothes needed movement. Without movement, the link broke; the equation failed. What then did a woman consist of?

In my stillness, in the vacuum left where movement used to be, I analysed how people behaved in front of mirrors. Every morning, you dressed your identity, picking clothes in an act of happy self-seduction; an age-old ritual in search of improvement, beauty, confidence and disguise. You put on the items which you hoped took you from what you were to what you would like to be. In moving, your identity was found – uncovered by your side step, your hair flick, your opening arms and your fluid, private twist in front of the mirror. The bond you had with your own reflection was lifelong and far more intimate than that with a lover. That autopilot drill: front view, then side profile, then the glance over the shoulder for as much of a back view as possible. Finally, the twirl back round on the heels, hair flick, chin raise – and the glimpse of yourself as you wanted to be seen. My relationship with the mirror used to be brief and fast. Sometimes just in order to say, *Yes, I still exist.* But most times, for speedy reassurance: hair OK; mascara unsmudged; damn, these boots are gorgeous; quick twirl; no dandruff; OK, that'll do, good to go.

All this was gone. There could be no disguise or reinvention through clothes. Clothes did not flourish in stillness, without sway or flow or hang, because clothes were about allure, about the body within. Whatever I wore, I always wore a wheelchair. Searching for a physical identity now in front of the mirror, I felt akin to a horse wearing blinkers. I could see in front of me, but everything to the sides and behind was hidden. I wasn't three-dimensional any more; I couldn't turn and glimpse myself in flight to check me out. I had no real sense of what I looked like. There was little communication in stillness and I was now, by definition, permanently still. How we walk, sway, tilt our bodies, wear our clothes, reveals everything – defiance, pride, comfort, depression, power, confidence, taste, ambition, disguise, seduction, aspiration, approachability. I had time to observe these things. I learnt that, once lost, the final twirl in the mirror was a glorious thing, a basic human freedom now removed. I learnt that I couldn't even remember how to twirl when I rehearsed it in my head. Silly, isn't it, that you could forget something like that?

I felt degraded. I could look *smart* – but I wanted to look *desirable*. Some mornings, I held morally dubious debates with myself. Perhaps it would be preferable to be blind. Then I could still dress proudly, knowing I continued to look nice. No need to feel embarrassed, or worry about pitying glances. Then I could sustain myself privately in the dark with internal, imagined pictures of myself. Then I could still dance, and make love. As it was, a sense of self-disgust was reinforced every day. When I ventured out, getting me in and out of the car seemed akin to transporting a large circus animal. Intimate, a bit sweaty. But not in a good way. And as I did my awkward, effortful slide across the transfer board from wheelchair to car and back again, I was conscious of all the hidden helpless bits I could do noth-ing about: my atrophied buttocks, my slumped back, my clothes, unfelt, ridden up like crop-tops. Burning in the ashes of my personal vanity, the internal dialogue. 'Apologies if this isn't very elegant, chaps. Apologies if my backside looks big in the baggy leggings. Because to be honest, I can't look over my shoulder to examine it in the mirror now and I'm sure it's not a nice sight. And to be honest I might even be presenting you with a less-than glorious builder's bum, but I have no way of knowing, because I can't feel uncovered flesh, and you'd be far too polite to tell me.' Physical pride. Femininity. I had to let them go, fluttering from the window, letting the past fall away.

It became a comfort to adopt reclusive attitudes: that tweak of the dial that said, stop trying, stop going out, make it easy for yourself. The party's over. Who cares what you look like? I ceased to worry that one pair of reading glasses was held together with Sellotape and the other so stretched I had to hold them on my nose. Would anyone notice if I didn't wash my face? Why bother with mascara, earrings? I stopped flossing my teeth and there were periods when I stopped brushing them. I did no kissing any more. It became apparent how serious self-neglect begins. I stopped getting my hair coloured. I lived and slept in the same T-shirt between weekly showers, wore jumpers riddled with holes and, perpetually, the scabby trainers. What did anything matter? I missed boots so much. Early in my time back home, I bought three pairs on the internet in blind hope, and none would fit on my watermelon feet even after being cut open. Paralysed feet were incredibly difficult for carers to force into boots. Do undertakers have the same problem putting shoes on dead people? So I continued in the size 10 trainers, two sizes too big, but that was the only way to prevent pressure points. Grey boats of protection, easy for carers to put on. The kind a middle-aged man with severe learning difficulties would wear. I didn't care any more.

Before my accident I had been in some of the best shape of my life, trimmed down to size 12 jeans – a statement which now rings with futile vanity, a pathetic boast. The When-I club. In hospital I became as slender as I'd ever yearned to be, although the bitter irony did not escape me. Once, in my shower chair in front of a small hospital mirror, I caught a first post-accident glimpse of myself naked – great bony shoulders, visible ribs and hollow armpits. That was the look I once craved, but never

slumped helpless in a chair. By then I could have got into a pair
of size 10 jeans, I realised, except it would have been physically
impossible unless I was suspended from the ceiling and a team
of carers pulled them up my legs as if they were filling sausages.
Now my carers dressed me in easy-to-put-on leggings, long-
sleeved thermal vests, old cashmere jumpers and fleeces, layering
to keep warm. As wardrobes go, it was a bit like being in prison,
or on a never-ending camping holiday. One evening Dave and
I decided to go out on the spur of the moment and I went to try
and change my top half, by myself, into something nicer. What
would in the old days have required a five-minute twirl turned
into a farce. A lovely French shirt was useless, because I couldn't
do the buttons. The velvet-trimmed T-shirt exposed a Buddha
midriff bereft of muscle tone. Eventually, I got stuck, half in and
half out of my favourite special tweed and satin jacket, one arm
jammed, the other armhole hooked behind me on the wheelchair handles. I couldn't move my chair and had to summon
Dave using the mobile phone round my neck to rescue me.
Trying to look nice, huh? My clothes were saying no.

At first, I felt furiously envious of women who look stunning
in clothes, whose bodies still signalled attraction. Who still had
everything I had lost. I tried to resist the inevitable lure of the
miserabilist high ground of disability: the sour voice that said
my incurable suffering trumps your trivial pursuit of a designer
label. You want Gucci? Me? I just want to walk. Later, those
feelings died and I began to appreciate women who were happy
in their bodies. It was wrong to be bitter – most women, like
me, just wanted to look nice. I was just glad they could.

Loss of control over bodily functions was another profoundly
desexualising thing. Under the laws of nature, double incon-

tinence was for babies, toddlers and the extremely elderly – it wasn't for adults. It was an anomaly, a weakness, a breach of the proper order, as far from attractive as it was possible to be. Shit ain't sexy. For Dave, in the early days, helping his wife onto a shower chair so that she could spend an hour poised over the loo trying to persuade her bowels to work, was not a turn-on. Neither were the dreadful times when I had bowel accidents, either in bed while he lay next to me, or dressed in my chair, when he had no choice but to help me out of soiled clothes and onto a shower chair. This was a man whose stomach, decades before as a young father, was too sensitive to allow him to change his children's nappies without retching. Not many people have seen severely disabled bodies with very few clothes on and certainly my own was the first one I saw. And I enforced the novelty of it on him. Not a pretty sight, not by contemporary standards of beauty. The human body was not designed to be immobile; neither was its sphincter meant to fail. My pee drained out from my abdomen just above the pubic bone, the antithesis of sexually alluring, and everywhere I went, my leg bag went too to collect it. Touch me, and you just might be grabbing a bag of cold piss.

Then there was the wheelchair itself, a cold hard metal appliance doubly antithetical to any kind of touch, let alone a sexual one. A wheelchair was a physical and mental stockade to keep you apart. Like a departing train. Stand back. Doors closing. Mind the gap. Easy, casual, precious human contact disappears once you are in a chair – all those loving pats and brushes and caresses of family life. When that spontaneous benign intimacy – bumping playful hips, falling asleep on someone's shoulder on the sofa, squeezing up together at the table – is removed from you, you don't half yearn for it. Touch becomes deliberate. You must organise it. When you want to hug those you love, they must bend out and down, cantilevering over your square metal skirts, your hard corners, while you reach up, try and sling your good arm over one of their shoulders. You kiss cheeks, feel their face on your collarbone perhaps, but you are denied the proper, lovely, torso-close, full-body experience of a full-fat, five-star bear-hug, lingering and comforting. 'One is always nearer by not being still,' wrote Thom Gunn in his poem 'The Sense of Movement'. And so touch became a new hunger for me. I watched the TV news, and everything I saw featured it – handshakes, back slaps, rescuers hugged by the rescued, protesters arm-in-arm, concert-goers swaying together, goal-scorers disappearing under a pile of happy, flailing bodies. Everything involving human events drama necessitated touch. Whereas I moved through life as a diver in a shark cage moves through a busy sea. I could stick a clawed fist through the bars but handshakes were insufficient to bond.

Disability taught me many things, but one was the tragedy of how risk-averse we were becoming about touch, even those not in wheelchairs. Human contact was being demonised by paranoia about abuse, to the extent that teachers, carers and adoptive parents were running scared of touching children. Collectively, something vital for human nurture was threatened. Life is made wonderful by touch, but we take it for granted until we lose it. Life is saved by touch. Literally. According to Francis McGlone, a professor of neuroscience who specialises in touch, premature babies who are stroked put on fifty per cent more weight compared to those who aren't, are able to leave hospital six days earlier, and a year later have better mental and physical abilities. This research is perfectly framed by a case of the premature twins, struggling for breath in separate incubators, who on their mother's pleading were reunited. They immediately put their arms around each other and began, dramatically, to thrive. They had been starving for touch. Without nurture and touch, or when locked in orphanages, babies die.

Infants bump and jostle with playmates all day. Children denied smart phones do the same. Adolescents, now wonderfully huggy and tactile, drape themselves around each other, link arms, take selfies cheek-to-cheek. Us Brits, we're getting refreshingly better at expressing the joy of being together. As they grow, the young become lovers and then have their own children, when the touching, hugging cycle begins anew, transformative – satisfying their babies' need for contact with their parents' skin, essential for them to thrive. Humans of all ages reach out and touch each other, tired or lively, insecure or confident, happy or sad, needing play or conflict. Team sport is the perfect antidote to isolation, the pre-match huddles, the celebrations, the fans. Other gregarious mammals are the same – dolphins, horses, cows. Watch them: they love to rub, jostle, play, lie down together, just like us taking pleasure from skin contact with their own kind. This is something much more profound than sex.

When you're disabled, however, this often vanishes. You join many other solitary people, spectators in lonely, uncomforted skins, unable to re-stoke their souls with the kind of non-sexual intimacy humans require. You hunger, then, for any kind of touch. Paralysis means you'll be hungry whatever happens. Normal skin sensation had been removed from eight-five per cent of my body. Only my right hand, the outside of my arms, my shoulders, neck and head could feel. I could lie in bed and Dave, who knew my heartache, would sleep against the length of my body, trying to comfort me, but I was unaware he was there. My skin didn't talk to his skin any more.

My self-esteem as a woman took a particular beating that first winter in hospital, when, exceedingly vulnerable and probably quite close to a breakdown, I let myself be used as someone else's emotional lifeboat. By the time I had moved into the single room, my fingers had improved to the point where I could use my mobile phone. This meant I was no longer guarded by Dave; and some people began to get in touch. Texting. Could they come and see me? It felt like pressure. I was a creature emerging from hibernation, a snail that had lost its shell. Everything was bright and fast and dangerous; it was as if I had lost my skin and had no protection from anything. Superwoman was now prey.

Out of the blue, someone I knew through the horse world texted me. He had always been a bit of a lame duck and I had been kind to him in the past. Now, at the precise point that the doctors perceived I was exhausted and advised me to stop writing, Gollum latched onto me. He started to phone me, in the afternoons at first, then late at night, long rambling calls about his problems, seeking emotional support from me. He had left his wife, he said. He was seeing someone else. He'd lost his job but found another. Tragedies from the past, always somebody else's fault, were pressing on him. The conversation was always all about him. Looking back, I don't think he once asked me how I was. He would phone drunk and I would still try and counsel him. I was too weak to hang up. Only later did I realise how unfair and wrong his behaviour was; you might even define it as a form of abuse. I was a complete mess and in that state the unlovely Gollum became almost the ghost of all I had lost. Who's gonna love you now? As I lay in the dark and listened to his incoherent ramblings, horrified by his presence in my life but unable to escape it, I pretended, briefly, I was still a desirable woman.

He came to see me once in hospital, a moment when reality was restored. As he stood there, boasting about his newly restored prosperity, and I dutifully listened, my bowels decided that they should come to my rescue, and they delivered me of a small, silent, wet fart. The faint but unmistakable smell ring-fenced my chair, humiliating me utterly, but it did mean Gollum left very quickly. His phone calls ceased. Who's gonna love you now, indeed. Thank you bowels. Now I knew the answer for sure. What a black comedy life was, indeed.

There was a Christmas party in the spinal unit and they brought in a rock band. In Glasgow, tribute bands are a thing apart. They attack the music with the disinhibition and volume of those who believe they *are* stars, not just those who pretend. This band were Kings of Leon, and of course their biggest hit was 'Sex Is on Fire'.

We sat, ringing the room, us poor souls in our chairs, our neck braces, our incontinence bags and our tubes, some of us with hands too damaged to clap. And then came the chorus, and the band raised their arms. They wanted us to join in the chorus with them, so they pointed – you! – and so the room full of terminally frozen bodies obediently chanted that yes, their sex was, er, well, maybe, on fire.

Sometimes nothing is ever too dark to laugh at.

*   *   *

With hindsight, fear of sexual annihilation was what made me a fleeting victim of Gollum. And fear of sexual rejection is another of the four primary causes of negative self-image among disabled women. That was another of those real No shit, Sherlock statements. If, when you were able-bodied, you never felt supremely attractive, then you can imagine that when you become profoundly disabled you're beaten before you start. No surprise there at all. A young woman, who had been disabled since she was ten, told me she had been stopped in the street by men who said, 'It's such a shame you're in that thing, you're beautiful.' The first few times she smiled sweetly and thanked them but now she ignored them. She was twenty-six and soon to qualify as a lawyer – an attempt to regain some of the status her disability had stripped from her. Poignantly, she said she had never been desired or kissed – 'damaged goods indeed'. Compared to her, I realised just how lucky I was.

In the spinal unit, rightly however, they took sex very seriously and were much more grown-up about it than we were prepared, or capable, of being in the immediate aftermath of our injuries. There were specialist out-patient fertility clinics for longer-term paralysed people. For us, as raw in-patients, just beginning our new life, there were education sessions on sex with a body which didn't move. Men and women separately.

'It is,' said the nurse in charge, a no-nonsense blonde, 'perfectly possible to regain your sex life after a spinal injury.'

Peony, sixteen going on thirty-six and more knowing about sex than most of us put together, rolled her eyes. She'd dived into the shallow end of a swimming pool in Spain and broken her neck.

'And paralysis does not affect fertility in women, so you must be aware and use contraception accordingly.'

There was me, in my fifties, and Periwinkle, who was older and had a disabled husband. Daffodil, forty-something, who had been injured in a car crash. Foxglove was a young woman who had come off a motorbike. We kept polite faces, refrained from scoffing. It was all true. Spinal injury does not affect pregnancy: lots of paralysed young women have babies and that's a fabulous thing. Generally, carrying a baby is easier every way if you're paraplegic rather than tetraplegic, less risk to your body. Given the extra physical complications of a high neck break, having a baby would be much more problematic. Once, I was contacted by an able-bodied man who said he was, as far as he knew, the only child born of two tetraplegic parents. And there was no doubt the subject held dark curiosity for many people, not just us. Later I met a woman who had broken her neck and become friendly in the spinal unit with a similarly tetraplegic man who made video porn films. He tried to persuade her to make a film together, her hoisted on top of him. 'We'd make a fortune,' he advised her. 'People pay big money for that sort of thing.'

When it came to the mechanics of sex for paralysed women, complete injuries were to be much favoured over incomplete, because of those soft and floppy legs. The intrinsic physical difficulties for people like me were what utterly defeated and therefore amused me. My legs were heavy and most of the time rigid with spasm. My adductor muscles clamped my knees together with a force that would delight the most demanding nun in a convent school. I was as unmanoeuvrable as your average second-row forward in a provincial rugby team – and, let's face it, about as alluring. I even had the same hairy legs because I couldn't reach them to shave. To get my knees apart would require a heavy-duty car jack. If making love was best suited to soft, supple, sensual, giving, eager limbs, then I was in the wrong movie.

To see sexual images for me, post-paralysis, was to see stories of a different human tribe: the ones who were still sexually viable, who wielded sexual power. I had no interest or curiosity in them. They were different to me. I felt like an anthropologist. By losing physical sensation, cut off from critical engagement, I had also disengaged mentally. Loss of sexuality hollowed me out as a woman, the memories too sad to stir. No more Roy Orbison or Bruce Springsteen singing about driving all night to be with a lover. I switched off films when they got sexy, if I was watching on my own; if in company, I drifted casually off to another room. They just made me feel empty. I had stopped reading fiction altogether, perhaps for the same reason. The other day I tried to remember what an orgasm felt like. I couldn't. Imagine that. Maybe lots of women feel this when they grow old. No skin in the game – both disinterested and uninterested. Somehow I doubt it. I don't think we ever lose our urge to be sexually attractive. However old you are, you can still feel young inside, still remember the tingle of being noticed. I'm certain that even at ninety, if someone flirts with you, the years melt away, the inner teenager stirs, the silly, potent daydream returns. No matter how wistful or how trapped by age you are, you're still susceptible to that mutual spark. The number of marriages in care homes supports this theory. But not for me. For me the magic of desire and of being desired – the sheer bliss of being found attractive – has been switched off.

There you have it – the core of loss. The stone heart of long-ing, envy and emotional shut-down which is a woman's self-defence against disability. Because you aren't fanciable and you won't be, can't be and never will be. Because the great game of sex, in all its hurts and joys and sleaziness and beauty, is no longer one you can play. That baton, that glorious burden of sexual attraction, has been passed on. Those rules that govern human chemistry, the language of wanting and being wanted, however crudely or elegantly expressed – they don't apply to you any more. The brutal truth about the mechanics of sex for paralysed and disabled people is that you've got to find some-one who fancies you to do it with. Those people aren't so easy to find, especially if you're a woman looking for a man. Disabled men have a much better strike rate copping off with their carers, probably because women put compassion and romantic love before sex. My husband wasn't like that. He loved me but he simply didn't, couldn't, wouldn't fancy me any more. He was blunt about that.

Loss of sexual identity was akin to bereavement. With it, unwelcome, also came jealousy, the nasty green eyed-monster, the scythe of betrayal – and yet also the basic dilemma born of fair play. Should our partners be condemned to sexual loss, just because we are? Does sexual infidelity count under these circumstances? Or is there space, and is there forgiveness? As Jack Nicholson once said to Angelica Houston, excusing his unfaithfulness: 'Toots, darling, it was a mercy fuck.' Perhaps it's something disabled people and their partners have to spend the rest of their lives working out.

*　*　*

Through disability, you learn other wisdom about being a woman. It's estimated that one schoolgirl in ten has an eating disorder. In some parts of the country, three in ten little girls are obese. The vast majority of the young female population spends an unhealthy amount of time in front of the mirror criticising themselves. An exceptionally beautiful professional woman I know, now nearing forty, admitted to me once that every single day she fretted about how unhappy she was with her body. Yet she had looks to die for. What a tragedy this is. Millions of lovely kids storing up a lifetime of unhappiness with their own bodies, bodies which are fit, mobile, creative, expressive. Bodies which are beautiful because they *work*. You struggle to square what you can see – a wrecked body, forcibly removed from the demands of being physically attractive – with the plight of healthy yet desperately dissatisfied young women.

So this is what you don't learn until it is too late. One is that a woman's relationship with her own body image tends to take the form of a totally unnecessary, destructive war. I used to be one of those teenagers too, negative about my appearance, yearning to be this, that and the other – slimmer thighs, curvier waist. We all know the drill, the drip, drip, drip corroding our self-esteem. Even before the advent of the internet, and Instagram, and the selfie, I wasted a spectacular amount of time and energy in thirty years of low-key yo-yo dieting, self-criticism, and worrying about how other people viewed me – and it's only now I realise what I've lost. If I could reclaim even half of that time, how much more creatively I would have spent it – dancing, running, learning, travelling, kissing, talking, laughing, reading, playing sport. Instead of trying to be thinner and sexier, I should have striven to be freer; braver; not to give a damn how others thought I looked; to relish every single second I had with a fit, healthy body. Had I known that I would end up with a spinal injury I would not have wasted a nanosecond on the width of my thighs, because these things, I now know, are infinitely irrelevant.

Hindsight is a cruel companion. How, from my disabled vantage point, do I bridge that chasm of wisdom? How to tell today's young women, so many of them psychologically crippled by the tyranny of aspiring to a sexy body image, what really matters? Instead of rejoicing in their health and opportunities, and the possession of a body which works, little girls are being schooled by their mothers, their peers, the internet and the media to find faults in themselves. More and more beautiful girls are being screwed up by the pressure to look like celebrities when they should be exploring the freedom to be themselves. Oh sisters, daughters, please turn off the soundtrack of self-loathing and get out there and *live*. Because the most sexy thing in the world is being alive, confident, active and interesting. That's what attracts other people to you, whatever their gender. When your body doesn't work any more, and you are sexually *hors de combat*, the concept of an ideal body image becomes as blackly funny as it is possible to be. So, too, does the idea of cosmetic surgery to put right wrongs which exist only in your own eyes. Physical imperfection is in fact lovely; we're all imperfect.

Without meaning to sound like a preacherwoman, disability has taught me to celebrate life and possibility. All that separates me from healthy, active people are the brutal seconds of my fall. Now, as a spectator, I find that I love watching bodies that work. I now perceive dizzying beauty in the simple movement of ordinary people. Sliding on and off stools on coffee bars, side-stepping, throwing out that first impatient stride when the green man flashes up at the junction. I feed off amusing, tender cameos: a few years ago, having received an honorary degree from Stirling University, I sat on the graduation stage and watched hundreds of young women totter across in front of me for their certificates, ninety-nine per cent of them on vertiginous heels, stumbling like endearing kid goats, but happy, happy, happy because they were going to look good in the pictures later. These girls brought tears to my eyes, because they were like kids raking in the dressing-up box for adulthood, one last time, a final rite of passage, before it was for real. They were more sexy and beautiful than they could possibly know, but not because of the shoes.

In the absence of any sexual future, my thoughts inevitably swayed towards to an earlier, much less complicated kind of affair of the heart. Horses.

CHAPTER ELEVEN

OF STRING GIRTHS AND RUNNING MARTINGALES

High up on the long hill they called the Saddle Back,
behind the ranch and the county road, the boy sat on
his horse, facing east, his eyes dazzled by the rising sun.
MARY O'HARA, *MY FRIEND FLICKA*

Ever since I could remember, I had been in love with horses
– and I mean love. An all-encompassing devotion, which
bewildered my parents, who had no interest in horses and
were far too serious-minded and austere to contemplate
indulging their children. They had been born in the Edwardian
age, met while serving on the team developing radar in the
Second World War, and decided to carry on being Edwardians.
Once the war was over, it seemed as if they transferred their
battle to all forms of waste or extravagance instead. We lived
in north London, in a tall, austere house with a big garden,
where I lay and made nests in the long velvety grass and my
father distilled spirit from fermented pears off the big tree. My
earliest memories were of horse-riding on the back of a vast
decrepit old sofa with a skipping rope for reins. Or roping my
amiable big sister round the waist, so I could drive her up and
down and around the garden. The afflicted will share these
universal memories.

At Granny's house, if it had
four legs I was in heaven.
Neddy the donkey …

… Polly the pony (with my
cousin Ann) …

… and even a rocking horse. Wishing Ann (left) would get off
so I could have it all to myself.

There were real live animals to base the fantasies on. At my grandmother's house in Northern Ireland, where we spent every summer, lived a donkey and my older cousin's pony, Polly. I fed her apple cores and, if I was good, I was allowed to ride her very, very occasionally. During the long days in between, I would stand at the door of the tack room, a walk-in cupboard, sucking in great breaths of warm, sweet, saddle-soap-soggy air, looking but not daring to touch, memorising the different components, the bits and accessories. That was what love smelt of. Hours were spent gazing longingly up at the forbidden treasures – martingales, bits, reins, double bridles, cruppers, crops, side reins.

Growing up horse-devout but horseless, in an era when riding was reserved for a cultivated elite, was hard. How I yearned to belong to that mysterious, unobtainable world. By way of compensation, I used to memorise equine body parts and by ten I knew as much about the conformation of the horse as your average vet student. And I read voraciously, cantering a thousand vicarious horses across the pages: *Black Beauty* by Anna Sewell, *My Friend Flicka* by Mary O'Hara, the horsey sagas by the three Pullein-Thompson sisters. Novels about little girls with ponies by Sheila Chapman, long forgotten now, the pages brown with compulsive re-reading, the corners of the covers quite worn away. My imagination thronged with legendary famous horse riders with splendidly exotic names – Pat Koechlin-Smythe, Lucinda Prior-Palmer, Anneli Drummond-Hay, Ted Edgar, Colonel Llewellyn and his great horse Foxhunter, a young Harvey Smith and David Broome. I borrowed their biographies from the local library and absorbed every detail of their starry lives.

Back at home after the County Down holidays were over, I drew my dreams compulsively on the backs of unwanted engineering drawings my father brought home. 'Daddy's got you more paper,' my mother would announce, and sure enough, there would be the fat, sharp-edged sheaves of A3, stapled into bunches, smudged blue diagrams of worm gearing, run off an early duplicating machine. More paper felt like Christmas every time it arrived, because when you turned the paper over – so the staples were in the top right corner – there were endless acres of fresh crisp whiteness waiting to be populated with horses: galloping, jumping, racing, rearing. I drew maps of fields and stable yards and filled them with different equines, like the cast of a dynastic novel – my fantasy pets, the black stallion who won every competition, the chestnut mare who was his best friend, their offspring who would win the next Olympics. I have a clear memory – we were still in London, so I must have been no more than five – of my teenage sister exhorting me to draw a horse for her friend. I was delighted to show off my prowess, proudly including the details I had studied in my cousin Patsy's tack room, and in the books I borrowed from the library. A carefully drawn snaffle bit. A plain noseband. My sister started giggling. 'Look,' she said to her friend, 'she's even given you a string girth.' These were all the rage in horsey circles in the early 1960s. I knew my stuff. I was slightly indignant that they found it funny.

Then there were my plastic horses, a herd of model animals and riders which, in the days before television, let alone tablets or electronic games, were my nightly playthings. They had names, backstories and lives that were utterly real to me. Blackie, Brownie, Whitey, Zebra (though his stripes wore off and I chewed one of his front legs badly), Sheriff, Thunder, Lightning. Ridden mostly by bandy-legged models called Pat Smythe and Colonel Brown. As an occasional treat, my herd was allowed to expand. I would go to Woolworths and buy a new one, eyeing up the others on the shelf, planning which I would get the next time, and the time after that. As we drove to my grandparents' house in Harpenden, we passed a shop, a rare equestrian outfitters, which had jodhpurs in the window display: I remember being on the back seat, pressing my face against the car window, peering through the raindrops and the dim street lights for a glimpse of them. They were jodhpurs like Colonel Brown had, with big flaps on the outside of the thighs.

My father, although wary of this strange madness, grudgingly fashioned a hobby horse for me, a plywood head attached to a broom handle, and my mother covered it with leather from an old armchair. It was immediately and inevitably christened Polly. We cantered everywhere together. With her, I felt complete; fulfilled; fused into a centaur which would paw the ground, neigh and prance and canter everywhere. Perhaps it is just as well I did not grow up today, an age of choice and gender fluidity for children, because for at least seven years I wanted to be a horse.

Indeed I *was* a horse most of the time, cantering, snorting, shying around the dinner table. When you live inside your imagination, all things are possible. On family journeys, one escaped from the boredom of the back seat of the car or the train to gallop across country alongside, soaring over huge hedges and ditches for endless miles. Every horse-mad little girl I know did the same. Horses set you free. When Polly disintegrated from wear and tear, I moved on to imaginary steeds.

With my brother and sister and Polly the hobby horse,
Barnet 1962.

Now I was bounded only by my imagination. In there I created
a vast stable of animals: blacks, bays, greys and chestnuts, my
plastic horses come alive. All shared the ability to jump over the
moon, for hours on end. Inspired by Pat Smythe's career, I
created Olympic courses in the garden – spreads, oxers and
triples built from flowerpots, dustbins, broom handles, canes,
hoes, shovels, upturned buckets. Hours were spent competing
against myself on different horses; I can't remember when I
stopped, but it may, tragically, have been into my early teens.
And that was only because I fell in love with Marc Bolan.

I wrote a long, illustrated story about a family called the
Riderds: calling them the Riders seemed much too obvious. My
mother, unable to assuage my longings, but a kindly soul, would
buy me an occasional copy of *Riding* magazine. I never thought
she had had any connection with horses but decades later, after

her death, I found pictures of her in the late 1920s, sitting on a blood horse, pigtailed, hatless, languid; her friend Sheila Denton alongside on another elegant hack. I saw a picture too, of my grandmother in a riding habit, looking effortlessly regal. Maybe my mother understood a little bit of my longing.

Once it became apparent that my parents considered riding lessons far too expensive, I had to resort to my own devices. Granny in Ireland used to send me a pound note every Christmas and birthday; I worked out that if a pony cost £50, I would get one eventually – but I worried about the cost of the farrier. All the books said they were very expensive. I laid more store on the Kellogg's Cornflakes Win a Pony art competition and put in two entries, convinced I would win. Meantime, while striving for my ultimate goal, I had other, more lowly dreams. Like a bike. Everyone else had a bike. You have to understand that all this was internalised: in my family, no child demanded anything. And because I was a surprise late baby, I was cotton-woolled. One morning, aged about eight, sitting on the downstairs loo, where I was banished every morning after breakfast to do a poo whether I needed to go or not, because it was good Edwardian child-rearing, I overheard my father talking to my mother.

'Shall I buy one with a crossbar?' he said.

And she said, 'Probably better with one.'

And I went off to school, fizzing inside with joy because I just knew he was talking about what type of bicycle to buy for me, and she knew I wanted a boys' bike with a crossbar because girls' bikes were wet. I was utterly desperate to be like my friends. We had set up a gang of bike-riding vigilantes, copied from the Q-Bikes in *The Beano*, but my membership was always on a shaky peg because I usually had to run after them on foot. I was just desperate to belong, to escape the reputation of my relatively elderly, old-fashioned parents, 1930s aliens washed up in the swinging sixties. But disappointment waited. After a few days, when nothing materialised, I plucked up the courage to sound out my mother about the time schedule on the bike. She was amused. 'Oh no, dear,' she said. 'We needed coat hangers and Daddy was discussing what kind to buy.' No bike arrived until I was ten and soon to go to grammar school, by which time it was a bit too late for my street cred. With hindsight, I see the old man was overprotective of me: he didn't want me falling off a bicycle and hurting myself. Any time I did fall, he reacted with such fury that I had to conceal my injuries, and hope he wouldn't notice the scratches on the bike. The old bugger always did, though. Just as well he was dead long before 2010.

The horse thing mirrored the bike thing, only deeper, a current of yearning to escape, to go fast, which flowed with me through life. It never left me and persists, darkened with the manifest irony of its consequences, to this day. I was eventually allowed the occasional riding lesson when I was about eleven and rode a friend's pony once in a blue moon as a teenager. The consequences were inevitable, I suppose, like any bad case of arrested development. Overprotected children tend to overreact when they gain freedom in young adulthood. Even having a boyfriend and a career didn't cure me: when I started my first job as a graduate trainee on a newspaper, immediately after leaving university, I went out and bought myself a horse with my first proper salary. A palomino mare, no less, flashy as you like, who I called Indiana.

'I'll take that sorrel filly of Rocket's; the one with the cream tail and mane,' said Ken. 'I've named her Flicka.'

Not being in possession of five thousand acres of Wyoming, I had to sell Indiana two months later because I couldn't afford her keep. After that, I got semi-sensible. I waited until I was in possession of a husband and a house with a field and a stable, and, then, conscious how book-learnt I was, enrolled on a part-time basis at a prestigious riding school nearby until I passed the British Horse Society exams up to assistant instructor level. I was going to make up for lost time and do things properly.

Thirty years of fun followed; numerous horses owned; foals bred and broken; horses despatched; riding clubs run; shows organised; competitions entered; lessons taken; rosettes won. I was never a serious player, because I was not rich and had neither time to spare nor money for expensive horses; I had a full-time job and a little boy; but what I managed to do I enjoyed greatly, always trying to improve, always taking safety seriously and doing things properly. It was only after my son had gone to university, and I had a little more time and money, and was fitter than I'd been for years, that I decided to go for one of my dreams: proper affiliated eventing. There is indeed no fool like an old fool.

In hospital after my accident, I had the unnerving experience of being contacted by a teenager, fourteen or so, who asked me if she should carry on cross-country jumping. Help. What does one say? Stop? And while you're at it stop cycling on the road, travelling in cars, eating polyunsaturated fats, going near build-ing sites, breathing diesel fumes, walking in the hills or drinking alcohol. Your life may last until you're a hundred and fifty, but it won't be everyone's idea of fun. People ask for my views on whether they should continue horse-riding, as if my risk analysis is somehow refined as a result of my experience. Should I tell them to carry on? I advised the girl to discuss it with her parents and a professional trainer; to be sure her horse was suitable for the job; and I said that for Christmas she should ask for an air safety jacket, which inflates if you leave the saddle. Also, learn how to fall. I told her that if she wasn't enjoying it, despite the precautions, she should stick to dressage. While I was in the spinal unit, I received a visit from one of my long-standing heroes, the event rider Lorna Clarke, who lived in the south of Scotland. For me, it felt like a visit from royalty, only much better. She was fun – wry, to-the-point, supportive, and very kind. Lorna, possibly one of the toughest eventers of all time, once rode three horses around Badminton. She was expert at calculating risk.

One never escapes it. Living is intrinsically dangerous. And horses, for all their gentleness, are intrinsically deadly just to be around. Probably as many people get hurt on the ground, kicked or crushed, as do from falling off them. Some years ago an academic called David Nutt was forced to resign as chair of the Home Office's Advisory Council on the Misuse of Drugs after saying that taking ecstasy was no riskier than 'equasy', a term he invented to describe people's addiction to horse-riding. He may have been tongue in cheek; he was also spot on. The debate is about choice and freedom; about balancing risk with sensible precautions. Even after my experiences I would defend to my last breath the right of anyone to choose life, excitement, sport and adventure. Accidents happen. I could have broken my neck tripping over a kerb. I used to console myself that at least my accident happened while I was doing something moderately exciting, however much, in the same moment, I wished to God I had been wise enough to give up jumping when I turned fifty and stick to dressage, where the odds of injury are lessened. I used to be a little scared doing cross-country jumps but the thrill was always bigger than the fear. Because it brought that sense of being alive, properly alive, pushing and scaring yourself; examining that implicit contract with the devil which tells you you're willing to accept the risks and suffer the consequences. As ever, the best piece of advice in life is the one you could have given to yourself, but chose not to.

One of the most moving letters I have received came from an experienced horsewoman, a stranger, who believed I had saved her life. 'Who would have thought that as my life flashed before my eyes it would be your name that was in my final thoughts?' the woman wrote.

'I followed your remarkable story from the silly fall onwards. I told people about it. I gave up hunting because of you. But at fifty-four I still felt that I was the right person to rehabilitate old racehorses.'

She told me one horse had retired and she got another. 'On a dull hack, out of nowhere, he produced the kind of monster buck that is the stuff of nightmares. Amazing how much time there is whilst in the air, even at speed, to work out the likely prognosis. But one thing I wasn't going to do was drop onto my head, and all because of the story you wrote about your fall. Every fibre made me twist and turn and take up those final moments to fall with my weight spread as much as I could onto my shoulder. And there was that moment of – '"Can I move? Oh dear I have got to try."

'It's been seven weeks and my broken shoulder is healing well, and I can't wait to get the strength back to ride again. But it won't be a thoroughbred, I am afraid, it will be a quieter native pony. It is very possible that it is only because of your story that I can even contemplate this.'

And so I sat within my ghost body, and tried to advise people to be sensible but also, whatever they chose to do, to do it with a light heart. They shouldn't worry or fret. One of my favourite quotes remained that of Sir Sydney Smith, 1771–1845. 'One great remedy is to take short views of life. Are you happy now? Are you likely to remain so till this evening? Or next week? Or next month? Then why destroy present happiness with distant misery, which may never come at all, or you may never live to see it? For every substantial grief has twenty shadows, and most of them shadows of your own making.'

That was the idea. Try as I might, though, my thoughts kept coming back to what wasn't there any more: action. The cruel dreams, the night-time liberation of the mind from the paralysed body, had not stopped when I left the spinal unit. One night I dreamt I was organising a ski race, not on a mountain but in a snow-covered car park, and the female contestants were all girlie types who shrieked and wobbled, teetering on the fall line afraid to let themselves go from the starting gate. Eventually, it was my turn; I launched myself, arrogant, able-bodied, but something went desperately wrong and my skis were sticky and my legs disobedient and I lurched, unwieldy as a novice, snow-ploughing to the finish. I also had a recurring dream where I was leading a horse in order to turn it out in a field. My dream walks were always slow and deliberate, methodical, but the critical thing was the fact my legs were working. That dream had variations; it featured different horses, some familiar, some unknown. One morning I dreamt I was leading Fergus, talking to him, walking shoulder to shoulder, his great head lowered to listen, and immediately upon waking I burst into inconsolable sobs, so strong was the sense of loss, of comfort snatched away. The reality of yet another morning shrink-wrapped to the bed was too much to bear.

How to begin to describe Fergus? Not easy. Horses are like boyfriends: memories of a very few stay with you all your life; the rest are a blur, inconsequential, names and faces faded. Some, the embarrassing ones, deliberately so. Just as you wince at the memory of kissing some frogs, so you try to forget some of the horses you gave house-room to, the ones which wouldn't box or stand or clip or eat or perform; the barger who you got impossibly cheap; the monsters like Horrid Dan with lousy feet who you bought despite yourself because he loved to jump and that was really, really, really what you wanted to do. But Fergus was epic, a huge presence; one of the chosen. He was also a minor national treasure, a police horse who came to me from the charity World Horse Welfare after doing nigh on twenty years of unbroken public service on the streets of Glasgow. He lived to thirty-six, setting the record (I believe) for the greatest longevity of his kind. I loved him to bits, as did the cops he served. They called him the banker, the one that never let them down.

Fergus, a 17.2 part-bred Cleveland Bay, understood most things. He looked at you with ineffably wise eyes that had seen everything; he obeyed without question. You could lead him without a rope or – though we never did – bring him in the house. Under saddle, meticulously schooled in the old cavalry school of policing, he could go backwards and sideways as fast as he would go forwards. He was an extraordinary mixture of boldness, courtesy and caution; a lion of a horse who was scared of absolutely nothing but would also, if necessary, test the ground with each foot before he put weight on it. Other horses deferred to him instinctively; they knew he was king. His iron will was forged through the heavy civil protests of the late 1970s and 80s: the miners' strike, the poll tax riots, student marches; the vicious cauldron of Glasgow football riots, all in unpaid service to mankind. He was like the eponymous hero in Rudyard Kipling's short story 'The Maltese Cat', one of those few horses everyone got truly sentimental about. The police, who should have put him down when his tendons went, aged twenty-three, instead patched him up for retirement. That's when he came to me. He was never an affectionate horse – after so many years of having to endure Rangers and Celtic fans and Glasgow drunks blowing whisky fumes up his nose: 'Haw, Trigger, gie's a kiss' – but his intelligence made him an honour to have around. He was also a supremely good listener. That's the magic of horses: they soak up human pain; they pass no judgement; they are a leaning post and a sounding board and solace for the soul. And thus, in my dream, as I walked I confided in him about my accident, about my stupidity in falling off, about the crushing guilt that burdened me.

There is an amazing equine life-saving story which involves Fergus, one that defies anthropomorphism, one I would not have believed had we not witnessed it, although I have since read about other remarkable incidents where horses have intervened to help their companions. When Fergus was nearing the end of his life, a frail old soul of thirty-four (human equivalent, about a hundred), he lay down on the side of the hill. It was something he did a lot, enjoying the sun, the freedom, the view. Only this time he made the mistake of going down the wrong way, with his legs facing up the hill. When he wanted to get up, he couldn't get the purchase to fold his back legs under his haunches. My husband saw him struggling and rushed to try and help, but as he got close he looked up to see my other horse, Horrid Dan, charging at him, ears flat back and teeth bared. Dan – the afore-mentioned crib-biting, flat-footed eventer – was a bad-tempered sod, talented but aggressive and extremely threatening towards humans, given half the chance. Dave, non-horsey but streetwise, did the only sensible thing and hurried away.

The fit young sports horse proceeded to attack Fergus. At least that's what it looked like. He pawed and nipped at him repeatedly on the ground, ripping his rug with his teeth. When Dave tried desperately to intervene, waving his arms, shouting, Dan threatened him again with bared teeth and heels. My husband retreated again, in shock, thinking he was about to witness murder. Would you call it equicide? Friends arrived to help and to their amazement realised they were in fact watching the opposite. Dan was in instinctive life-saving mode – he knew, as a fellow creature of flight, that being stuck on the ground meant death. He was determined to get his companion back on his feet. When the pawing and nipping didn't work, the younger horse did something remarkable. He grasped Fergus's ear in his teeth and then reversed, like a dog pulling at a stick, until he had dragged the stricken animal down and round, through ninety degrees, so his legs were pointing downhill. Horses' ears are particularly sensitive. Fergus squealed with pain, but as soon as his legs were facing the right way, he heaved himself to his feet and shook himself off. The two horses, both saver and saved, touched heads and then, cool as you like, wandered off to graze together.

That was the kind of magic that horses could give you, a depth, a fascination, which lay beneath the thrill of riding. How was I now, cerebral-me and useless-rest-of-me, to give this up? How did I deal with a love affair with horses? It was like being asked how you felt about the man you adored who had betrayed you and ruined your life. Do you see him again? Do you even start to explore your feelings at all? Do you stalk him on Facebook, and humiliate yourself by begging his friends to tell you who his new woman is? In the early days in hospital the horse issue was blanketed by shock and emotional numbness and I think I was a little bit like that deranged loser in love. I

Horrid Dan ate fences the way he ate people ...

had a subscription to the weekly magazine *Horse & Hound*; Dave brought it into hospital and I read it, even quite enjoyed it, passed it on to another patient, a riding instructor who had had a spinal tumour. Besides, I had been so touched, after my accident, to receive a card signed by the staff at the magazine wishing me well. In much the same way, I saw paralysed motor-bikers reading bike magazines; young paralysed women reading fashion magazines. Several friends asked me, hesitantly, what my attitude was to horses, hedging around it, trying to find out if it upset me to talk about it; or whether I wanted to ride again, should such a thing be possible. Other people assumed I would slam the door on the horsey world. My big brother, seeing me reading *Horse & Hound*, gave me the incredulous stare of he who visits the asylum and leaves in despair and bewilderment at the madness he finds.

'I don't like to say anything … but how can you enjoy that kind of stuff now?' he said.

Dear rational Andrew, the gentle giant who had suffered such distress when his beloved little sister, who he'd mentored all his life, had hurt herself so gravely. He lived on the West Coast of America and had been unable to reach me for weeks after my accident, because of the ash from the Icelandic volcano. Now he crossed the globe frequently to support Dave and me in any way he could. But he wasn't horsey, and he was very logical and sensible, and he struggled to see me still interested in horses. He had a very valid point. Untouched by the passion. I suspected Dave, too, loathed horses now, but was keeping a tactful silence.

Try as I might to avoid it, the issue managed to ambush me. When I was on a weekend visit home from hospital my dear friend Kate, who has since died of a brain tumour, offered to help sort out my clothes. She brought bags of them down from the upstairs bedroom where they had been stored for nearly a year and she and I had begun the by-then-familiar game of Keep-or-Throw when, unexpectedly, the next item in the pile was a pair of riding breeches. She held them up and she and I stared at each other wordlessly for what seemed like a long time.

'I just don't know,' I said eventually. Another long silence. 'Shall we keep them just now and see what happens? You could put them right down on the bottom shelf out of sight.'

She nodded, carefully expressionless, and did as I suggested. Ordinary clothes were bad enough, beset with loaded imponderables. At that point I hadn't a clue what fitted my shrunken, sexless, uncooperative frame or what it might one day be capable of. What kind of trousers could I wear – and how did I find out, other than an exhausting lying-down trying-on session? But riding clothes were another league altogether of poignancy. Bad enough the acute bereavement for jeans and smart pumps, lost for ever; but the sight of breeches and jodhpurs and riding jackets, the unattainable desire of that small girl in the back of a car forty-odd years ago, craning at a shop window, was profound.

At that point I simply didn't know what I felt or what I wanted, so I equivocated, telling people I'd like to reach the stage where I had a choice about whether or not to ride again. Only when I had the potential would I choose. Part of me yearned to be close to a horse again, to bury my face in its neck and inhale that sweet, heady smell, just as you would your ex-lover. But the hurt, the sense of loss and powerlessness, the knowledge that nothing would ever be the same again meant the idea was terrifying. And besides, I felt it would be utterly selfish to put my family, after what they had already endured, through the additional worry of seeing me mount a horse again.

Addicts are so called because they're addicted. They go on the wagon, but then they lapse because they are left with a void which needs to be filled. My void in the beginning seemed all-encompassing. When I got home reminders of a horsey life-style were all around: the stables, the riding arena, the empty fields, the vanity pictures of me jumping hanging on the kitchen wall. If I wanted to escape memories of horses, then the only thing to do was live elsewhere. Like a big fat weevil in my brain, the relationship between dangerous sport and its retribution bored away. It posed a deeper question, too, one I had difficulty addressing. Could paralysed people ever find real beauty and compensation elsewhere, once movement has been taken away from them? Despite everything, that was still what I craved.

That's the glorious obsession of all risk sport; the degree of passion held; the capacity for madness within us all. People who crash fast cars want to drive again. Lone sailors who capsize return to sea. Mountaineers can never resist the lure of mountains. Nobody stops wanting to be liberated. And such people can be really cavalier with fate. I am reminded of my friend Ian, a climber, high on Denali, Mount McKinley, in Alaska, who made the decision not to go for the summit because he knew he would lose his fingers to frostbite. And who watched, in horror, as others went on, and did so. Later, back in the frontier town nearest the mountain, he had a distressing encounter with one of them, an elderly Czech climber, who held out his rotting hands, too far gone to save, and begged for help.

On the good days, when I was feeling strong, I started to contemplate riding again. I wanted to revisit that old lover, see his face one more time. I told Dave and he shook his head and smiled wryly. He was aware how strong the addiction was. Months earlier, the chief executive of the charity Riding for the Disabled Association had emailed me, offering to help facilitate this should I ever want it. Now I wondered if it was physically feasible. Did I have enough torso strength to support myself once in the saddle? Could I be hoisted onto a horse again? Apart from anything else, someone had told me that the walking action of a horse was said to stimulate the core muscles and hips of riders. And on days when my bravado was high enough to allow a daydream, I contemplated doing paradressage. I had heard of another former inmate of the Scottish spinal unit who was now a successful dressage rider, using Velcro pads to keep her legs on the saddle. My friend Annie was less keen on the idea of disabled riding. After the glory and the speed of whizzing cross-country, she said, she didn't fancy going back to plodding around a dusty indoor arena on an old cob, held in the saddle by helpers. That was true; I didn't fancy that either, but I wanted to go there to find it out for myself.

My first task was to get up close and personal with a horse again. Fifteen months after my fall, I went to visit Tammy, a gentle old mare with kind eyes, a liver chestnut coat and sun-kissed blonde highlights. I think her owner, my friend Gillian, was more nervous than I was. We both cried a little, of course, while I got as close to Tammy as it was safe to, and she loomed over me, burying her rubbery lips in the crook of my neck. She sighed deeply, exhaling a sweet gust of grassy breath down my T-shirt, her whiskers tickling my cheek. Jane Smiley, the novelist, said that the eyes of a horse always told you something a little bit beyond your comprehension. They always asked more of you than you were able to give. For Smiley, the horse was life itself, a metaphor but also an example of life's mystery and unpredictability, of life's generosity and beauty, a worthy object of repeated and ever-changing contemplation. And, I could now add, a bringer of cruel harvest. I was pretty sure that the kind mare was aware of the tension and grief inside me. She didn't ask anything; she simply rested her nose near my face and offered profound, silent comfort.

I had never been sentimental about horses – they live, they die, some like Fergus were special and you cried over them, most were not and you didn't – but having them around was always a joy. You can be entirely rational about pleasure. They weren't my babies and I was far from anthropomorphic about them, but I loved their smell, their beauty, their grace, their generosity, the thrills of riding them. Some people needed to wear nice clothes or drink alcohol to forget or be happy; I needed only to stand in the darkened stable at night, listening to that primitive sound of big, placid creatures munching contently at their haynets. It used to make me feel at peace with the world. The moment with Tammy, of reconnecting with one again, the creature of my dreams, the slayer of my dreams, was an emotional occasion; a moment of intense bitter-sweetness. Going to visit my own horse, the one I had fallen off, was not an option: Terry was far away, in a happy hacking-only home, and it would have been too upsetting to see him. I never did. The woman who bought him sent me two sensitive emails to tell me where he was and how he was doing, and then backed discreetly out of touch. I was very grateful to her for that.

Still determinedly rational, in the cool shadow of Tammy's barn, I also realised exactly how limited I was around horses as an immobile tetraplegic. Even touch, that most elemental communication with them, was compromised by my inability to straighten my fingers. I couldn't offer a Polo mint on the palm of my hand. I couldn't grip her lead rope, or reach her neck, let alone have the endorphin-sparking satisfaction of a long, smooth caress down her shoulder. An affectionate rub with a clenched fist at the point where her leg joined her chest was my only option, and it really was second best. There was no way of leaning in and pressing my face into her coat for that unforgettably sweet, heady scent of grass and leather and warm horse, because I couldn't get close enough. The diver in the shark cage, unable to escape the metal skirts around her. The golden rule of being around these equines, for anyone, was always be ready for the unexpected and never, ever sit down or kneel next to them, at risk of being trampled or kicked should they startle. Stuck in a wheelchair next to a flight animal, I was utterly vulnerable, there totally on trust. I looked up, appraising the height to her withers, and quailed. How could I possibly ever get up there? From a wheelchair vantage point, she was impossibly tall and narrow. I wasn't capable of lifting my back-side high enough to slide up a board into the seat of an SUV, let alone standing and swinging a leg out from my hip. Once again the physical isolation of my condition was reinforced, the denial of proper, reciprocal touch with anyone or anything living.

Five months later, I was sitting in a saddle on top of a horse again.

CHAPTER TWELVE

WHEN MELLY MET NELLY

We had sold our horses in our fathers' time
To buy new tractors. Now they were strange to us
As fabulous steeds set on an ancient shield.
Or illustrations in a book of knights.
We did not dare go near them. Yet they waited,
Stubborn and shy, as if they had been sent
By an old command to find our whereabouts
And that long-lost archaic companionship.

EDWIN MUIR, 'THE HORSES'

The hoist tightened round my thighs and ribcage and scooped me gently into midair, backside dangling. Both my body and mind had entered a kind of private ice age; I stopped breathing some time ago. I was trapped in a most improbable confusion of present and past lives, swinging powerless in a hoist, as in hospital, but on a deliciously familiar horsey stage – cold echoey indoor school, earthy smells, dirty anoraks, the whispered shuffle of heavy hooves, creaky leather. As I was swung out into space I glimpsed below me, impossibly insecure and narrow, the waiting back of a horse. Then the hoist whirred again, and I was lowered onto the saddle, which I couldn't actually feel. I just felt a new sensation of perching, wobbling; and the helpers were gently stretching my legs down Nelly's sides. The mare was relaxed, uninterested; just a normal day in the office for her. The hoist was removed and I was upright, miles high it seemed, teetering, unsupported but for my hands wedged in a strap in front of me, beset with paralysis and anxiety.

'Breathe,' advised Sara Smith, my new mentor at the Riding for the Disabled Association.

She grinned up at me. 'It helps if you breathe.'

You know that kind of weird, detached sensation you sometimes get, as if you're an observer instead of a participant in your own life? As if things are happening to someone else, not to you? That's how it felt. Two worlds had elided. I was back, but in my new body. Twenty months after the fall, I had returned to the saddle and I didn't know if I was brave or crazy or a bit of both. Deep down, I was aware that, childlike, I was

On the hoist. Keep looking at Sara and
pretend not to be scared.

hoping that it had all been a bad dream and that horses might offer some strong magic to reawaken my old life. At the very least, I wanted to make reality a little better. Riding could do that.

Then there was the practical aspect. My recovery had progressed to the point where this had become possible. From alive-but-deader-than-dead Asia A, I had developed some power in my torso and much better balance. The emotionally loaded horse question had turned itself into a personal physical goal. It became an unspoken part of the challenge: not just to get on my feet again, but to see if I would ever become strong enough to sit in a saddle, hold myself upright in it, balance, stay on board, swing my legs. The stories of physiotherapy benefits from horse-riding were impressive – children with cerebral palsy who had revolutionised their core strength through being on the back of a horse. I wanted to see if I could do it. And there I was – not, sadly, poised in my dressage saddle, but flopped upon a wide flat treeless one suitable for disabled bottoms. But I was on a horse again.

Nelly was a twelve-year-old, 16.1-hands-high bay mare, one of those wise, easygoing, multi-talented horses who gift them-selves to the service of humankind. She'd been destined for eventing but proved too lazy. Nothing much bothered Nelly: she served as a vaulting horse for the disabled kids, cantering in slow, rhythmic circles while they leapt and somersaulted on and off her. She did a reasonable dressage test with a competent disabled or special needs rider; and she carried tense, very crip-pled people like me in ordinary lessons without turning a hair. That first time, I stayed on her back for a very short time. Initially, those first few minutes, I was terrified, not of falling off, or hurting myself – I was, with hindsight, stupidly cavalier about that – but of failure. What if I couldn't balance? What if I made a fool of myself and wasted everyone's time? What fools pride makes of us all.

Sara suggested we try a little walk around the arena and it struck me, as we readied ourselves, that to the outsider we must have had a certain timeless quality, the foot soldiers clustered around the badly injured comrade, ushering them from the field of battle aboard some requisitioned mount. I was starting to perfect that random, fly-on-the-wall perspective, watching myself with detachment. Sometimes self-mocking, sometimes in self-preservation, it was a way of making sense of the unfamiliar situations I faced. So there we were, a medieval grouping, with the horse ambling in the centre, dreaming of her haynet, and at both of my knees people designated as side-walkers, ready to grip a leg to hold me on board. One of them was my friend Tanya, who had driven me to the stables, and now was faintly grey with anxiety, hands hovering to catch me. Someone else was at the front, leading the mare; Sara was floating, the officer commanding the troop. After the first lurch, as the horse began to move, when I almost retched with alarm, it got easier. Even in that first brief taster, the feel was enticing: the sway of my body with the horse as she walked; the sense of connection and rhythm. I was a sack of potatoes by able-bodied riders' standards but I could, to my delight, hold myself upright, grasping that strap over the front of the saddle.

As soon as I could, I returned to the stables and sat on Nelly again: the second time felt so much better. My legs relaxed and I breathed. I got a glimpse of how much good her movement could do me in terms of physical and mental rehabilitation. My torso and hips swung with the horse's stride, mimicking walk-ing. Once again I was in touch with, communicating with, a living creature. I was forced to use every fraction of remaining active muscle I had to keep myself upright – exhausting, but possible in short stretches. The mind-wiping effect, though, was profound – there were brief snatches during the thirty-minute session when I concentrated so hard I simply forgot I was paralysed, something I never thought could happen. Sara, a woman possessed of a special quota of serenity, smiled at my improvement and said simply: 'Muscle memory is an amazing thing.' She'd seen it all before. Tanya, meanwhile, joked that the London Paralympics dressage might just be a little too close, but offered to groom for me at the next Olympics in Rio. The blood fizzed in my veins. Now I could have ambition and dreams again, although back in my wheelchair my emotions slumped at the old realities of the unhealed, unhealable body. But I tried to take my lead from the animals. Don't fret. Don't analyse. Accept. Be. Live placidly in the now. Therein, perhaps, lay peace and a greater wisdom. When a *Times* photographer came to take pictures and Nelly was asked to stand motionless, me balancing on her back inside a circle of flashlight umbrellas on stands, she earned even more respect. She snorted the first time and her skin flinched when the lights flashed; otherwise, heroically, she didn't move a muscle. Just out of shot, Sara hovered, poised to grab her reins.

The riding, like so many things I attempted to do, was always marginal. By that I mean I could only just manage it, pushing myself right to the edge of my physical limitations. The rigid tone in my legs was a real problem. To combat it I took a near enough maximum dose of baclofen. It reduced the worst of the spasm and made life more liveable. (Though God knows what it does to your brain or your body long-term. I once asked Dr Mark Bacon, the scientific director of Spinal Research, what the long-term side-effects were. 'Nobody knows,' he said apologetically.) Spinal injury's a bit like that all round: you make the best of it in the here and now. Don't ask too many questions. Don't look into the future. Don't make plans. You're lucky to be around.

In addition to a steady diet of baclofen, I started to use another drug, clonazepam, to soften my hips. Clonazepam is one of the family of benzodiazepines, sedatives and muscle relaxants (including Valium), much abused as street drugs and very addictive, but of serious practical value for spinal injuries. In hospital I used it to ease my telegraph-pole legs and allow me to put on my trousers when I was fighting FIM. Now, as the drug was quick-acting, I would take a quarter of a tablet once I had arrived at the stables, ten minutes before getting on Nelly, so that my hips would open enough to let me sit upright in the saddle, legs apart.

In the paralysed rest of my life, though, away from the escapism, other things were going wrong with my body. Only now was I beginning to grasp how fundamental guts were to all-over health; indeed, that they were probably responsible for much of my nausea, oedema and spasm since I left hospital. When your guts go wrong as a tetraplegic, daily life tips into out-and-out war, trying to combat bowel accidents at any time of the day. I went to extraordinary lengths to make sure I'd be safe on riding days, contorting myself for hours on the shower chair. It was a daily, gruesome form of torture. Mornings were indescribably hard. Later, when a mammogram showed I had developed atypical ductal hyperplasia (ADH, a kind of pre-pre-cancerous condition) in my right breast, I was absolutely convinced it was as a result of trauma caused by straining over the arm of the shower chair to reach my bottom. At the stables though, I could be released from ill health and hurt.

The sessions with Nelly were going so well that Sara carved out two lunchtimes a week when I could come. By now I had gained enough confidence and fluency in my car to be able to drive myself to the yard, another huge frontier conquered. In the car, there was free movement, autonomy – I found I could forget, however briefly, that I was paralysed. On Nelly's back, I felt the same liberation. I became the centaur, moving free again. Good RDA horses are amazingly steady, tolerant and forgiving. They wait. They endure. I had seen Nelly being ridden by the able-bodied staff, when she had leapt sideways and tanked off, mouth set against the bit; but when disabled riders were on board she was a saint. Or so I convinced myself at the time.

So often, the riding took away the spasms. Sometimes at the beginning of a session I had to prop my arms against the mare's neck, fighting to stop my body doubling up, but after five minutes of being led around the indoor riding school, I was able to relax my arms. I would still feel like one of those wooden dolly pegs with which our mothers used to hang out the washing in the 1960s. Then, after another ten minutes' walking, my pelvis would start to unlock and swing with the horse's movement. Then the spell would start to work. As soon as I softened, Nelly would walk more freely; and suddenly we were in tune, horse and rider as one. In a practised procedure, the side-walkers slowly fell back, giving us more space. Then it was just Sara leading the mare, and then she dropped physical contact and simply walked at her head, no lead rope. From nowhere, a little enchantment settled on us.

Subsequent weeks saw progress. I arrived one day to find Nelly tacked up in a normal saddle, instead of a treeless one. To my paralysed body it felt like swapping a seat astride a sofa back for one balancing on a wooden pole. Help, I cried inside. That saddle looked tiny. Hoisted aboard, the staff tucked my legs back behind the knee rolls and my pelvis automatically tilted forward, holding me erect. No spasm, no slumping now. I felt astonishingly secure, so much so that I could take my hands off the safety strap and wave my arms around and turn my torso. Three-quarters of the way through my allotted time, I glanced down at Sara and said, 'This is amazing. I could trot.' Her eyes lit up. She was an extraordinary mixture of patience and go-for-it elan. She made you feel anything was possible. She was a former British ski team racer, who once went downhill at ten million miles an hour. 'Well, if it feels right, it usually means it is right,' she said and while my jaw was still flapping she took hold of my knee, nodded at Matthew, the other helper, and asked the mare for trot. We did three strides: a bizarre, fleeting flashback of another life, another body.

Soon I was riding balancing just on my seat bones – hands holding the reins instead of clutching the safety strap. By now the staff were standing back much more, letting me be the one in control of Nelly. I began to trust the mare more and more, controlling her with my hands hooked into special loops on the reins.

Aside from the emotional solace, riding was proving to be remarkable physiotherapy. Nelly's walk did indeed mimic a human one; my pelvis swayed with hers. I could sit up straighter for longer. On one occasion, after I was winched off her back, my legs were so loose that I could lift them into the car myself – normally I need someone to do it for me. Suddenly, riding started to have some resemblance to how it used to feel: studying my position in the big mirror on the wall; trying to lift my upper body; keeping my shoulders back; pointing, to use the vulgarity beloved of riding instructors, my tits at the horse's ears. In the mirror, concentrating fiercely, I saw just me on a horse, striving for self-carriage and lightness, as in the old days.

For Dave, who came to watch me just once, it was poignant. 'It was just like seeing the old you riding at home,' was all he said. But if relationships work, at their deepest level, it is by generosity and he was delighted to see me so thrilled. Happiness is so often the result of trying to make someone else happy, or at least help them to be happy. Nelly was proving immense therapy. Increasingly I rode with Sara merely walking at my left knee. Then came the day she stepped back a few paces, and finally I started to ride independently, just me and the horse, a partnership based on balance and trust. When I got off, soon afterwards, my legs were actually floppy, my stomach muscles no longer in spasm. I was high as a kite, and it was nothing to do with any drugs. I gloried in the motion and the empowerment, steering Nelly around the school, my hands trying to establish a relationship with her mouth. Like old times. My hands, funnily enough, were softer, in the horse rider's sense of being sympathetic, than they had been able-bodied. Using a long stick in each hand to touch her sides, replacing the commands from my legs, I was able to persuade Nelly to relax her jaw and perform dressage moves – tight, ten-metre circles;

changes of rein; semicircles and loops. I built up to a serpentine, a multiple 'S' movement, pretending that I was normal, imagining that I was bending Nelly around my inside leg and allowing my outside leg to swing back behind the girth. Maybe, just maybe, the muscles would start to remember. A riding arena is marked with letters. Circle at B. Change the rein H to F. That alphabet was my release from prison – my weekly forty minutes of escape, forty which felt like five, it went so fast – me and her: slowly weaving our way around inside the chill indoor school, my mind wiped clean of anything but my communication with her.

The divine madness continued. In one session, from the moment I was hoisted onto Nelly's back, I could feel something slightly different; a loosening around the hips, the tiniest glimmer of a memory of what riders call a seat, a softness and connection. For the first time back on a horse I was able, by trying to wiggle my thigh, to achieve flickers of movement in my right calf, bringing it back against her side on the girth. I couldn't see it happening, which made it difficult, but Sara was my eyes on the ground. When my legs moved, the mare moved obediently sideways, or forwards, depending on my fumbled instructions. I was riding independently every session, and even starting to attempt shoulder-in, a lateral dressage movement where you ask the horse to walk forwards but with its body angled; its front legs on different tracks to its back legs. The centaur, within her little fantasy world, was getting ambitious.

Some time earlier, I had gifted the centre my dressage saddle – that powerful symbol of the past – and, by sheer serendipity, Sara found that it fitted Nelly's back. Thus I sat, snug within my own prized possession, the deep dressage seat holding me in an upright position, opening up my hips at the front and straightening my legs.

'When you ride you don't look like a paralysed rider any more,' Sara told me one day. 'We have crossed a line. Up until now, I taught you with my eye on your vulnerabilities, always ready to intervene. Now, I'm teaching you as I would any horse and rider, trying to create improvement. We've been set free.'

Despite what was to unfold, I still regard that as one of the nicest things anyone has ever said to me in connection with my riding. We all had to be patient in our dream chasing, but oh, I was so upbeat. We were kindred spirits, Sara and I, both unable to resist a challenge. She entered me for my first dressage competition as a tetraplegic. The test was at Level 1a, walk-only, for the most physically disabled riders, and the occasion was a Riding for the Disabled Association regional qualifier, fortuitously being held at her centre.

As a spectator sport, it was at the watching-paint-dry end of dressage – no trotting, no cantering, no music and most certainly none of the extravagant movements you see in dressage at the Olympics: piaffe, passage, half-passes, flying changes, where high-trained horses display a kind of supreme, controlled but explosive equine ballet. No, from the ratings point of view, this was the opposite of spectacular. All I had to do was to get my carer to dress me in riding clothes, wedge my oedema-plump feet into jodhpur boots, and then be judged ambling around an indoor riding school: a grey-faced spectre, frozen but for the flappy elbows, steering a placid horse in diagonal lines, circles and smaller circles.

My dear friends got me there on time and turned me out well, grooming the old stains off my riding jacket, tying my stock tight around my neck for me. They admired my substitute breeches, a pair of £4 oatmeal-coloured leggings which Barbara had sourced in Primark, because proper breeches weren't stretchy enough to fit a urine bag down the thigh. And lastly, before the hat, they put my hair in a net. Hairnets, a relic of the elegant, haughty Victorian horsewoman, mounted side-saddle, with a habit and a veil.

I had a flashback, fleeting, stabbing. The neck brace. My dinner-plate-sized view of the sky. Moving away from the whirling rotor blades and there was the A&E doctor's face, the pretty blonde one, leaning close; warm, friendly, warning me I was about to go into resuscitation. And then, amused, she was disentangling something from the top of my head, dangling a cobweb of nylon into my field of vision.

'What on earth is this?'

'A hairnet,' I explained. 'To keep my hair tidy under my hat.'

Tidy above an exploded spine. How silly, how eternally poignant, the minutiae of normality alongside utter, screaming catastrophe.

That competition day with Nelly, the glory was to participate. For many of the vulnerable people who attend Riding for the Disabled, it was as great an achievement as any Olympic medal by an able-bodied athlete. To my amusement, I found out I was the only person entered in the walk-only class, therefore the most solitary humble of the humble. Unless I really stuffed things up, it seemed, I might be about to win my first ever dressage class. Sara would be there to call out the movements to me but, like a child sitting a music exam, I had conscientiously learnt the test myself. My judge, I was told, was to be Lady Hope, whom everyone called Mary, a woman much loved in the horse fraternity. I had heard complimentary things of her in the past, but you were always slightly scared of dressage judges; they could be terrifying. She wanted to meet me beforehand and I remember her drawing up a chair next to me in the hall outside the riding arena, exuding warmth. It turned out she read my newspaper column.

'I'm so thrilled to meet you,' she said. 'I know I shouldn't tell you this when I'm about to judge you, but I'm your number one fan.'

Still smiling from the encounter, I was hoisted off the platform onto the gleaming, polished Nelly, mane plaited, hooves oiled. The girls had worked so hard on her. There was a potential for drama. Nelly was in season, a female on edge and at the mercy of her hormones, and in order to keep her settled during the competition a small pony, a gelding, was brought into the indoor school as her companion. In human terms, you might describe him as a walker, the kind of non-threatening, asexual manfriend a famous woman might take to parties while she hunted for prey. Grey-haired and testicle-less, he stood bored in a corner, oblivious to Nelly's bottom-wiggling.

And then everything was up to me, to my voice and the give in my hands, and the cooperation of a good-natured big animal. Heart thumping, very alone under the fluorescent lights in a big empty arena, we entered the stage. She who had lost her body could once again, in partnership, create free movement again; she could put on the show required for the judge and the small audience watching from the benches at one end.

Live in the now. Breathe.

Enter at marker A, at X halt, immobility, salute. Keep breathing.

Proceed in medium walk, track left at C.

The discipline of remembering the dressage test and riding the mare with what function I had left erased my mind of corrosive things. Frozen hands made suggestions along narrow reins, and Nelly answered. The body continued to balance. And the mare held calm, a little bored, going where I asked in a rhythmic walk in a nice shape. I had never felt more alive, out in the middle of the arena, beyond help. The funny thing is, I didn't feel at all precarious. Unbeknownst to me, Zen Master, my friend from the spinal unit, was by sheer coincidence in the small audience. His daughter was a competitor too. Afterwards he emailed me:

> I wonder if that's a world record; two dozen people simultaneously holding their breath for four minutes. Frozen until your final salute. At first you seemed so vulnerable up there, but then I saw a horse striding with absolute concentration, so aware of her huge responsibility to you, and also to the rest of us audience, readers and medical staff who have shared your anguish over the past two years. A glass of water would not have spilt on Nelly's quiet back. An achievement to have done it; yes indeed, but by far the greater achievement to have arrived to Enter at A at all. Four minutes of a dressage test – less than the sum of its parts. Well done Melanie; admit and enjoy the sheer scale of what you have achieved.

He saw it, of course. He was aware that only by the good grace of the horse was I balancing on her back, something I had chosen not to dwell on. Only Nelly's good behaviour, and my

Finishing my first tetraplegic dressage test, both first and last.
Bottle the look of happiness in my face.

trust in it, kept me aboard her. My vulnerability was absolute:
if she had moved unexpectedly, sideways or forwards, I had no
power in my body to respond or grip. My hands alone could
not hold me on.

Evidently, we made a sufficient combination for the test. I
was delighted to show more promise as a disabled rider than I
ever did able-bodied and Lady Hope gave me 69.4 per cent, a
respectable score; in fact, one of the best I've had in my life.
And of course, as the only entry, Nelly and I came both first
and last, a suitable commentary on the state of my life. The red
rosette still hangs in my kitchen, as does the one for sixth place
which we won in the subsequent Scottish RDA dressage

championships walk-only class. I was beginning to dream big and Sara was encouraging me.

Where my body was concerned, I had reached a state of strange duality: although my internal health was deteriorating because of my guts, there were definite improvements on the muscular and neurological side. Bad and good thrived together. Bad, I was all too aware, dominated. At the spinal unit, I asked Dr Purcell to refer me to a colorectal surgeon – I had decided the only way out of the daily torture was a colostomy, rerouting my intestines out of my stomach and bypassing the stasis of the lower bowel. Graham Sunderland was a doctor with an evident sense of humour, which struck me as rather essential in his job. His was well-paid, vital work and he was hugely in demand, but it was not the most glamorous end of life. Either you were consulting, and your time was spent wearing a sympathetic face and listening to lengthy tales of gut ache and jobbies, or you were elbow-deep stitching up coils of intestines. As the song went:

We praise the colorectal surgeon
Misunderstood and much maligned
Slaving away in the heart of darkness
Working where the sun don't shine.

He agreed with me that I had reached the end of the road and was a candidate for a colostomy. I was entering new territory, and it scared me, but I told myself it was reversible and if a miracle happened and my innards started to function again, I could revert back. The date was set for the operation.

Meanwhile, despite the nausea and the oedema, my optimism about my neurological recovery was high. It was by then almost three years since my accident and I was still noticing improvements, infinitesimally slowly, unpredictably – but unmistakably. With the self-carriage that the riding required, my torso muscles were flourishing, to the extent that two weeks before the date for my colon surgery, I had a breakthrough with my walking, and I use that loaded word deliberately. It was extraordinary. Everything came together. Legs, torso muscles, stamina. I found myself walking up and down the living room, turning, pausing, pushing the Topro Taurus frame myself with ease, full of breath, confident, unstrained. I felt light. It was all I had dreamt of. A phased leap in recovery, Kenny the neuro-physiotherapist acknowledged. Like all of his profession he was cautious verging on sceptical about spinal recovery. I did so well we tried again, this time with Dave filming me on my iPhone. That thirty-second clip is now a precious snippet, a window that opened – there I was, leaning with my elbows on my frame, but walking forwards all by myself, slowly, rhythmically, independently, calmly, my torso strong enough not just to support me but to create forward momentum. In the background Kenny lurked with the wheelchair, a large incontinence pad on the cushion as a reminder of my fragility. I have never managed to walk better since, or to push the frame of my own accord like that, and I am in no doubt that it was the therapy from horse-riding which strengthened and suppled my torso. And who knows how much more I could have improved if I could have continued riding long-term – another poignant 'what if' to keep me warm on a winter night.

Shortly afterwards, ten days before I was due to go into hospital for my colostomy, I heard that I was to receive an award. The trustees of the Riding for the Disabled's national organisation wanted to present me with the Birt Spooner Cup, awarded periodically to someone who had done an exceptional amount for riding and disability. I was supposed to go to London to be presented with it, but my underlying health was such I could not travel so far. It was determined that the cup would be couriered up and that the Scottish head of the charity would present it to me at the stables when I was there for one of my lessons.

So much pitch-black irony abounds now, when I look back, that I quail in the face of it. Even me, with my darkest of dark humour. The Birt Spooner Cup, it turned out, was enormous: a solid silver extravaganza about a metre high, an ornate fussy monster of a trophy straight from a long-forgotten age of ostentatious display. Unfortunately, in transit, the cup had been dropped and badly bent: when propped on its stand – and we could hardly lift it; it was so heavy – it listed far to one side like a drunken relic. The whole thing was a little ridiculous and over the top.

'Never mind,' said Sara, chortling. 'I'll get it mended so it can grace your sideboard.'

The plan was that after my normal half-hour lesson, the four of us – Nelly, Sara, the charity lady and I – would do a quick presentation and pose for photos. The cup, meantime, was placed on the spectator benches of the indoor riding school, propped on a horse rug to stabilise it. The charity lady sat beside it, a pleasant person who wanted to watch my lesson. My cup, you might say, awaited me, though not quite yet overfloweth.

The routine was familiar. Nelly was led in; I was placed in the hoist and then lowered onto my dressage saddle, thinking, fleetingly, how much I looked forward to this now, compared to the apprehension of that first time, sixteen months earlier. As a standard warm-up in my lessons, I would do a couple of circuits with Sara walking at the horse's head, after which I would ride solo. The three of us moved away from the hoist.

And that's when Nelly decided there was a monster lurking behind the doors, and took off.

CHAPTER THIRTEEN

IN BED WITH A WALRUS

No matter. Try again, fail again. Fail better.
SAMUEL BECKETT

One of the popular definitions of insanity, usually attributed to Albert Einstein, is of doing something over and over again and expecting a different result. I don't think I would ever be classified as insane, but I was, with hindsight, naïve to convince myself that getting back upon a horse was without considerable risk. Aware in my rational brain that I was vulnerable, I preferred not to explore the consequences of another fall. Lightning was unlikely to strike twice. I chose merely to trust and hope and enjoy.

Nelly was not having a good day. With hindsight, she may have come into season, and her hormones were making her skittish. Or maybe there had been a first flush on the early spring grass, unnoticed by the staff, and she was a little intoxicated with sugar. Either way, she was not her normal relaxed self, and within a few strides, as we passed the doors of the indoor school, she became jumpy. Sara was at her head, controlling her by the mouth, talking to her. But the mare suddenly became electric, certain there was something terrifying behind the entrance she had passed a thousand times. As I clutched the saddle strap, and Sara struggled to hold her, she shied to the right and exploded into canter. Now, when half a ton of horse panics and decides to go, it goes. There is a finality to the act; several millennia of equine survival distilled into an instant, the instinct of a creature liberated from all reason and training. Horses have no weapons, they escape predators by running away. They have lightning-quick responses, the fastest of any domestic animal, in order to live another day. To flee is to survive.

I think I stayed on her for the two strides it took her to mow Sara down under her front legs, but on the third stride I felt myself going. Or rather, I felt my head and arms going. Watching in the café, behind the glass divide, one of the stable staff said she saw something pink flying through the air. That was me in my favourite microlight duvet jacket. And just as I had felt only my head and shoulders take off, so they were the only things I felt land, some agonising, bewildering, empty seconds later. My left shoulder blade hit the rubber-chipped surface first, then the back of my head with a thump. The rest of my body landed too and was, well, still attached, but insensate.

In the shock and embarrassment that followed, I clawed myself up onto my left elbow, gazing down my unfeeling body, declaring to anxious faces: 'My neck's all right.'

My right thigh was slung across me, on top, as if I had been put in a recovery position.

Those words. The ones Dave hates so much.

'I'll be fine,' I said.

Bleakness and reflection, however, were for later. Lying there, the immediate priority was to get back in my chair. I had the self-composure to instruct them how to scoop me back into my wheelchair from the floor, an art drummed into me in the spinal unit. You lie on your back, your legs are elevated, and the chair is tipped over so its back, mimicking your shape, so it can be slipped under your hips. Then, with enough helpers, you and the chair can be lifted as one, the axles doing most of the work, the frame turning round the unbraked wheels. Subsequently I found myself in the café drinking sweet tea and telling them repeatedly I was fine and yes, I was OK to drive home and no, I didn't want a lift and no, I most certainly did not want to go to hospital to be checked out.

We even went into the yard with the drunken, lopsided Birt Spooner Cup and posed for pictures, me balancing the damn thing on my knee, smiling through the shock and still pretending, as hard as I was able, that I was OK. The alternative was unthinkable. And I did feel mostly fine. Oh, I knew I was jarred up – the right hip felt uncooperative, and it hurt enough to make me gasp transferring into the car. But I hadn't landed on it, there had been no impact, so how could it be broken? Once home, I transferred into my recliner chair to rest it. It ached. True, I felt a little queasy.

'How are you?' asked Dave.

'I'll be fine.'

It wasn't until I was trying to get from wheelchair to bed, quite late that night, that the pain kicked in as I moved. Pain that had me crying out and vomiting helplessly. I saw my husband's face turn into a mask. And I saw how swollen the hip and thigh was, the skin starting to go taut and shiny.

* * *

You reach a point when so many things are going wrong that there is nowhere to retreat to, not even your own head. I knew I had to take control of the situation, because as a tetraplegic I needed specialist care. I had an absolute dread of ending up in a general hospital where spinal expertise would be lacking. I weighed the odds of a 999 call, at 2 a.m., against waiting a few hours and asking my GP to instruct them to take me to the hospital in Glasgow where the national spinal unit was. In hindsight, it was risky, but it paid off. By nine the next morning the paramedics were putting the patslide under me, transferring me from bed to stretcher, and I was driven back to the same A&E I'd come into three years earlier. By now my hip was vast. Once again, I entered the familiar cacophony, the soundtrack of the NHS in trauma mode. Groundhog day. As ever, my perspective was that of the beetle on its back: the handovers from ambulance personnel; the checks; the forms; the cotton bud up the nose to check for MRSA; the smell of antiseptic hand gel. And how much easier it was the first time, when I was barely conscious, for this time I had the job of having to explain my plight. The exquisite embarrassment of being laid low by horses once more ... and repeating the story over and again to registrars and nurses and consultants who looked at me as if I was not just stupid, but *spectacularly* stupid.

'You were tetraplegic from a horse-riding fall, and you went back to riding?'

'Yes' – gibbering – 'but to Riding for the Disabled. It was for rehab. It's very safe.'

'But you ... fell off again?'

'It was a freak accident.'

But they'd already made their private judgements, and they'd put on that mask of studied neutrality which emergency staff wear when dealing with pitiful street drunks and overdosed addicts and foolish affluent middle-aged sporty types and vomiting Hooray Henry students, every social class finding its method of self-destruction. Their faces spoke of pity and exasperation and weariness, honed to a patina of blandness. Meanwhile, I continued to avoid meeting my husband's eyes and fantasised that the hospital trolley might slowly fold up and devour me, make me disappear, like a carnivorous plant. I would have really loved that to happen. Then I imagined a cartoon, in the first frame the image of a vengeful, sardonic God, glancing down over a low cloud, with a speech bubble coming from his mouth.

'I told you to stop horse-riding. No really, I TOLD you to stop.'

And in the second frame, the finger pointing, the bolts of lightning: 'Kazam!!!' 'Boom!!!' 'Take that!!!'

The operation was quite a complicated one. I had broken my trochanter in two places, which made it a less than straightforward procedure and, as a result of my failure to go to hospital to be checked out immediately, the bones had been churning around for twenty-four hours. I had lost two litres of blood. The trochanter is the segment of bone at the top of the femur, the part that turns the corner from thigh bone to ball joint. It's a junction bone. Burning with a sense of desperation about the need to keep control of my body, or what little there was left of it, I described to the surgeon how, even though I was tetraplegic, I had learnt to walk a little bit again, after a fashion, and pleaded with him to repair me in a way which would allow me to continue mobilising. I was not usually a forceful person but I knew I had to be my own advocate in this. I'd heard horror stories of other paralysed people who had broken their hips post-paralysis but, instead of being operated on, had been left to heal as they sat.

My surgeon inserted something called a gamma nailing, a ferocious-looking bit of ironware resembling a long poker with an handle jutting out at the heavy end, the top. The shaft went down the inside of my femur to the knee, presumably by screwing or hammering and brute force – one really doesn't want to think about these things – and the handle bit screwed into the ball joint. Thanks to a combination of paralysed nerves, a sedative and a low spinal anaesthetic, happily not a general, I slept throughout the procedure.

Afterwards, it's fair to say, I was a physical mess. My haemoglobin level was low and over the next three days I struggled to talk or lift my head as I was transfused with seven units of blood. And most of all it hurt more than any pain I've felt before – despite the fact I was paralysed. My new bedmate was a walrus, a vast, shiny-skinned mountain of sea creature, taut to touch, grafted onto my waist where my right hip and thigh used to be. At least when it was there it meant I wasn't alone. The walrus wept from a twenty-four-inch scar, studded with dozens of staples. Eighty-four actually; I counted them when they came out. Every single movement I made hurt, including the pain of the cannula twisting in my arm as I lay at night watching the dark syrup drip through it down into my veins.

The thing was, once again I couldn't resort to self-pity. Once again, my ills were totally self-inflicted. I had been exceedingly unlucky, yes, but I had put myself into a risky situation consciously. I couldn't even be bothered telling myself that it wasn't fair. It wasn't – but that changed nothing, and anyway horses have no sense of fairness. Yet again, I was the mistress of my own destiny. Rather than cry, I beat myself up for being such a fool, for causing my loved ones yet more grief, for giving myself more physical suffering, and for embarrassing myself profoundly. Once again, I fought the seduction of the morphine and tried to plot a way back for me and the walrus. Paralysed people broke bones all the time, post-accident, and were unaware of it until their limbs went blue and started swelling, I reasoned. It happened. It was routine. You went for it, because you had little left to lose. Or rather, you *thought* you had little to lose until you lost it, and only then you realised how important a 'little' was. The logic of risk seemed impeccable beforehand. Forty-eight hours later, after an urgent operation and a hip rebuild, there was no bravado left, just blinding physical and emotional misery. Blurry, relentless. Like looking through a car windscreen in a rainstorm.

Being back in hospital was ghastly; a reminder of how precious home was. Post-op, I was put on an acute surgical ward. Mixed, men and women. During the night it was desperately hot, airless, and I felt the wriggling, itchy texture of opiate on the inside of my eyelids. I tugged my theatre gown up, and pushed the covers down to the bit where the walrus started.

'Try and cover up, pet. There are men on this ward,' called the tough voice of a female auxiliary nurse.

Out of nowhere, anger flared. As if it was *my* fault if a bare chest upset some shitty man? As if somehow in the gloom a glimpse of my sad still carcass with its empty breasts would inflame passion or propriety? What a great metaphor: it's a man's ward; it's a man's world! Cover up, all pets, all females, lest you evoke evil desires. Briefly, silently, pointlessly, I seethed with rage, the blood pressure cuff tightening on my arm. All those decades wasted fighting that mindset. Did she want me to wear a bloody burka?

Then, amid my lathered internal diatribe, I remembered where I was: I was back on my back; back in the system. I had a master's degree in surviving the NHS system, if not a PhD, and the way to do it was to lie low, go with the flow, befriend the overworked staff. Chill. Cool your jets. No fancy stuff. No fuss. I pulled down my gown obediently. Life was ordinary. I'd done what hundreds of frail, compromised or elderly people do every day: I'd fallen and broken my hip. That's not to say I didn't have to be assertive. In the morning, I explained to the overworked staff that one of them would have to empty my bowels manually. Otherwise I could die. They looked blank.

'You have to do it, I'm afraid,' I said. 'I can't.'

'But we're not allowed to. That's abuse,' they said.

'It's not,' I said. 'That's a myth.'

'Sorry, we can't.'

Spinal-injury nursing is a very specialised area and when I had first gone home I had encountered this problem with one of my rota of district nurses, who regarded putting her finger up my bottom of a morning as abuse. I could understand normal reluctance – it's no dream job – but I had been startled by the implicit suggestion that I was asking her to cross some ethical line. Thereafter, she had been given special outreach training by someone from the spinal unit using a plastic model called Betty Bot. But evidently the myth was and still is to this day widespread among young nurses; and ignorance kept it in circulation. Here it was again. Wearily, I asked to see the senior nurse, and explained that if they couldn't or wouldn't do it, they'd have to phone the spinal unit, a hundred yards away, where this was a routine chore, and ask them to send over someone who could. I'm sorry to be difficult, I said, but it's critical for my care. As I lay and waited, I reflected that mine was a strange world indeed, where I must spend the morning negotiating with a group of complete strangers over the necessity and intricacies of having a poo.

It actually became almost fun, because a senior staff nurse I knew well came over from the spinal unit and gave a tutorial in bowel evacuation to the acute ward staff, clustered around her at my back.

'You see, I've widened your skills base,' I told them. 'You should be very happy.'

I'm sure several of them still privately thought it was abuse.

Word of my second fall spread and the head of the spinal unit came to see me; it was like getting a visit from God. Another God, not the cartoon one with the finger firing lightning at me. David Allan was always so fabulously quirky, almost perverse, in his views. He wasn't judgemental at all about my second horse fall. Far from it.

'In fact, I see it as a success story because it means your rehabilitation was going so well.'

He cheered me up hugely. Only an orthopaedic surgeon could say something like that. He explained that my trochanter must have been broken in a pendulum motion: as I hit the ground on my left side the right leg had whiplashed across the front of my body and, well, basically snapped itself at the top. I was very grateful to him for his moral support. As I was to my spinal consultant, Mariel Purcell, who snatched time to come to my bedside and dropped her usual cool detachment, expressing real dismay and sympathy. I pleaded with them both to persuade the colorectal surgeon that my colostomy should proceed, as planned, within a few days. I was in the right hospital, after all. My experience that first morning had convinced me that I had to fight for this as hard as I could. The senior nurses had already warned me that more surgery was an unthinkable infection risk while there was an open hip wound not far away. But I decided that consultants were far more flexible than the bureaucratically hidebound nurses and administrators: they were my only chance of making it happen. Graham Sunderland, the colorectal surgeon, came to see me. I pleaded with him; I tried to explain how my bowels had become impossible to manage and I simply could not go home like this, not now, not back to the daily torture on a shower chair when my mobility was even more compromised.

'It's too short a time between operations,' he said. 'It's a risk.'

'Please don't postpone it. If you lived in this body, you'd understand ... please.'

He stood up. 'You're a madwoman.'

He smiled and touched my shoulder fleetingly.

'OK,' he said. 'Let's do it.'

Looking back, it was one of the most humane gestures I have received from a member of the medical profession. Later, I found out that he was a lieutenant colonel in the TA and had done a long stint at Camp Bastion during the Afghan War as a trauma surgeon, saving the lives of soldiers dreadfully injured by IEDs. He was a man who knew that sometimes situations are less than perfect. Risks were in perspective for him.

On the fourth day after the hip, and six days before the colostomy, a physiotherapist arrived at my bedside, a steely look in his eyes. It seemed unthinkable, but he was going to try and manoeuvre me and the walrus out of bed and into a wheelchair. As it turned out, some things were not yet quite possible. With a mouthful of strawberry-flavoured morphine gel and two people's assistance, I got as far as legs over the bed, propped from behind in an almost sitting position. The right foot didn't reach the floor but hung in the air, twisted inward by trauma, several inches above it. One gets used to physical symmetry; how strange it is to look down and see when it is taken away. Braced on my feeble arms behind me on the bed, unable to bend in the middle, I felt the world spin around me and the nausea rise.

By day five, I could sit on the side of the bed by myself; and then, with many expert hands and the use of a wooden transfer board, I managed to slide across into my wheelchair. It was as terrifying as a ship-to-ship transfer in a Force 10 must be, because the hip pain seemed biblical – there was the anticipation of it, which was worst of all, followed by the electrical jolt of its arrival. But from where I was right then, mentally and physically, the simple, successful change of position felt epic. It told me I could at least recover enough to be able to transfer myself into a wheelchair again, something I had secretly feared lost. Perversely, then, it was a corner turned: there is nothing like a double dose of disability to make you yearn for a single dose, nothing like two thumps in the face, or two sessions of torture, to make you appreciate just one. It was too much to ask to be healthy, I knew that, but a bit of a miracle to allow me to return to being just four-fifths crippled would be great.

By day six, I was able to get in my chair just with the aid of the nurses, and I started to wheel myself around the bed. There was slightly less pain every day. In the chair I could also access the back of my head with a brush for the first time: by now my bedhead didn't just resemble an eagle's nest; in this one you could hear the chicks hatching. Sara, as a kind of penance, came to see me with a tub of detangler and tamed it into a small, severe Jane Eyre ponytail at the nape of my neck. She showed me some of the bruises she had received when the mare mowed her down.

'What did happen with Nelly?'

She was one of the most experienced of horsewomen, the coach of coaches, a highly rational woman. And utterly direct.

'When horses go, they go.'

Both of us knew it really wasn't worth saying any more. The horse world is rather cluttered with people who always know best, who freely pass judgement on everything and nothing. Ignorance holds sway a lot of the time; and blame is a cheap horsey commodity, easily thrown. Sara and I were both wiser than that. When horses go, they go. Nelly went. I just wish she'd chosen a different day.

A word here about blame. Sometimes, in the early days after my neck break, people who didn't know me very well would ask me if I was going to sue. Someone, anyone. I found the concept strange. Why ruin someone else's life as well as my own? I can well imagine the trauma that the instructor who was teaching me that day must have experienced; indeed, much later, from a third party, I learnt of her distress. I was sorry that she got hurt too. All this came rushing back to me at the time of the famous rescue of the Thai boys from the cave. The football team had been taken into the caves by their coach, Ekapol Chanthawong, and the Western media was straining at the leash to blame him. The response from the parents exposed the beauty of the Thai culture against the ugliness of our own. 'If he didn't go with them, what would have happened to my child?' said the mother of Pornchai Khamluang, one of the boys in the cave, in an interview with a Thai television network. 'When he comes out, we have to heal his heart. My dear Ek, I would never blame you.'

By then I was able to transfer from bed to chair without any fast-acting morphine at all. The sickening bolts of pain had gone and the physios produced a special power-assisted frame to get me upright. Crying out at the shock of seized joints being wrenched open, I managed to stand up for a few brief seconds and my left knee straightened a fraction. The surgeon told me I could start weight bearing on my repaired hip but so far the knee was too crooked to let the foot reach the floor. Just before the second operation, as if to reassure me that, however bad things were, they could always be worse, I was transferred to the female orthopaedic trauma ward. In reality, it was a geriatric hip-repair ward, where tiny old ladies, white-haired sparrows, lay in serried ranks with their broken hips, confused and plaintive. Of all my time within NHS walls, this was the saddest place. This was where they came, the demented and the rambling, when they fell in care homes and broke their bones. Often, when I heard nurses being harshly criticised, I wished their critics could spend the night on one of these wards. Listening down the cavernous empty spaces of the small hours, when the misery ratcheted up and the soundtrack soured. That was when, unseen behind those same thin curtains, many of the patients turned into aggressive banshees, goaded by dementia and pain.

Here were yet more unwritten comedy scripts, humour at its blackest, the foul-mouthed Glasgow grannies turned comic assassins. It was rather wonderful hearing women swear like this.

'Yer fucking bastard, get your fucking hands off me. Aaaaaargh, yer fucking bitch, you're hurting ma leg.'

And the calm, pleasant voice of reason: 'I'm not actually touching your leg, Jeannie, please mind your language, now if you could just roll a little to the left.'

'Away tae fuck, yer fucking pest.'

'Jeannie, please stop trying to hit me and roll to your left.'

Simultaneously, there were other conversations going on. Full volume.

'Yes, Mary? You buzzed.'

'What's your name, dear?'

'Linda.'

'Brenda?'

'Linda.'

'Brenda?'

'LINDA!'

'What time is it, dear? I need to go home.'

We never hear about this, when standards of compassion in the NHS or in care homes are criticised. We never read in reports about the effing and blinding and theatre of street abuse – or hear the sounds of bashing and crashing as the patient flails at the nurses. Humanity at its most raw and painful. The other little old ladies and me, those of us still in possession of at least some marbles, cowered beneath the blankets. Then morning came and I found myself being prepared for the colostomy operation – my insides flushed, my consent sought, my watch removed. On one side, the aching long hip scar, but now there were fresh body maps – black marks inked on my tummy, guidance for the surgeon as to where to fish out my guts to the surface. Go in here. The dreaded black spot. And then, in what seemed only ten minutes later, I was back in bed but had a bit part in *Blue Planet*, exploring a whole new exotic underwater world. The friendly walrus was still there, in place of my hip and thigh, and he'd been joined on the other side by a bright red sea anemone, as rare and perfect as anything ever glimpsed through a diver's lens, which blossomed on my stomach.

It was housed in a clear bag glued to my skin. I lifted the bedsheet and sneaked glances at it, watching for signs of life. Occasionally, it burped dreamily at me from behind the plastic, just like a sea creature. That, I realised in slow wonderment, was what in a former life was once a fart. But what was it like, that former, healthy, thoughtless life? I could barely remember it now. Two days after the colostomy operation, I was shattered, perhaps justifiably after two major operations. My body was so battered I felt at times like giving up control and letting it drift completely into the hands of others. Stop trying. How tempting that was. Everything hurt. The orthopaedic physios got me standing, weight-bearing, both knees straight, both feet flat on the floor, but the pain was such I only lasted a minute, then maybe another twenty seconds, before the grey mist and the nausea swirled in.

I felt it was a victory to have managed that much, however, and perversely, according to the gospel of Pollyanna, I took some comfort from the fact I was feeling pain. The nerves were most certainly not dead. Every day came tiny improvements and the walrus was taking its leave, my thigh shrinking back to ordinary size. The wound ached, the knee rolled inward, and the pelvis was like piano wire, but the agony receded. By now I was on a new learning curve: visits from stoma nurses to give me lessons in how to manage my new acquisition. Happily my damaged fingers could do it. My stomach resembled the Pompidou Centre, all my vital service ducts down the outside of the body.

Nobody lingers long in the modern hyper-managed NHS, where beds are so precious. Only the old ladies with broken hips log-jammed. Some were operated on but lapsed into confusion from the shock and an inevitable urinary infection, and you could see them starting to slip away. Most were waiting for beds in care homes. Some would never stand again; never return to their own homes; within a few months a horribly high proportion would die in hospital or in a care home. One woman in her nineties, in the bed diagonally opposite me, had the imperiousness of a retired academic, or a former headmistress when she arrived. Her broken hip had initially been misdiagnosed: such was her tenacity, her scorching resilience, that she had been dragging herself around her flat for a week before she had eventually convinced them something was seriously wrong. Her desire to live was magnificent: she gazed around like a hawk, listening to conversations, tidying her possessions on the bedside table, establishing control in her new settings.

She overheard me explaining yet again through gritted teeth to a new physiotherapist how I was already a tetraplegic from falling off a horse, and yes, I'd fallen off again, but I was determined to keep walking.

'Are you the writer Melanie?' she called, crisply, after the physio had gone.

'Er, yes,' I said, embarrassed. 'Probably.'

'I read your articles.'

'Thank you,' I said, for want of anything else.

'You've fallen off another horse, then?'

However I tried to explain it, it sounded more unconvincing every time.

She appraised me with fierce eyes, and talked no more. Shortly after that she was taken away to be operated on. The next day, she lay, hardly visible under the blankets, a lost soul, deflated, demented, passive, her flame snuffed out by the ordeal and a urinary infection. Later that week I wheeled to her bedside and tried to talk to her, but she was just a shell. Just another statistic. I have no idea what happened to her, but it makes me sad to think.

To see it first hand, to share the distress and confusion of these old ladies through the nights, and witness the difficulties the staff had nursing them, was a deeply humbling experience. The reality of the NHS, though, is that entertainment is never far away. On my ward the only other patient under seventy-five apart from me was a woman my own age who was by her own admission a frequent in-patient. She was in constant need of drink and fags. She was being kept in for observation because she was suffering bad intestinal pain, but had been told she must stay in bed and shouldn't go out for a smoke. She didn't like that.

'This place is doing ma fucking head in,' she cried repeatedly.

Mine too, I thought, and yet again we only had our lifestyle choices to blame. We take our risks in different ways. Later, after she'd sneaked off for a fag and her son smuggled her in some alcohol, she was more content. As everyone else in our bit of the ward was away with the fairies because of urinary infections, she turned her attention to me.

'Ah'm fucking bored, hen. Have you got any magazines to read?'

I gave her all I had, which was, genuinely, a copy of a Sunday supplement filled with Gwyneth Paltrow recipes for a detox lifestyle, mung bean soup, balsamic-macerated berries, quinoa granola and spelt flour. My neighbour didn't talk to me much after that.

Soon after that I went home. My pelvis and lower back had seized up and now, morphine free, I was in constant pain; a new kind this, buzzing red hot from the waist down with a mixture of neurological spite and muscular-skeletal venom. Every time I tried to move I could feel one bit grinding against another; my body was like some decrepit piece of machine left to rust and now far beyond the reaches of WD-40. I felt very sorry for myself.

Pollyanna had had a bruising time, but her small voice endured. Just about.

CHAPTER FOURTEEN

AM I HUMAN OR
AM I DANCER?

I'm out of bed and dressed – what more do you want?
BANKSY GRAFFITI

It was going to be a long road back. Even Robert the Bruce's spider, I suspect, would have said, *Bugger this for a game of soldiers*, and gone off to find somewhere easier to build a web. 'Your body has endured two major assaults. Write off at least a year,' said one of my consultants. Everyone else agreed: *Please give your body time; it's been through a lot and it's understandably mangled.*

Spinal injury started to feel too big an enemy; it seemed determined to break me. It or me. A never-ending tie-break in the final set and I was facing yet another advantage point against me. A prison sentence with no hope of parole. The expression 'life-changing injuries' was the discreet euphemism used when someone had suffered brain injuries or broken their spine. What I was only beginning to grasp was that life-changing injuries led to further complications which changed your life even more. Ill health created more ill health. For every action there was a consequence. For all that I was paralysed and supposed to be unfeeling, the skin around the hip scar ached like bad toothache. At the colostomy site my tummy bulged, lopsided, my body out of alignment like a beaten-up teddy bear. Plus, the physiotherapists' adage that there was a 4:1 ratio of muscle loss to length of layoff haunted me. Every one day I failed to do any walking, however minimal, what pitiful muscles I had were wasting and would take four times as long to return. I started to wake in the middle of the night and convince myself that I was dying of all kinds of hidden nasties. Maybe other things had gone wrong – with my luck, they would, wouldn't they? – and I would be dead by morning. But because I was paralysed I couldn't tell and I would just whimper my last in the dark. I began to live in constant fear about my health and my brain grew tired with worrying. I was certainly losing my grip on my assumed identity, Mrs Happy Smiley Make-the-Best-of-it Tetraplegic. I was sick of being disabled and angry that I couldn't find a way out.

Much of this I had to internalise. Dave, poor guy, was supportive and non-judgemental. What he told his mates in the pub may have been different. He did not get angry with me; and my reciprocal duty, I felt, was to pretend that I was cheerful and getting better speedily. So I hid my sense of hopelessness. I said 'I'm fine' a lot. I was getting good at damage limitation where my family were concerned. Hopefully I managed to conceal the worst of it from Dougie too – I broke the news of the fall to him in a phone call after the operation, making light of it, playing down the pain, emphasising the black humour, trying to spare him worry. Certainly he didn't have to make any mercy dashes to hospital. He was facing his finals; he had enough on his plate, but he was immensely kind and in that heart-wrenching parent–child role-reversal, he made me promise to phone him and talk stuff through, any time at all I needed to, if I was ever feeling really miserable.

Helen Gray, the wise and warm district nurse who had supported me ever since my initial accident, and a woman who had become vital to me, gave me a stiff talking-to. After she'd got me into my chair in the bedroom one morning, following my monthly catheter change, everything got the better of me and I started howling. I couldn't do this in front of my family. She hugged me and let me sob on her shoulder. Then she sat on the corner of the bed and appraised me.

'Take the extra-strong pain relief. Stop imagining stuff. Give yourself time. Most of all, stop dwelling on the unfairness of it all.'

She opened her hands, palms up.

'We are where we are,' she said.

Of all the truisms of healthcare, I thought that was the best. It helped me. I wondered in passing how often she had said it to palliative care patients. What had happened with Nelly and the events that followed had really crushed me, dealt a much bigger psychological blow than I admitted to anyone. Out of loyalty to Sara and Riding for the Disabled, and to a certain extent because of my own embarrassment, I could not write about what had really happened in my newspaper column. I made oblique mention of a fall – after all, as I now knew well, falls came in a wide and diverse variety. Only family and close friends knew the truth. I had seen how the real story would be perceived by the outside world and I felt stupid and defeated enough.

For the first time, I started to acknowledge that everything which had fuelled me – all the fighting and the physiotherapy, the perseverance and defiance – was maybe a waste of time. Up until that point, I had stubbornly proceeded on the basis that I was going to regain more function, that my trajectory would be upwards, that my health would improve. This positivity was the strand that linked everything. Every time I had an operation, I used to quiz the doctors about whether it was reversible. The procedure to drill the hole into my bladder. The colostomy. 'Yes, yes,' they said, 'these things can all be reversed.' My bluff had been thumped out of me when I hit the floor of the riding school. Whereas before I had half-believed my own publicity and bluster, now I had to recognise that I was very vulnerable, and moving deeper into the permanence of disability. A new feeling of isolation ambushed me in private moments. There were occasions when I wept with the intensity of a child lost in the supermarket, crying for my mother to come back and make it all OK again. Like Tolstoy's Ivan Ilyich, my misery made me regress to the place where I could be petted and pitied like a child.

Hope faltered. Reversible operations would never be reversed. When I pulled apart my clothing, top from bottom, I looked down at an abdomen which was now a fully occupied waste disposal area. An industrial depot. Close to my left hip, the sea anemone of my bowel, stitched to the surface, mobile behind plastic. To the middle, the cursed catheter tube, gateway to a vital organ and repeated infection. To the right, a large patch of Tegaderm, transparent sticky plastic which stuck the tube to my skin and guided it towards the drainage bag on my thigh. (Made, I had been fascinated to discover, by 3M, the same people who make Post-its; I mean, who knew?) All in all, a less than alluring landscape. Who's gonna love you now, huh? I mean, really?

An email pen pal, Jeannie in Australia, cheered me up with admirable brevity. 'Isn't it marvellous how brave we can be when we really don't have any choice apart from topping ourselves?' It is indeed.

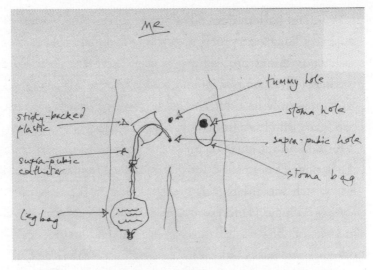

Who's gonna to love you now? My abdomen was a crowded
industrial area. (After John Callahan)

It took me a couple of months to understand how the colostomy had revolutionised my life, handing power over my
bowels back to me. I could manage the functions of my own
body, sitting fully dressed in my chair. I would have to wear
stretchy-waisted trousers for the rest of time, but it was a price
worth paying. Gone was the unbelievable torture of hauling
myself onto a shower chair every morning and sitting over the
loo; gone too were the bowel meltdowns which had been
making my life unliveable and turning me into a hermit. Now
I could, with help, simply wash in bed every morning; I was
liberated to travel to places overnight without taking a shower
chair and a special carer: and I could stay in accommodation
with less than perfect disabled facilities. Not only had my
misery quotient been slashed, but my life had to some degree
been returned to me.

A certain pattern descends when you come as an adult to disability. You have a problem, you learn how to manage it. For as long as things proceed on an even keel, that's fine. You become a little complacent and relax a bit. Then more things go wrong, only in a different way, and you're forced to raise your game and learn from scratch how to handle them as well. A forced learning curve on the graph, always lifting away from the flat line of normality. Thus it was one day at the hairdressers. Which was the bigger torture: getting my hair done or leaving it dingy? Hairdressing salons uniformly had fixed seats in front of their wash basins, all of them too low for me to transfer onto, but in order to cheer myself up with some blonde highlights, I had to get my hair washed on the premises. One place where a friend went had an electric seat for arthritic elderly ladies, which slid out and raised up in front of the basin. There I ventured and, after the laborious procedure of getting foils put in and waiting for the dye to work, I had to transfer from my wheelchair to the wash basin. But the seat was not ideal, the nylon cape I was wearing caught under me and trapped me; my hands slipped and I flailed and tipped backwards. As happened when I got flustered, my body went into spasm, and my legs stuck straight out. Alive but helpless, I was six feet of rigor mortis on the brink of sliding onto the floor – and without company because Dave had left me at the salon. He knew I'd be fine. Ha. But there I was, on my back, half off a chair, shrouded in black nylon, and blinded by great folds of silver paper hanging over my face. The young assistant tasked to wash my hair stood back, eyeing me with horror, unsure what to do.

'My nan manages that seat OK,' she said helpfully.

Other clients in the salon averted their eyes to the circus but watched covertly in the mirrors.

'Bend up my knees so my feet are on the floor,' I pleaded. She was just a kid; she didn't want to touch me.

'Now stand there and block my knees.'

In situations of obvious helplessness, you change the atmosphere in a room. You're embarrassed barking orders. Normal people are equally embarrassed, anxious, unsure what to do. You are making them feel uncomfortable. You are exerting a horrid kind of power over them. They wish you'd go away. People with mental ill health, behaving oddly, create the same aura. I thrashed around a bit more until I managed to sit up and balance. She washed my hair and I was able to transfer without incident back into my chair, anxiety levels at maximum. I thought I'd be fine now, but I wasn't. Back in front of the mirror, I was assailed by the pervasive smell of poo. I hitched up the cape surreptitiously and peeked. The miracle of the stoma bag, the thing that had changed my life, had failed. Come unstuck. I hadn't realised such a thing could happen. But there I was, with wet hair, and quantities of nervous poo spilling out of my stomach under my clothes.

What does one do in such circumstances? Where lies shelter, or a shred of dignity? They didn't teach me about this in hospital. The salon did not have a disabled toilet. Desperate, desolate, mortified – the smell was intense – I excused myself temporarily and managed to get myself out of the shop and onto the pavement. I began to wheel back to the car. I phoned Dave, who fortunately was not far away, and he fetched a bucket of water from the salon. Cold, in the mop bucket, because he's a man. We reached the car and I huddled into the gap behind the open driver's door, wishing the earth would swallow up me and my lapful of poo. It was at that point, in the timing of a comic script, that a tall distinguished-looking man in an overcoat and a hat, who had been hovering, approached us.

'Excuse me,' he said, coming right up to the door.

I looked up at him, cowering like a seal pup.

'Are you Melanie Reid?'

'Er, yes,' I said, jaw clenched in despair.

'Forgive me.' Oh no – he was leaning over the door. 'I just wanted to say how much I admire your writing and your tenacity.'

As my mother would have said, always be polite. Courtesy under extreme duress. 'Er, thanks so much,' I blurted. 'Really kind of you … er …' And forced an embarrassed, pleading smile. Thinking, *Please go, please, please, please.*

He paused there, as if hoping I would say more. Maybe he read the desperation on my face. He took his leave.

Despite the situation yet to be dealt with, when he was out of earshot we burst into mildly hysterical laughter.

'Now that,' said Dave, 'is what you call fucking incredible timing.'

Huddled in the lee of the car door, using the cold water, I did the best I could to clean myself up, sluicing water over my bottom half. It reminded me of sluicing down the legs of a horse after a competition, or after a sweaty journey in a lorry. Like a cub scout going wild camping for the first time, I did an al fresco change of stoma bag, then loaded my lap with jackets from the car, and returned, apologising, to the hairdressers to get my hair cut. The easier option would have been to go home but I couldn't bear to have come this far, gone through such trauma, and fail in my goal. Besides, by now the germs would be washed everywhere, reinfecting me; there was nothing I could do about that, either. A certain peace comes with resignation.

'Please tell me if I smell too bad,' I whispered to my stylist, a sweet girl, but also young.

'Yeah, OK,' she said, round-eyed, and I could see her wondering why she always got landed with the nutters. There were later embarrassments with stoma bags coming unfixed, but never anything quite on that scale or with such dramatic flourish.

The Nelly fall had one devastating consequence for me. It closed the door, for ever and a day, on riding horses again. It taught me that I was simply too paralysed and too breakable ever again to risk getting on the back of a live creature with a mind of its own. After what I'd been through, even fools start to parent themselves. The dream was over; the longest, unbroken love affair in my life was finally ended. This left me back with the void again. Horses had roamed such a big part of my head for so long that the sense of loss was profound. Disability was going to be acutely boring, I suspected. What could I possibly do now that would engage me, exercise me and stimulate my brain? I was an alcoholic looking for something to replace drinking. The comparison was not frivolous.

In addition, I was forced to address the footprint of that life. What to do with my horsey kingdom? My tack room, my loose boxes, the endless paraphernalia which I would never use again. The tack room in particular was a shrine. To each their hobby, their temples, their divine objects. For all sports, for rugby players, skiers, cyclists, painters, climbers, it is the same: the smell of mud and changing room, the incense of tyre rubber and derailleur, ski wax, oil paint, rope coils or saddlery. Lifelong intoxicants. But what does one do with the accumulation of cherished but old-fashioned stuff when the game is over? With hobbies, the sad fact is that what you've got is never enough. You never stop acquiring. Hobbies blur the line between need and want. Nobody ever entered a bike shop or a climbing shop or a saddlery shop and left empty-handed. My tack room was stuffed with almost everything, except an air jacket to protect my spine.

And so my eyes feasted sadly on that thirty-odd-year fairy-tale, the hoarded treasure of so many bridles, even more nose-bands, snaffles and pelhams and gags, breastplates and martingales, fetlock boots and cavessons, leather hole-punches and hairnets. The esoteric trivia of a very small obsession. The horse corner of the barn was still in frozen animation, deserted since the day we never came back. Everything not in the tack room – dandy brushes, buckets, feed bins – was coated with an inch of dust and dead daddy longlegs. In the riding arena, baby sitka spruce and buddleia sprouted out of the rubber and sand, marking the years that had passed since I had been turned to stone by the evil spell. Immediately after the accident, my friends had sold my trailer, but had carried out no final house clearance. It was like a death but nobody had wanted to presume anything – and now, still living, I was some weird equine Miss Havisham, queen of a derelict domain I had once been so proud of. I had worked so hard all my life for my barn and my riding arena, and it was all I ever wanted. And now it was a lost playground.

Something had to be done. We decided to rent out the stables, field and riding arena with our former holiday cottage, because it seemed a step away from the past, and because we needed the money. I laid down some stipulations. I couldn't bear to have someone use it as a competition yard, with big glossy horses clattering up and down horsebox ramps. That would have destroyed me. We found tenants who were perfect – a kind couple with two Highland ponies who liked hacking. I carried out a wobbly hand-over – 'It's a handy set-up; I hope you and your ponies enjoy it' – and then, to my own fury, started to cry in front of strangers. I told them to bundle up the old stuff to the back of the tack room, out of the way, and I gave away as much as I could. I took my favourite Stubben bridle up to the house and hung it by the kitchen door. For the next couple of years or so, I would put my face against it and sniff the leather every night on my way to bed. It's still there, though I don't stop to smell it any more.

As John McEnroe once said, the older we get the better we used to be. I was never a great horsewoman, but I was humble and aware; and looking back, I was always trying to improve. One day around that time, in the office, I came across a box file with notes from my dressage lessons, an attempt to pin down those brief, addictive seconds when you achieved 'feel' – when mind and body and horse melded in softness, lightness and understanding. When it happened you wanted to capture it so you could do it again. It was the same as a sports person finding the sweet spot on a tennis racket, or pinging a golf ball four hundred yards without trying, or a professional dancer entering the place where the conscious and unconscious meet, and letting loose their soul. 'Between the idea and the reality/ Between the motion and the act/ Falls the Shadow,' as T.S. Eliot wrote in 'The Hollow Men'. The magic in between. The tantalising glimpse of why we all strive. In the file, stored away, were notes and certificates from decades ago when I took British

Horse Society exams, along with notes from various intensive riding courses as I tried to improve my lightness of being. Every lesson, every instructor, I took away a nugget and wrote it down. God loves a trier. Or perhaps in my case he didn't.

There were notes from the summer I took Horrid Dan to a famous riding centre in England and was introduced to the concept of the four stages of competence. An instructor used it to illustrate the subtle, invisible art of shifting the balance of your seat bones to ask a horse to canter. Sitting reading those notes, I was back there – in a hot indoor school with the dust motes dancing in the sunbeams; in the pleasure in losing myself in an all-consuming mental and physical challenge. Anyway, stage one – for anything: chess, parenting, ballroom dancing – is in a state of unconscious incompetence. We don't know how to do something; we don't even recognise what it is we don't know how to do. Once we acknowledge our own deficit, we move to the next stage, conscious incompetence – when we realise how much we have to learn. Did I remember how I strived to pick up that canter stride invisibly? In my wheelchair, my limbs twitched wistfully, reprising the memory: the minutest pelvic slide, the tiny shift back of the outside leg; the subtle lift on the inside rein. Occasionally during those lessons I got it, everything came together and the horse rose up into canter, but it required body- and mind-sapping concentration in the hot dust. Horrid Dan was a horse who knew most things already. Gradually, as a rider, I learnt which of his buttons to press and entered stage three, conscious competence: you know what to do and how to do it, but it's still exhausting.

Sadly, we never reached stage four – unconscious competence: the place where experts reside, between peace and concentration, where you have practised so much that the skill becomes instinctive. It remained the unfulfilled dream of my life: Dan got navicular disease in his feet, became chronically lame and was put down. I bought Terry, whose heart was never in jumping, and the accident happened. Horrid Dan never refused a jump; he ate fences the way he tried to eat humans.

And there too, pitifully, I found the notes from my riding lessons in spring 2010, the days before my fall. The happy esoteric jottings of someone who would soon, to all intents and purposes, be dead.

14/3/10 – pretend to carry a tea tray as I ride. Bent elbows. Shoulders back back back. Look at horizon. Outside rein, inside leg. Then turn using nothing else. Come off track 5m loop, then counter canter. HE DID IT!!

20/3/10 – 15 metre circles= jog a few strides, then walk, then jog. Sink legs. Higher I sit the better the transitions. ***_Tricia told me I looked like a pro!!_*** On right rein I have to try so much harder to lift my body up … it collapses.

28/3/10 – jumping lesson with Mandy. EYES BEHIND HIPS ON APPROACH. FOLD HIPS NOT SHOULDERS.

And then five days later my hips folded all right, but the wrong way, up my back towards my shoulders, when Terry refused a jump and my eyes nearly drove into my brain. And all the dreams died. If nothing else, I suppose, my notes are a fair

summation of my riding career: shows passion and commit-
ment if nothing else. And the saddest resonance from those
notes is that within seven years of my accident those instructors, Tricia and Mandy, good women both, had died prema-
turely of cancer. And I, wrecked though I was, lived on with a
void that screamed to be filled. After that I grew used to seeing
the great solid grey bottoms of the Highland ponies plodding
from field to stable, and hearing once again the sound of horses'
feet around the place. But it satisfied nothing.

Old passion gnaws at you. If addicts can give up heroin, then
I could surely give up horses, couldn't I? Or, if I couldn't ride,
was there some way I could still remain connected to them? My
problem was that it was the actual riding which had fulfilled me
– the freedom, and action. I wanted my mind wiped, my body
and brain engaged. After my accident Nelly had given me
movement, empowerment, independence, connection, intense
physiotherapy. Just for a few precious minutes, a couple of
times a week, she removed the pain of my existence and gave
me legs again.

Kindly people urged me to try carriage driving. The first
time I did was back at the same Riding for the Disabled centre
– I confess I didn't go anywhere near Nelly's stable – in the
shafts behind a black cob who resembled an ocean-going
tugboat: low-slung, broad of beam, with legs like oak trees,
and a backside the width of a small car. Sara was the driver and
my chair was bolted alongside; she handed me a second set of
reins. And it was a lovely jaunt, along quiet lanes, the cob
steady as a rock. The last time I was in a pony and trap was in
County Down, age six, with my big cousin, clopping down the
Hillhall Road to buy sweets. I remember the jauntiness, the

fun, and the always good wind that blows between the ears of a horse.

One of the doyennes of disabled carriage driving persuaded me a couple of years later to join her in the south of England at purpose-built facilities for competitive paradriving, where she handed over the reins of her experienced pony and we whizzed around an indoor course of gates like a timed jump-off at the Horse of the Year Show. It was seriously fun and fast, but deep down it did not compare to the fulfilment of riding. The sense of feeling the horse's mouth, but having no contact with its body, was disconcerting. One felt detached, unconnected, unconsumed.

'Probably not dangerous enough,' sighed Dave.

In place of the physiotherapy I had received from Nelly, I even tried being hoisted onto a mechanical horse. Sara's one at the RDA was an elderly thing which only rocked like a

Driving Rogan the cob at Riding for Disabled. It was fun.
But not a patch on riding.

cantering horse, but you sat in a proper saddle. Physiotherapy-wise, it was good to prise my pelvis open and straighten and loosen my torso, and it had the benefit of being unlikely to take off with me, but it lacked all the subtleties of communicating with a real animal. I would have carried on using it, but the centre was forced to end its tenancy and close, and the option was taken away. I still dream of finding somewhere with a sophisticated mechanical dressage horse, capable of lateral movements and mouth-responsive, fitted with a hoist for riders without any mobility, but sadly I haven't found it yet. Gradually, I began to distance myself from the horse world. It hurt too much.

Little else physical was left to me to escape the crushing passivity of the wheelchair. I was picky. Few things appealed, mainly because they involved the help of so many people, and I sought to be independent. I had tried disability skiing at an indoor slope but found it an intensely bitter-sweet experience. Too many memories of past good times in the Alps. At the top of the slope, I ached to push off and gather speed, swooping freely, but I was trussed like a turkey in a sleeping bag on a sit-ski, with someone snow-ploughing behind, steering me. I would never have sufficient arm function to sit-ski by myself and I would always be that much-attended, fussed-over, disabled skier whom we've all watched idly from the chairlift, patronising with a 'Wow, isn't it amazing what they can do?' I was too proud and arrogant and fussy and ungrateful and shitty and masochistic to do that. I wanted to be alone, doing it by myself. An angry conscious incompetent.

I craved to be active in some way. Shortly before my accident, I'd been the fittest of my life – that dreadful creation of the Saturday supplements, the fifty-something who was reliving her thirties. I had gone to a boot camp in Somerset, pushing myself to extremes under the tuition of former marines. At home, at weekends, I ran in the forest. One evening a week I went to the local village hall for a Pilates class followed by an hour of riotous hard-sweating step class which I relished to my marrow because it made me feel so alive. Our instructor used to play an extended work-out re-mix of the famous Killers anthem, 'Human', about ten minutes of unadulterated, full-volume, soaring escape, as we joyously stomped out the answer to the song's question about whether we were human or dancer.

Years passed before I was able to listen to that song again without weeping, because whenever I heard it I was right back in that hall on a cold winter night, joyously springing up and down. Because I could. It amuses me to read on the internet that the song's lyrics are regarded as some of the most opaque and mysterious – for me, post-accident, they made total sense and had absolute, cruel synchronicity with my life. I knew the answer to the question all right, cold hands, vital signs and all. Once a dancer, now I was merely human – they were two separate tribes and I had passed from membership of one to the other, never to return.

Every action has a consequence. Although the hip healed and the pain from it receded, I was far less physically active than I had been. I began to put on weight, and that made me eat more. Sometimes the only rational response to your circumstances is to be depressed. There was bugger-all pleasure anywhere else in my life. But then the tendons in my shoulder started to rub against the bone, worn out pushing a heavier body, a job they were never designed for. Night times were the worst, when, like toothache, my shoulders constantly interrupted my sleep. Then a hernia blossomed at the site of my colostomy, evidently kinking my gut. Oedema and nausea returned and, within a few months, the bulge developed to the extent I went back onto the waiting list for more surgery to get it repaired. A year later, I was back in hospital for that ordeal. I was due shoulder surgery as well, but after the operation was cancelled because of emergencies, I decided I never wanted to go back into hospital, and put up with the pain.

For a good while, it was hard to avoid feeling sorry for myself: it seemed that whatever I did, and however hard I tried, something would thwart me. Although I was still taking anti-depressants, it didn't feel as if I was. I would binge on sweet food and then spend several hours a day in deep, depressed, uncomfortable sleep, slumped in my chair, my neck bent cruelly forwards, hands clenched in misery, control and hope abandoned, not at all interested in waking up.

I flailed around for a meaningful life. Long-term coping seemed to be dependent upon finding enough distractions to stop me thinking too much. It was as if paralysis had erased most of what my life had used to consist of – sport, interests, pleasures, travel, my image of myself. In my writing, I still had the concept of work, although changed and somewhat limited. But while my cerebral life was rich, I couldn't possibly spend the rest of my days reading or painting or watching films. I felt as if I had stopped accumulating proper experiences. Going anywhere new became an ordeal. I graded places not by their visual splendour or the nice food, but by the accessibility of the kerbs, the minutiae of the ground. I looked down, not up, and ate weary meals at rendezvous in shabby roadside places simply because the parking was flat and generous. I learnt about being a helpless victim of diesel fumes – at waist height, child-height, buggy-height you have no idea how foul city air is. My memory bank of movement, my former, mobile relationship with places, was receding into the past. My cognitive dissonance between old self and new self meant I could no longer inhabit and enjoy old memories of what I had and did. Even my sense of touch had changed. My entire independent life hung upon the thumb and forefinger of my right hand, which had developed enough grip to enable me to muddle through the day – my own small private miracle. The other fingers were clawed, unfeeling, and useless. But essential as my finger and thumb were, I couldn't trust their judgement. Subtle messages were absent or false. I could touch my hair, but never again would it feel silky or soft or clean or greasy: it just felt coarse. Likewise, the skin on my face grated when I ran my thumb over it. Because I couldn't unclaw my hands, I would never again stroke properly a horse or a dog. Just one of a thousand daily bereavements and daily signposts removed.

Some people, disabled as adults, claim to accept their handicap quite quickly. For me, it was a period of mourning which was to take years, the long, slow, lingering death of one person while someone else with the same name tried to make sense of the changes and reorientate themselves in a foreign landscape. I seemed doomed not to accept. In this compulsion to probe and analyse my situation, I irritated myself. But I needed meaning; I couldn't just resign myself to stasis. Why couldn't I just get on with it? The late John Hull, an academic who lost his sight as an adult, wrote: 'My desire for coherence … impels me to probe the experience, to grapple with it, to strip off layer after layer from it, to find meaning within it and to relate that meaning to other parts or aspects of living.' I knew exactly what he meant. I used to secretly envy the patients in the spinal unit who were entirely passive. Their heads went down from day one, they didn't engage, or go to the gym. They existed. Perhaps once they got home they would anaesthetise themselves with drink or drugs or food. But I couldn't do that. Alcohol held no appeal to me; I rarely drank and then only socially. Drinking was associated with being young and letting go a bit, having fun, feeling sexy and irresponsible, dancing. Now staying in control was my preoccupation. I was eternally watchful over my own body, delving, analysing, making comparisons. At some bewildering point, I passed the watershed where I forgot what it felt like to be normal – forgot how to sit up in bed, throw my legs on the floor, and get up and go to the bathroom. Now I could watch others, and think, how does she do that? And try to remember what it felt like to reach a high shelf, or wash my face under the running tap.

The boys rescued me from my gloomy introspection. Dave needed me in a state of positive equilibrium, otherwise he couldn't go to the pub without feeling guilty. In motivational mode he reminded me of Sir Alex Ferguson, the legendarily brusque Scottish football manager who was so successful with Manchester United, though he never swore or threw things at me. We're back, he said, on the first rung of the ladder on the snakes and ladders board. And you're going to get back on your leg bike and your standing frames and get up that ladder and head for the next one. We're going to stay optimistic. Disability, we decided, required this, tempered with realism. It wasn't naïve or stubborn to keep working on my body as long as I accepted there would be no miracles.

Meanwhile, after his graduation, Doug moved his stuff back home. It was lovely to have him but it felt temporary; he was like a big, sweet migratory bird, too large to be cooped up, stretching his wings, feeding himself up, preparing for the season to change so he could fly off. But what to do and where to do it? He had a master's degree in engineering but confessed that he couldn't bear to spend the rest of his life sitting behind a computer doing calculations. He was too much of a doer, too restless. He spoke to me about jobs in marketing or selling, based in Scotland, and without anything explicit being said I realised that he felt under obligation to stay nearby to support me, although almost all his band of close friends had moved to London. At exactly the same stage in my life I recalled my resentment when my parents, who had retired to Scotland, put me under moral pressure to stay north of the Border after graduation. As a result I turned down a job offer in London which I'd regretted it all my life, another unwanted 'what if'. Fantastic as it would have been – for me – to have Dougie nearby, as a superman, driver, fixer and moral support, it was not what was best for him.

Go south, I said, don't worry about me, you don't have to hang around for my sake, and I told him what his grandparents had done to me. Move to London, I said. Get a job there, explore what you want to do. Live. Life is short. Be happy. I'll be fine. And as I said it, two things happened: I could see the weight lift from his face and his shoulders; and I also committed myself to get on with things for the sake of him. It was best that the parent–child relationship was kept the right way round.

Meanwhile, the stories I heard from other walkers and almost-walkers with damaged spines gave me nuggets of hope and information. It was a kind of Incompletes Anonymous. A neurophysiotherapist gave me a comforting image: she told me that what she did was like pushing a pea uphill with your nose. Slow progress was the norm; frustration was inevitable. One man who wrote to me had suffered an incomplete spinal cord injury in his neck six years earlier at a broadly similar neurological level. He wanted to bust some myths. 'Firstly, the two-year so-called neurological "window for recovery",' he wrote. 'I was told this too. While I know that we are all different, and albeit infinitesimally slowly, I have continued to improve. In fact over the past year, the pace of improvement has increased markedly compared with that over the first two years.' Four years after his accident, he met the neurological surgeon who carried out the operation on his neck. The surgeon was impressed with his gain in arm and hand function. The last time he had seen his patient, he had no triceps function, no wrist extension and no finger/thumb pinch action. My reader asked him about the two-year window of opportunity. 'Ah well,' said the surgeon. 'We've changed our tune, we now believe that the brain can create new neural pathways to bypass the damaged area and that recovery can continue indefinitely.'

The patient wondered whether the two-year period might be a self-fulfilling prophecy, simply because most people give up as a result of the received wisdom. He urged me to keep going with exercise. 'Even if it takes years we will improve – although we don't know what the end result might be. One thing's for sure – if we don't keep trying we certainly won't find out. We have to make our endeavours an art form, a culture. I believe that a cure for spinal cord injury, whether from stem cells, nanosurgery or robotics, is going to happen. We must therefore keep flexible and stop contractures setting in.'

Another man was an incomplete C4/5 tetraplegic, coming up to his eighth anniversary. 'I am totally addicted to rehabilitating myself. As a result of continually abusing my body I have biceps and triceps, I can stand independently and walk various distances with gutter frame, Zimmer frame, parallel bars and a gym treadmill (.45 of a mile last time out). My consultant said I would plateau in two to five years, where have I gone wrong?'

Said another woman, hit by a virus which damaged her neurologically. 'Fourteen years ago I couldn't move at all, or smile, or talk, now I can do all three … I have to say from long experience that doctors, nurses and physios often predict wrong, they all said I would make no recovery …'

One woman told me: 'I had a major stroke nine and a half years ago – and I mean major. I'm still getting changes now. I do plateau for ages sometimes and obviously sometimes I feel I'm wasting my time. Somehow, though, I don't know how to stop trying. I was originally told my window for improvement was six months. It's best to ignore experts when they say something you don't like. It helps to be bloody-minded.'

Another of my post-accident friends, Annette, was paralysed after she fell off a horse and damaged her neck at C6. After years of intense, and expensive physiotherapy, she was walking with a stick, swimming, skiing upright. She regained proprioception. And then there was Reiver, my old partner in crime and hope from the spinal unit, who was told he would never walk again, yet within four years was walking on a pulpit frame in the house. Even Snafu, I read in the paper some seven years later, had regained enough mobility to walk on parallel bars.

As time passed, and my body settled down from its second hiatus, it did continue to improve in numerous tiny, slow-motion ways – a process that goes on to this day. My left shoulder, which had been very restricted since the original fall, loosened up a little. I regained more strength, movement and a modicum of grip in my left thumb. With my left hand, formerly useless, I could eventually lift a mug of coffee safely to my mouth. My right hand became much stronger than it had been. After several years, my fingers softened to the extent that I could interlock them and clasp my hands into a cat's cradle. At night, instead of a sliding transfer from chair to bed across a board, I began to use the Topro Taurus stand, getting to my feet, turning forty-five degrees and then sitting down on the bed. My adductor thigh muscles relaxed and my legs no longer acted like scissors: when I walked on my frame, always now for safety with two people in attendance, I could place my feet deliberately without wearing ankle splints. With slowly increasing stamina, I found I could stagger up to a hundred metres, and climbed all ramps the length of the house in one go. With increased exercise, and more cautious eating, I began to lose weight again.

Around my body, as the years have passed, there have been minuscule easings as nerves tried, however imperfectly, to rejoin. Often these changes were so small that I tortured myself I was imagining them. Waiting for nerve damage to repair is the longest long-game in the world. Ask anyone with a brain injury, or a damaged spinal cord, and they will express the same frustration about a wait that never seems to end. Skin and the flesh underneath, I came to understand, had different nerve supplies: firstly, I realised I had recovered some sensation under the skin – when poked in the ribs, for instance – and next, after seven years or so, I noted the return of some form of long-distance skin sensation over the whole of my body. It's what a healthy person might feel, perhaps, if someone was stroking them through two or three thick duvets.

Approaching a decade post-accident, this is where I am. None of it means I am in any way a functioning human being: I am still doubly incontinent, the motor functions controlling my main muscle groups are effectively dead, and my life is still that of a profoundly paralysed person, spent in a wheelchair. I am buggered, and I always will be. But it's a long game. I can't allow myself to be too cynical. If I need reminding of this, I tap my chin and feel, in some strange nerve anomaly, a tingling in my feet. There's definitely a signal of some kind running down my spine.

Often, I call up the visual image of Zen Master's little army of brilliant technicians working away inside me, trying to fix the wiring. I will believe in them for as long as I have a shred of evidence that neuroplasticity is an ongoing process. That little injection of hope – let's call it extreme hoping – every now and again makes this grotty life much easier to live.

A sports coach called Matt Fitzgerald wrote a book about triathlon called *Iron War*, suggesting suffering in extreme sport wasn't a negative, but a positive. Triathletes belonged to a 'pain community', people who cultivated an inexhaustible appetite for voluntary suffering in pursuit of the triumph of the spirit over the flesh. Fitzgerald wrote: 'Our earthly lives are doomed … in the billion year perspective utterly meaningless, yet we muster courage not just to survive and bear suffering but to create meaning ... we can't resist trying to see what we can do. Human beings ... try when it's hopeless, when it doesn't make sense any more ... we are heartbreakingly beautiful in this way.'

Heartbreakingly beautiful? Has he seen me slumped on a shower chair, all tubes and bags and purple swollen feet? I wonder if Fitzgerald includes in his pain community those who have cultivated an inexhaustible appetite for *involuntary* suffering. The chronically ill and disabled, who have to create meaning for ourselves because we have no choice.

I fully understand the addictive qualities of extreme sport, but I'm wary of the fashionable notion that suffering is essential. I suspect it's a conceit of the healthy, a leisure indulgence developed by a society which has never been safer and healthier – or less aware of that. Jordan Peterson, guru and preacherman to the millennial generation, lectures students on YouTube that pain's vital, pain's the norm. And there's that other comforting quote: 'Pain is temporary. It may last a minute, or an hour, or a day, or a year, but eventually it will subside and something else will take its place. If I quit, however, it lasts forever.' Who said that? Ah yes, Lance Armstrong, the greatest sporting cheat in the world. The glory of suffering might be humankind's biggest, ever-recyclable con trick, played upon itself.

There were always days when I got sour and sick of my handicap. Then I'd feel resentful watching the unthinking, unknowing able-bodied masses walking around – upright on legs that obeyed them, with perfect, happy rounded buttocks; watching them unconsciously spring to their feet, lean over, reach, balance, hop, run, jog, dance. I still avoid watching people dancing; it makes me too jealous. And some days, I have little sympathy for heavily overweight people, spoiling their wonderful bodies; or healthy people comatose with alcohol, seeking oblivion for fun. Every disabled person, I guess, is entitled to open those valves of bitterness occasionally and mutter, 'If you don't want to live – I mean live, really live, appreciate every damn moment of being free and able – give me your body.' There is no shame in it. We are unlikely saints.

I think back to poor old Aunt Averil. Oliver Sacks, who worked such poignant magic with L-dopa on locked-in victims like her, appreciated the ultimate courage, approaching the heroic, of those who were imprisoned by the illness. They were ordinary people made great by their endurance, he said, with their lack of complaining, their inexplicable affirmation of life in the face of inconceivable depths of suffering. He quoted Friedrich Nietzsche: 'Only great pain, the long, slow pain that takes its time … compels us to descend to our ultimate depths … I doubt that such pain makes us "better"; but I know it makes us more profound. In the end, lest what is most important remains unsaid: from such abysses, from such severe sickness, one returns newborn having shed one's skin, with merrier senses, with a second dangerous innocence in joy, more childlike and yet a hundred times subtler than one has ever seen before.'

Would that this was true. I don't feel newborn, or profound; I'm not heartbreakingly beautiful in my suffering, or a triumph of the spirit over the flesh. I just want the cheeks of my bottom to stop aching and the bloody clock turned back. 'You desire to know the art of living, my friend? It is contained in one phrase: make use of suffering,' said the melancholy nineteenth-century Swiss philosopher Henri Frédéric Amiel; like Nietzsche, obviously a forefather of Jordan Peterson. Only by constant struggle, a daily fight to 're-climb a thousand times the peaks already scaled, and reconquer the points of view already won' was peace to be found. Oh really? From my perspective that isn't wisdom; that's just a bone-headed battle hymn of maso-chism, a post-justification of shitty events. Don't people who've had tough lives and dealt with tragedies always say things like that to console themselves? On the whole, thank you very much, I'd prefer to have gone through life shallow and healthy, untouched by both suffering and deeper insights, looking after my loved ones, playing with my horses, doing step exercises to The Killers. Lots of people do get through unscathed, the lucky complacent buggers. But I didn't. I was forced onto another path.

CHAPTER FIFTEEN

A POCKETFUL OF DIAMONDS

Hope is contagious.
BARACK OBAMA

It was the summer solstice, the shortest night of the year, in the mountains of Scotland. Only four hours or so of total darkness and I had continued to walk through it, cautiously, methodically, eyes down, stepping into the small pool of light cast by my head torch on the path. Deep in Glen Falloch, with a sense of mountains rearing on either side of me, and the throaty, incessant roar of the waterfalls, I found myself alone. Time had absented itself and I was disembodied with tiredness. Eyes, mind, breathing – everything focused on the path, steps slower but rhythmic. There – one foot in front of that stumble stone. Now there – next foot on a welcome gravelly bit.

In 1803, on the very same hillside, Dorothy Wordsworth wrote: 'We heard, as if from the heart of the earth, the sound of torrents ascending out of the long hollow glen. To the eye all was motionless, a perfect stillness. The noise of waters did not appear to come this way or that, from any particular quarter: it was everywhere, almost, one might say, as if exhaled through the whole surface of the green earth ... William says, if we were to name it from our recollections of that time, we should call it the Vale of Awful Sound.' A picture of her came to mind, valiantly trudging with voluminous ankle-length skirts, poor girl. Cocooned by the exact same sound, sucking on the same cold Highland air, I was a hair's breadth, a tiny swerve of time, away from Dorothy. I had by then been plodding stubbornly for twenty hours on an endurance charity challenge. A little delirious with fatigue, I began to wonder if in fact I was standing still. Perhaps if I just waited, both the dawn and the finishing gate would come to me. I did not know which to expect first.

How to capture when night becomes earliest dawn? I think I was distracted by the faint smell of wood smoke and I lifted my head, scanning the darkness. When I turned my eyes back down to the path I realised the pool of light from my head torch had softened, and around me the darkness was in retreat. I could almost sense the textures and shape of the grass rising out of the ground. Attempting to pin down the exact moment was impossible, like trying to capture rainbows or bottle clouds: night became day in a drift of split-seconds. I looked up, and could now see where the mountains ended and the sky began. Below, on the riverbank, I could make out the shape of a tent and a suggestion of white smoke drifting from the remains of a camp fire. When I brought my eyes back to the path, the light of my head torch had vanished, conquered by daylight. Fumbling, vaguely out-of-body, I switched it off, blinking at the mystery and sheer exclusivity of it all. It was all mine. Strung out across the miles, lost to time, I had literally stepped across that gap between night and day; that place where the divide between the real and the spirit world was the thinnest. I felt I was the only person in the whole world.

The memory has become an allegory of sorts. In my forties, the years before my accident, I had fallen in love with exercise. Walking, especially in the mountains, had become one of the most satisfying, primitive, reassuring, liberating things to do. Walking was to be human, to rediscover ancient things. Walking always took you somewhere and walking sorted you out, made sense of problems, and made you feel good. Sometimes Dave and Dougie came too, sometimes my girl-friends, and we went for a week. Ambitious walking was like regressing to childhood: you left behind the twenty-first century, your car keys, your mobile phone (because more often than not where you were going it wouldn't work) and your responsibilities. Like a kid, all you had to do – your adventure – was to put a bag on your back, and get yourself on foot to the place where you were staying at the end of the day.

So I walked a lot in the hills when I could. And then after the accident, when the most obvious thing that paralysis took away was the ability to walk, its restoration became an obsession. The ability to stand supported, wobbling on numb legs, and the fierce will first to make one foot to move, then the next, was powerfully symbolic. When despair threatened to wash me away, it held me together mentally.

In reality, such a fierce focus on mobility, although it was exceptionally good physiotherapy, was less kind to my mental health. Constantly striving, delving and analysing my body was exhausting. It was also very easy for others to misinterpret it as some pointless masochistic drive for heroism, when deep down, I just wanted to be ordinary again. As the months turned into years … four, five, six … I became a bit stuck, as if becalmed at sea, waiting for winds that never came and stubbornly determined not to move on with my life. *I'll wait until I'm walking better* became a refrain. A retired medical consultant, also an incomplete tetraplegic, wrote to me, urging me to accept that I was crocked and to start enjoying life. Life's what happens while you're making plans, and all that. He was plainly exasperated by my hair-shirtedness. 'Buy yourself an all-terrain scooter and get out into the fresh air and live! You can't sit inside waiting for ever.' But when I did go anywhere, in those first few years, I would look up at the mountains and waves of bitterness would wash over me, because all I could think was, I can't climb them any more.

Janis Joplin sang that she'd trade all of her tomorrows for a single yesterday, and that was still how it was for me.

Something happened, though, gradually, along the highways and byways of wheelchair life. Getting a serious spinal-cord injury is like rebirth as a new, unfamiliar, radically altered person. You're starting again in a strange world and you have to grow up all over again. From infant to dependent child, to self-conscious adolescent to some kind of maturity – this stuff doesn't happen overnight, psychologically or physically. You don't wake up the day after ground zero and say, *Right, that's just the way it is, I'll just get on with it* – not unless you are devoid of imagination or are some kind of passive, secular saint. Were I to be happy and mature in my new identity, whatever that might be, I had first to accept my injury. And in a funny way, that happened while I was unaware. Just as I had stepped across the mysterious gap between night and day that June morning on the mountain path, body and mind separated from each other by fatigue, the same thing has happened to me now. First there was the darkness of denial, and then the unpindownable dawn of acceptance, so that when I raised my eyes I could look at the mountains and think, well, actually, I'm rather lucky to be here to see them.

I have made a dignified peace, finally, with the dilemma so beautifully encapsulated by John Hull about his blindness. 'If I were to accept this thing, if I were to acquiesce, then I would die. It would be as if my ability to fight back, my will to resist was broken. On the other hand, not to acquiesce, not to accept, seems futile. What I am refusing to accept is a fact.'

In life there are golden ages, but the frustrating thing about golden ages is that you don't appreciate you're in one when you're in it. It is only later, looking back, that you understand what you had. There are golden ages in offices, when a team of talented people, well-led, spark off each other, laugh a lot, go to the pub together, and produce the highest-quality work. Friendship groups have golden ages, when serendipity decrees that everyone you know and love is living in the same flat, or the same city, and you spend great times together, relishing the company and the fun, convinced this is so good it must somehow last forever. Families have them too, decades unmarred by death and divorce, bolstered by prosperity and love; and of course as individuals, we have golden ages of health, achievement and romance. You can have a golden age with a wonderful, kind horse which is never sick or sorry; or a dog that is more special than most. The art of living well, I think, is to understand how swiftly you get old, and to learn to identify golden ages as quickly as possible. And the real secret is not to be always looking forward, plotting the fulfilment of tomorrow, the job you haven't yet got, the perfect partner you haven't met

– or indeed the amazing horse that would do everything effort-lessly and the bigger horsebox you'd need to take it places. Instead, focus on what constitutes your life at the time and love what you already have.

Now, I try very hard to do that; to understand that I am actually, despite the wheelchair and the lost body, existing in a golden age of sorts. No person has ever felt more loved than I do; and I am liberated to tell people how much I love them, which is a powerful thing. I have been fortunate enough to squeeze, as it were, into the back of the church at my own funeral, to read the cards sent to my anguished husband, smell the flowers, and catch some of the loving words and warm trib-utes. Wisdom can be hard won. I've learnt that we can choose to find happiness, whatever our circumstances. Most people, noted Abraham Lincoln drily, are indeed as happy as they choose to be. Or as Anne Shirley of Green Gables preferred it: 'You can nearly always enjoy things if you make up your mind firmly that you will.' By the nature of what has happened to me, I have, along with anyone else with long-term health issues, a ringside seat in this debate. The misery of paralysis could have blown away my family; could have destroyed me. Together, inspiring each other, Dave and Doug and I chose a different route. In writing, I found a form of salvation: I had no religious or spiritual roadmap to follow, no role to adopt, just a blank page of biographical narrative to create. I could only be myself, navigating a new, alien, terrifying landscape, trying to dodge the clichés and the maudlin, seeking for a way to laugh, however darkly, because it stopped me crying.

When you have a serious health condition, there is pressure from all sides, including yourself, to fit the hopes and gloss over the fears of others. You have to evaluate a medical system which does not have the resources to take you as far as you might like to go, and which is therefore constructed to damp down expectation. You will experience immense generosity of skill and character from health workers and medics but you will also encounter other disabled tribes and lobby interests, who have appointed themselves the tyrants of How to Be and regard you as a traitor if you don't fit their mould. You will make your own mind up. John Callahan, the quadriplegic cartoonist, once drew two sheriffs in wheelchairs drawing their six guns on each other: 'This town ain't accessible enough for the two of us.'

Staying alive, in the beginning, was the hardest thing I have ever had to do. Funny, after Glen Falloch, I remember telling people that the mammoth endurance walk which led me there was the hardest thing I'd ever done, both mentally and physically; and that I would never do anything like it again. I nurtured that achievement as a personal treasure, a mental trophy for extreme endurance. How ironic, in the light of what followed, that exhaustion and bad blisters should impress me so much. And how fortunate it is that we have no concept of what our future holds. When you confront your own death, and but for the smell of roses attend your own funeral, you emerge with a more vivid understanding of what it is to be alive – what Andrew Marr, post-stroke, described as the pungent loveliness of life.

I coped in the beginning by deciding that false hope was better than no hope, on the grounds that if you don't aim for the stars you'll never reach the top of the hill, or if you don't shoot you'll never score, and a whole host of similar corny truisms. Isn't that what you have to do with identity theft

– never give up looking for traces of your stolen self? Hope has never left me, but it coexists with acceptance. And now I can appreciate what I still have. My transcendence, my subsequent night to dawn, has been to go from being alive to living. Too much of a healthy life, when you take it for granted, is spent in a whirl of plans, achievements, expectation and wanting, trying to bend time to your will. Only when this is taken away from you do you start to understand the simplicity of being where you are, with what you can see, and the wind you can feel on your face. Buddhists, of course, have known this for two and a half thousand years; and, in the twenty-first-century West, the mindfulness movement has borrowed some of their tenets and turned reflection into a billion-dollar industry, but really, it's unnecessary: you just have to stay still, focus on the beauty of ordinary things and let the world spin on without you.

In that spirit, then, Dave and I appreciate that for all we have lost, what we still have is precious. We are growing old together, the gap in our ages wiped out by my disability. When I can, I try and cook for him. We find happiness in sitting in companionable silence together, or watching the news, or perhaps meandering down the track with Pip, laughing fondly at her. She is a dear sweet old dog now, but still incorrigible. Life may be smaller, but life is still immeasurably good.

And then there is Dougie, who after he went to London got a job in a shop on Carnaby Street for the winter and sofa-surfed with friends while he tried to find a career. He hid it well, but it was a tough time for him and he was a little lost. I worried, because he had already had to cope with so much. I longed for things to be easy for him, for a good job or an interesting career to fall his way – as every mother does, but in my case perhaps more keenly. I had transgressed the natural order of things: the mother who had caused her son grief which he did not deserve and she could not redress. Again, as when he was a student, I could not spontaneously jump on a train or in the car and go and see him, take him out for supper and cheer him up. He never read the Pollyanna books – I spared him that – but my son was nothing if not resilient – hard times do that to you, I think – and he had the support of wonderful friends. His dream was to become a commercial pilot, and that's what he eventually managed to do: after months of dogged application he was accepted onto a training scheme, took out an eye-watering personal loan, and learnt to fly.

Now, some years on, he has found his own golden age. He's done it, and I am alive to see it. He's a first officer for a big airline, flying out of London. He sends me pictures of buildings and European cityscapes on WhatsApp, with the message 'Guess where I am?' I hear happy snatches of his news in

'I can see our house from here.'

London, that frenetic, fun-filled, friends-rich twenty-some-thing life. For me, it is blissful. Earthbound, wheelbound, I have seen him grow wings and soar, just as the cliché of parent-hood suggests one should. My guilt, about my impoverished ability to be a proper mother, eases.

One day, as I was finishing this book, he messaged me to tell me to look out at 5.15 p.m. for the landing lights of his plane; he was on a flight plan with an approach to Glasgow which came in over the hills several miles to the south of our home. When he was smaller, we used to watch the lights of the inbound aircraft, lingering in the night sky over the Campsies. I sat at the end of the garden at the appointed time and – There! There! – for about seven seconds, along the horizon, was the tiny black dot of a commercial jet making its descent. Dougie in the cockpit. I'd seen my boy piloting a plane, albeit from ten miles away. A sweet, private, heart-burst of embarrassing proud mother syndrome.

At home, those distant hills, the sky, the trees, all bring daily comfort. With my acceptance of my situation slowly came the compensation of nature, the slow and quiet kind that you miss until you stop moving yourself. The writer and birdwatcher Simon Barnes says the wild world is full of attainable miracles. 'Life in the twenty-first century is like being perpetually stony broke, unaware you have a pocketful of diamonds.' And I have chanced upon those diamonds by sitting very still, moments of breathtaking fascination watching tiny things move around me. The thrill of the minutiae. All you have to do is stop and look, but so few of us do – heedless of gardening and the buds that come from the cold soil, happier to crush a beetle underfoot than watch it try to negotiate the kitchen floor. Becoming a born-again birdwatcher meant I was privy to precious theatre – a tawny owl which one memorable night came and sat under the outside light about seven feet away from the French windows. As we watched, holding our breath, it examined us with its wide, ruthless face, then casually floated down, three times, to swallow mice – whole, wriggling. It was as vivid, as intimate, as the best of David Attenborough. I had a ringside seat for a sparrow hawk on foot stalking around a shrub just outside the window, like a Nazi trooper, trying to locate the robin it had struck but missed in flight. And then, one autumn, I witnessed an extraordinary twenty minutes of frenzy and clamour when a flock of redwings descended on the rowan tree at the front door, heavy with red autumn berries, and stripped it like locusts. In my old life, I realised, I would have jumped out of my car and I might have noticed, in passing, that the tree was suddenly denuded. Now I was catching the secret dramas. These were close to privileges of a kind I could never have imagined.

In this way, you learn, very slowly, to rediscover joy. You may not be dancer, but you are human. You are here for moments when you think: well, actually, life's not that bad after all. You tell yourself: not only are you still alive to have seen such wonderful things, but, yes – admit it, and I'm not good at this – you appreciate it more than you might otherwise have done.

None of this is to say that I'm yet skilful at being disabled; in fact, I can see I'm still not much past stage one, unconscious incompetence, and not yet at stage two, conscious incompetence. The inner superwoman is not dead. She still lurks inside me, a truculent spectator; I can find myself hawk-like, observing and silently micro-managing people in my head, consumed with the knowledge that I could once have done what they're doing much better than them. What a delusion. The fool doth think he is wise, but the wise man knows himself to be a fool.

'The thing is,' says Dave, looking ineffably superior, 'is that I know I'm stupid. You, on the other hand, have a long way to go to accept your frailties.'

Slowly, very slowly, I have started to reintegrate with society. It's not easy. Going out in public in a wheelchair is physically difficult and psychologically demanding. The feeling of slowness and vulnerability is intense. I dislike when I enter company and everyone makes a fuss, standing up and rearranging furniture around me. The barrage of incoming How *Are* You-s? People are just being kind, but the end result feels like they've used the Tannoy: 'There's a cripple in the room!' Can you imagine trying to socialise in a crowded room in a wheelchair? It's impossible. You just get jammed in one place, parked always at fart height, neck bent back, aching with the strain of looking up. You cannot mingle. Accordingly, all conversations in wheelchairs outlast their natural lifespan. Small talk is replaced by overly heavy talk. Your radar for the people you'd prefer to avoid is rendered useless, whereas you yourself are the most obvious person in the room. Your body language is neutralised. You can't do what everyone on two feet does, which is to dance the subtle waltz of social gatherings, bouncing and drifting from person to person, ducking and diving, seeking lightness, laughs, gossip. Going to the loo becomes a crowd-parting performance – the Tannoy blares again: 'Cripple heading for Ladies! Make way!' – rather than a useful way of escaping from a conversation which has run its course. Or maybe, of course, I'm just an anti-social git. There is definitely an element of that.

These feelings I have learnt to internalise, to the point where they don't bother me so much any more, and the smiles and gracious thank-yous which I hide behind are less forced than they were, because people have nothing but goodness in their hearts towards me. And yes, of course, it is lovely to get invited to things. And yes, inevitably, when I venture out there are times when I do need help getting through doors or up kerbs, and then I am profoundly grateful not to be ignored when I ask for help. Perhaps, in a wheelchair, you always want it both ways. Of course you do. You want to be ignored for your chair, and treated as you would be on your feet. Yet you expect subtle special treatment. You want to meet sensitive people who understand your plight instinctively. You want every door, every slope, kerb and car park to be so wheelchair friendly that you can zip through life without drawing attention to yourself. You want to socialise, but on your terms.

After about eight years in a chair, I felt grown up enough to go to London by myself on the train – a long journey from Scotland but a manageable, calculated risk that nothing too bad would happen that I couldn't cope with. When you travel in a chair, you book a space for it to park in and you book special assistance at the stations – expert helpers to get you on and off with ramps. And the system works very well. You're placed next door to the loo and the buffet brings you what buffets bring – remember, life is too short to moan about food. The only thing you can't do is move anywhere else in the train. Or legislate for who might sit opposite.

On one particular journey a man got on at Birmingham (I was lucky; it could have been Carlisle) and from behind put a heavy hand on my shoulder.

'This seat free, mate?'

I nodded. Offended at being touched, but by definition powerless.

He was the train companion from hell. He was drunk, but holding it together in that menacing way that heavy-duty alcoholics can. The smell of booze from his body pervaded our end of the carriage. A Londoner, a big powerful tattooed white man in his forties, he had the hardened flintiness of someone who could survive on the streets or in prison. You wouldn't want to cross him, let's say. Worst of all, he wanted to talk. Jesus, I thought, darkly amused, it's like being back in the spinal unit. It was almost funny, except it wasn't, because I could go nowhere.

At first I managed to avoid catching his eye and so he pestered the passenger opposite, who was with his wife and new baby. He was talking nonsense, but it had an edge – he demanded a response. He knew he was a pariah and he wanted his presence acknowledged. The father humoured him briefly. My opposite number consumed two cans of super-strong lager and two whisky miniatures, in swift succession, and then fell asleep. Aware I was clenched with tension, I relaxed.

Half an hour out of London, he woke. He leant across the table to me.

'Good book?'

'Er, not really.' It was a proof copy I was reviewing. Immediately I realised it was the wrong answer.

'Why you reading it then?'

I half smiled at him, ducked my head immediately. Rigid.

'Is it your job then?'

'Sort of.'

He smiled wolfishly. 'I knew that. You're not reading it like normal people read.'

I kept my head down. I felt totally invaded. He was pathetic, but he was also scary. It was clear he had identified in me someone lower down the food chain than he was. Had I had legs, at this point I would have got up and moved away. The silence grew, and I was aware he was studying me.

'What's your job then?'

I kept my head down, re-reading the same line over and over again.

'Don't want to talk, then? Not going to tell me?' He sounded menacing. 'Why not?'

For moral support, I started texting my friend Helen, who was meeting me at the platform.

My companion began a slurry monologue. 'Well, why should I care, I'm back in London and London has the best pubs in the world and as soon as this train stops I'm going to be in the first one I see.'

The moment he got up and left, of course, I felt prissy and snotty. But in the strange equivalence of human interaction, of unconscious power play, he had turned me into a victim and made me feel trapped. Me, who would hand control to very few men, and then only when anaesthetised. What should any disabled woman have told a man like that? Fuck off, mate? I don't want to talk to you? I simply didn't know. As I said earlier, I don't think I'm yet adept at being disabled.

Perhaps I will grow more relaxed about these things, but it is a lengthier and more complicated process than I ever imagined. I do keep trying. The fact is, drunks on trains notwithstanding, every time I have made the effort to go to something, no matter how much I have dreaded it both beforehand and initially, I have by the time I leave come to enjoy it. I have rarely gone home and felt anything but uplifted and glad that, despite myself, I made the effort.

Physically, I am much more at peace. Despite everything, I still manage to achieve more than the doctors ever thought I would. Every morning I stand up and do my faltering, non-functional stagger up and down the house, leaning on the frame, hovered over by people who love me and whose time I impose on. Some days it's easy, some days it's hard. There is no conventional linear progress, except in the sense that each year my stagger is marginally less haphazard than it was the year before, demonstrating that my neurological recovery continues in tiny ways. Short of the cure we must believe will come one day, the spinal cord, however, once damaged, remains damaged. There are no miracles. To all this I am reconciled.

There have been several near-misses, brushes with disaster, when I have fallen again, both literally and metaphorically. But I'm still going, trying, living, loving, laughing, driving cars in the fast lane, listening to the occasional piece of music at full volume like a teenager. Attempting to find merit and dignity and meaning everywhere I go and in everything I read and hear. I'm glad to be alive again: more patient, less judgemental; better at listening to the quiet people. As a full-time conscript in that army I never knew existed – that parallel universe of disabled, ill and suffering people – I now understand how relatively selfish and complacent I used to be, healthy and zooming around at a hundred miles an hour. Perhaps life, inevitably, is like that – until it happens to you, you have no concept of how everything could disappear in seconds. We all lack perspective

MELANIE REID

on what matters. So please, pause and appreciate exactly what you *have*. Don't get angry about discarded socks or wet towels dumped on the floor or traffic jams – these things are irrelevant. Don't waste time and energy moaning about your job, your relationship, the weather or your unfulfilled aspirations. We only have one life and, take it from me, we should never waste it. So get busy living or get busy dying. Cherish the people you love, change your job, tilt up your face and kiss the rain, follow your dreams. Because you *can*.

EPILOGUE

The moment I press the button to open the rear doors of my disability van, the smell overwhelms me. In an instant, I am Mole in *The Wind in the Willows*, nose in the air, quivering, transfixed, aware of the invisible little hands pulling and tugging, all one way. I am Mole on that winter walk when he cries out, with anguish in his heart: 'Please stop, Ratty! You don't understand! It's my home, my old home! I've just come across the smell of it, and it's close by here, really ...'

The aroma of a horse yard is unmistakable and intoxicating – that indescribably hearty, fermented reek of haylage, mixed with sweet clean sawdust and background notes of dung and sweat and stable dust. Almost a decade has passed since my neck break, and another four years since I fell off Nelly, and I have deliberately not been near horses for a long time – distancing myself from the emotions and the memories, disentangling from the love affair. But, in a mere breath, I am time-travelled, heart-emptied, back there, mud on my boots, beet pulp ingrained in my fingernails.

I have planned this visit as a positive farewell of sorts, but also as a distraction, because another early calendar Easter is looming, inescapable. Like tinnitus, the bitter little tape has already started playing its annual loop in my head: Good Friday, huh? Out of all the days of the year open to you, you had to go and bloody fall off on the one which two thousand years of the Judeo-Christian tradition had decreed as the most important and unforgettable, didn't you? Good Friday, that eternal label of mankind's spiritual salvation, of bank holidays and chocolate eggs, forever floodlit as your worst of bad Fridays. Spend the rest of your life savouring the irony of that one, you godless creature you.

The idea is to fill my head with nicer noise, with beauty and hope and the story of Jo Barry, an elite dressage rider who also tumbled down a rabbit hole into the nether world, but has wondrously managed to climb back out again. In December 2014, four days before Christmas, Jo was in the outdoor school exercising one of her top horses. Corchapin, a chestnut gelding known at home as Colin, was a younger half-brother of Valegro, the Olympic champion. Jo and he were in a very happy place. The partnership had had a great year, scooping several national championships, and they were fast-tracked for greater success on the UK Lottery Performance Plan. Jo, a former junior GB squad member, several times ranked Rider of the Year and a protégée of the Olympic gold medallist Carl Hester, felt her dream of getting onto senior GB teams was within touching distance.

She finished the schooling session and eased Colin into walk, letting him stretch and cool down on a long rein. Jo patted him. The session had gone well.

Nobody will ever know what happened next. Although there were people around, no one witnessed the incident. Jo was spotted lying motionless on the ground, Colin standing nearby, sand on his saddle and knees. Had he stumbled? Had something spooked him? Had he fallen on her? The priority was to call an ambulance and get Jo to hospital as quickly as possible. Once there, it became evident she had sustained serious head injuries. Scans revealed compression of the pons region of her brain. The pons is part of the brainstem at the base of the head; it's the bridge for communication and coordination between spine and brain – possibly the most vital of the vital bits.

When she woke after ten days in an induced coma, Jo could remember nothing. In the weeks to follow, she learnt the extent of her injuries. She couldn't walk, her speech was very limited and quiet, and the movement on the right side of her body was severely compromised ... It was as if, she says, it had gone into a deep sleep. She had double vision. She left hospital after two months, walking by then, but horrendously weak and with all her fitness lost. Her life had been saved by her riding helmet but her career, far from going stratospheric, seemed doomed.

It's just over three years later and I sit in my wheelchair by the edge of the same outdoor riding arena, watching the same Jo Barry training one of her promising young horses, already a winner at lower levels. When they pass me, so close I could almost touch them, they suck out my breath with the magic of what they create together: the sheer presence of the horse, the gleam of his coat, the creak of tack and soft thud of his hooves. And on his back, Jo, impossibly slight and still, holding the power together with her hands and legs and poise in the saddle. In their wake, as they pass, the air swirls. It is a kind of velvet violence, the same sensation you get from being really close to a professional ballet dancer performing on stage, when you glimpse the enormous power and self-carriage needed to create art. That place between idea and reality, between trying and not trying. When Jo asks, unseen, through her legs and hands, the young horse throws out his limbs in controlled grace, learning how to stretch and collect and move sideways, his neck arched in soft submission. Rider and horse as one. My all-time fairy-tale. I find myself in a little-girl reverie.

Dreams are often lost but dreams can be found again and I am here, a witness to their turning. Jo's catastrophe had a much happier ending than mine – fantastically happier. Every day after her injury, she dedicated her energy to getting her body and brain back. Four months after her accident, heart in her mouth, she got on a riding school horse. Her right side wanted to curl up and she had little control of it. She could hardly believe how difficult she found the basic requirements of riding; it was something she had started as a three-year-old and she was now in her thirties. How could it be so hard? She spent the next three months riding friends' steady horses, battling the fatigue and allowing the movement in the saddle to rebuild her core strength and connections to her limbs. Sometimes she wondered if a comeback was possible. But muscle memory kicked in and her nerves started to reroute and reconnect. Riding at any level, but supremely so at hers, demands that the brain marshals and coordinates every bit of the body. Her sport, by sheer chance, offered her the most perfect all-body physiotherapy for neuro-logical damage.

By summer, she was back on her dressage horses again. By autumn, she was competing. Her recovery was stunning. So was her dedication. Three years on, in every sense, she appears whole again and is back at the top, winning with younger horses, training with Carl Hester, creating art every time she asks a dressage horse to perform. Like everyone who has had

Jo on Humphrey winning again. A triumph
of neurological recovery.

damaged wiring, she monitors her body constantly. She's a
perfectionist. She says she's not yet back where she was, but she
nearly is. Her speech, when she's tired, can be a beat slower, and
she feels her right side is still marginally weaker. But her body
is still improving; she gets hours of physiotherapy on horseback
every day.

There are strange symmetries at work here although, horse-
wise, Jo and I inhabited different worlds. The level at which she
operated, a driven professional, was light years beyond me. Yet
we were both victims of random chance and we know the
implications of life-changing injury. And in our struggle to
recover our bodies afterwards, we are both steely and committed. Neither of us, I suspect, knows when to stop trying.
Perhaps she is one of the few people who really understand why
I risked getting back on a horse.

Our accidents have had different outcomes, but hers is a remarkable triumph and mine ... well, mine is not a tragedy. I've finally worked that out.

Afterwards, we sit talking in the barn between the rows of stables. One of the livery horses is reaching over his door. I allow him to explore my hair and my wheelchair with his rubbery, prehensile lips, dropping strands of haylage in my lap. His touch closes my throat and makes the roof of my mouth clot with emotion. I want to tell Jo about the beauty she creates with a horse, want her to know I understand her struggle and give her my blessing to go on to greater things. To ride on, although I can't. But the words don't come. They sound silly, corny, too fey.

Instead, I remind her that it's only been three years since her accident. 'That's nothing,' I say, surprised by my own intensity. 'Nothing. Neurological recovery keeps going. It just takes its time.' I tell her that it's been eight years since mine – and only recently the toes on my right foot regained some feeling, while my foot placement is still improving.

She breaks into a rare, quiet smile. She gets it. And I caress the horse's nose as best I can with my fist, then say goodbye.

Ten days later, Jo makes an astounding comeback and does what she thought she would never do again – winning the GB national winter championship with one of her young horses. Since then, her career has taken off again in an extraordinary fashion and she continues to sweep the board at major competitions, often achieving around the magic eighty per cent score. Hers is a story of fierce optimism, which gives this book its best possible ending.

SPECIALIST SPINAL NOTES

There can be no realistic self-help manuals for life with a bust spine. No how-to guides on living with knackered bodies, numb fingers or clouded minds. No pamphlets on ways to stay patient, hopeful or alive. The complexity of neurological damage defies generalisation. We're all variously stuffed in our own way and we have to learn how to cope. Here's what I've found out.

1) Your hands will improve and will continue to improve. They will get stronger and less clawed. You will learn to cope with what you have better.

2) Get in as much gym as you can before you leave hospital. You won't realise what you've lost until it's gone. Private specialist rehabilitation is expensive.

3) Remember your shoulders will wear out. Take up wheelchair sport by all means but remember shoulders are not designed for propelling bodies. To preserve them, choose the lightest chair possible. Keep as thin as possible (it's bloody difficult), and consider getting some kind of power assist if you're pushing big distances.

4) Be assertive about being pushed in your chair by the well-intentioned but ignorant. Don't let people move you around without asking. But do seek help when you need it. The vast majority of people are very kind once they understand.

5) Manual chairs are better if you can get by with one; obviously paraplegics can, but tetraplegics too. They're easier, neater, lighter, less hassle, more flexible, less problematic on steps. Try power-assisted add-ons for manuals like dynamo wheels, SmartDrive, PowerPack, PowerGlide, etc., before you go for a fully powered chair. Lots of different devices around, like the Firefly or Batec motorised scooter attachments. See (9) below.

6) Power chairs are great if you have to travel any distance under your own steam but they can make you feel more paralysed and disabled. Plus they wreck the house, banging into things, and it's much harder to get close to worktops, beds, etc. The choice is a minefield. Get specialist spinal advice. See (9) below.

7) Go to some of the big disability exhibitions – Naidex is the main one – and look at the gadgets, aids and inventions. It's the best source of finding out who's doing what. Technology is racing ahead and we must be hopeful. See (9) below.

8) I tried an exoskeleton (the Rex) and it was fun but bulky and utterly impractical for day-to-day life. For specific jobs, terrific – some surgeons and dentist with spinal injuries are apparently using them to continue working.

9) In the early days, don't rush into buying the latest device/ chair/mobility aid. All of us, a few years down the road, have lurking in the garage something expensive and unsuitable which we bought without enough experience, now gathering dust.

10) Get a colostomy if you're a tetraplegic. Don't wait until things are desperate. Do it as soon as you can. It's life-changing; the single best decision I made. Wish I'd had it done before I left the spinal unit.

11) Remember you know your body best. Better than newly qualified district nurses, A&E staff, most general nurses, your GP. Tell them loud and clear what you need.

12) Indwelling catheters and bladder infections. My life was transformed by an open-ended catheter which ended six years of recurrent bladder infections. At time of writing, that situation holds. Touch wood. Qufora or LINC Optitip are available on NHS in 2018 – there will be more developments – researchers are now trying very hard on the catheter front. Keep pushing, keep asking the specialists.

13) D-mannose supplement. I started taking two pills a day at the same time I started the open-ended catheter. I haven't had an E. coli infection since. D-mannose might be the reason, it might not – but I'm not stopping it to find out. There's some scientific evidence supporting it, and several incontinence professionals have urged me to use it: it's a sugar which is not absorbed by the body, but as it passes through the bladder it is latched onto by the ever-present E.coli bacteria, and the two

things are harmlessly excreted together. That's the theory. I like it. I'm going with it. I don't cut down rowan trees either just in case I upset the fairies.

14) Life as a para or a tetra evolves. It is like starting a new life and growing up. Where you are now is not where you will be in a few years' time.

15) Please support the charity Spinal Research. There *will* be some kind of cure some day; the more we fund-raise the more likely we are to see it in our lifetimes. In 2018, research pioneering gene therapy to dissolve scar tissue within the cord is showing genuine, serious promise, funded by the Medical Research Council, Spinal Research and Wings for Life.

16) Ignore other people's timescales, especially if you have an incomplete injury. Conventional wisdom says you plateau and recovery stops after six months, or a year, or eighteen months. Nearly a decade on, little things are still improving in my body.

17) The attitude prevailing in spinal units and the NHS is one of stifling expectation about neurological recovery. They don't have the staff or budgets to do otherwise. They could be sued for giving patients false hope. Always bear that in mind.

18) If you like black humour, and let's face it, you'll never have a better excuse, study the cartoons of the late John Callahan. A movie of his life, *Don't Worry, He Won't Get Far on Foot*, came out in 2018. 'I try not to dwell on paralysis,' John once said. 'Unless I want a Chinese takeaway and the person with me

doesn't want to go out in the rain to collect it. Then I subtly bring the conversation round to the fact that I'm quadriplegic. That way, I know I'll be looking at egg foo yung quite soon.' His fans included Richard Pryor, Bob Dylan, Robin Williams and Bill Clinton, but the disability rights lobby don't like him. 'When you see someone laughing like hell and saying, "That's not funny,"' P.J. O'Rourke once wrote, 'you know they're reading John Callahan.'

19) If you're young, be disabled and proud. Normalise it, be militant, embrace identity politics. Society will allow it. Don't be like me. Happily, younger men and women with unconventional bodies are operating in a world where kindness and inclusivity are powerful social forces. They're able to write a new narrative about the beauty in disability and flaunt it on catwalks. They don't want to be able-bodied. They want to be seen as ordinary and one day they will.

20) The politics of incomplete spinal injuries are complicated, but chances are you may be incomplete if you're reading this – more and more people in spinal units are there as a result of improved emergency protocols. When I was an inmate, one of the mentors from the local spinal injury charity was a man who walked on sticks. All the other mentors were complete injuries in wheelchairs. Within the spinal world, at least at that time, the focus was very much on catering for the needs of the latter and there was a certain attitude to those with some mobility. They were called – and the label had a certain edge – walkers. At Stoke Mandeville, where I once swam in the inter-spinal unit games (I came last by an embarrassing two minutes) I

heard a woman who won a race bitchily dismissed as a walker – by implication, a bit of a cheat. Some in the wider disabled community regard anyone who seeks to leave behind a wheelchair as some form of betrayer. Their identity is firmly in a wheelchair and those who strive to escape it are letting them down. On some internet spinal forums, for every dozen messages exhorting the need to work hard and never give up, there will be at least one from the wheelchair user who reacts with weary cynicism to the evangelism of exercise. Could anything be more damaging for public perceptions of paralysis, one poster asked bitterly, than 'someone hobbling up on stage and telling the audience that through hard work and perseverance, they were able to overcome?' This emphasis on effort and willpower would make the public look at people in wheelchairs and assume they just weren't trying hard enough, otherwise they'd be walking too.

21) It took me ages to realise how many of us are neither complete nor walkers, but exist in a non-functional torturous limbo in between. Our bodies were irrevocably damaged, but a lot less than some. But there's nothing to do about it but try and keep what function you have going and hope science gets a move on before you get too old.

22) And the final secret weapon? A Dyson hairdryer. Spilt pee, leaking bags: sooner or later, every single spinal patient gets their trousers wet. The best by far secret weapon is the ridiculously expensive Dyson – immensely powerful, fast, and light to hold. Can't face the hassle of getting people to change you? Pee not too smelly? Be rescued in seconds.

ACKNOWLEDGEMENTS

Snatches of this book will be familiar to those who have followed my journalism in 'Spinal Column' in *The Times*, but most of what's here is the previously untellable story. In order to protect the identity of NHS staff, and my fellow patients in hospital, I have disguised most people, changing backgrounds, gender, injuries, and names. Suffice it to say that no fiction could do justice to the craziness, camaraderie, humour and utter despair of a spinal unit. My grateful thanks go to my fellow inmates in the unit in Glasgow, now part of the new Queen Elizabeth University Hospital. All of us were in our own way trying to make sense of a foreign land. In this account there is, unavoidably, a fair amount of bad language, bodily detail, pee, poo and vomit, most of it mine, but that, I'm afraid, is the unvarnished reality of chronic illness. Much though I wish it was, this is not a miracle story. Its message is not that everyone with a spinal injury, with enough hard work, will recover some function. Some won't. Every single injury is different. There are no generalisations, no judgements. No one is less brave than anyone else. We all endure paralysis in different ways. My experience is that neurological improvement is more long-term, more persistent and possible, than the medical profession is able to allow. No one should ever give up hope. Equally, no one should be condemned for not trying hard enough. When you exist in the world of chronic ill health, hard work is a given – every hour, every day, whether seated or stumbling.

Gratitude beyond words goes to my beloved family – my husband David, my son Dougie, my brother and sister and their families in the US and France. While love gave me reason to continue, the NHS enabled me to do so. It seems invidious to mention anyone from a huge cast in Glasgow, but Susan Gilhespie, Mariel Purcell, Leslie Wallace, Christine Eden and Gillian Irvine did more for me than they will ever realise. In the immediate aftermath of my accident the St John Ambulance and crew of Royal Navy SAR Sea King XZ920 delivered me to hospital far faster than seemed possible. My then editors at *The Times*, James Harding, Magnus Linklater and Anne Spackman, were amazing, facilitating my emergence as a magazine column-ist and saving my life in yet another way.

I am grateful to Martin Hunter for allowing me to use his photographs and to Greater Glasgow & Clyde Health Board for the MRI image of my neck. Revisiting the last nine years has not been easy and I would like to thank my editor at 4th Estate, Helen Garnons-Williams, my agent, Jenny Brown, and my copyeditor, Rhian McKay for their sensitivity and quiet encouragement. Countless small acts of kindness changed my world. My dearest friends know who they are, proven kindred spirits.

Especial thanks though to Judy, for proof reading, Carrie and Kathy, the emphysemic gym assistants, Janis for sending me a postcard every week for a year, and Eilidh, Sally, Mona and Susan for stocking the freezer with food for Dave. When I was due to come home, local farmers, unasked, arrived in a fleet of huge tractors to repair the farm track to our house. Annie

Maw, herself paralysed, was a stranger who rescued me from despair, Gregor Fisher became the greatest of allies. So too Tanya Alexander and Sara Smith, who got me back on a horse, even though it ended badly. Thanks to Paul Lough for getting me driving again, Dennis Stevenson for mentoring and Angela Mudge for being supremely matter-of-fact about everything. Dr Judith Sim from Edinburgh University gave me insight into medical sociology, and Peter (Andy) Wrate taught me a valuable grounding in Buddhism. In the unlikely event I ever succumb to religion, it will be to Buddha. My readers from *The Times* have been heroically loyal, supportive, kind, clever and amusing, sustaining me through thick and thin. To John Witherow and Nicola Jeal, my present editors, thank you. At home, I could not have done without Janice, Barbara, Anna and Sarah; my now retired district nurse Helen; and my present and former GPs, who have gone the extra mile for me despite their workloads. Through the friendship of Mary Hope, I am honoured that the dressage rider Jo Barry chose to share her story of neurological despair with me. And finally, thanks with ribbons and bows on to Andrew Marr, an old pal, long-time hero and sadly now fellow crock, who has been kind enough, in the face of a vast workload, to write the foreword.

PICTURE CREDITS